'Few biblical interpreters have delved as [...] brain as Joel Green. Here he draws upo[...] Scripture to put forth a fresh picture of human existence, one that makes sense from both perspectives. He does not shy away from hard questions, especially those about life and death, body and soul.'
Patrick D. Miller, Charles T. Haley Professor of Old Testament Theology Emeritus, Princeton Theological Seminary

'In this outstanding work, the author provides a scholarly and thoroughly biblical analysis of human personhood in dialogue with the neurosciences. This book is likely to provide the definitive overview of this topic for many years to come.'
Denis R. Alexander, Director of The Faraday Institute, St. Edmund's College, Cambridge

'If you think nothing new ever happens in theology or biblical studies you need to read this book, an essay in "neurohermeneutics". Green shows not only that a physicalist anthropology is consistent with biblical teaching, but also that contemporary neuroscience sheds light on significant hermeneutical and theological questions.'
Nancey Murphy, Professor of Christian Philosophy, Fuller Theological Seminary

'Joel Green serves as the vanguard of interdisciplinary research on this topic. No one combines the requisite background in theology, biblical studies, and the natural sciences as adeptly as Green, and with the critical thinking needed to move along the interstices of these disciplines. Indeed, he succeeds at closing the gaps between these disciplines. In this volume, we see him examining the biblical data afresh from his monist perspective, surveying the convergence of biblical studies and the neurosciences on a number of conclusions, and exploring the implications of monism for the church and for our understanding of salvation, mission, and life-after-death. This "progress report" is another timely and welcome contribution from Professor Green.'
Bill T. Arnold, Paul S. Amos Professor of Old Testament Interpretation, Asbury Theological Seminary

'Some are students of the Bible. Others are students of neuroscience. Joel Green is both and more. He's also a student of the human condition. Oftentimes students of the Bible and students of the neurosciences tell radically different and ultimately irreconcilable stories about human nature – *what* we are, *who* we are and what we're made for. In *Body, Soul and Human Life* Joel Green helps us to listen more attentively both to the Bible and to the unfolding music of the neurosciences. What you hear may surprise you. Far from telling different and irreconcilable stories about human nature, Joel Green helps us to see that these two sources – the Bible and the neurosciences – actually tell mutually enriching and complementary stories about what it means to be fully human, and fully alive. I heartily recommend it!'
Kevin Corcoran, Lecturer in Philosophy, Calvin College

STUDIES in THEOLOGICAL INTERPRETATION

Series Editors

Craig G. Bartholomew
  Redeemer University College
Joel B. Green
  Fuller Theological Seminary
Christopher R. Seitz
  Wycliffe College, University of Toronto

Editorial Advisory Board

Gary Anderson
  University of Notre Dame
Markus Bockmuehl
  University of Oxford
Richard Hays
  Duke University Divinity School
Christine Pohl
  Asbury Theological Seminary
Eleonore Stump
  Saint Louis University
Anthony Thiselton
  University of Nottingham
  University of Chester
Marianne Meye Thompson
  Fuller Theological Seminary
Kevin Vanhoozer
  Trinity Evangelical Divinity School
John Webster
  University of Aberdeen
Jim Kinney
  Baker Academic

BODY, SOUL, AND HUMAN LIFE

The Nature of Humanity in the Bible

JOEL B. GREEN

B
BakerAcademic
a division of Baker Publishing Group
Grand Rapids, Michigan

Published by Baker Academic
a division of Baker Publishing Group
P.O. Box 6287, Grand Rapids, MI 49516-6287
www.bakeracademic.com

Baker Academic Edition Published 2008
ISBN 978-0-8010-3595-1

Previously published by Paternoster

Printed in the United States of America

Library of Congress Cataloging in Publication Control Number: 2011276311

CONTENTS

To
Jim Holsinger
"A human being fully alive . . ."

SERIES PREFACE

As a discipline, formal biblical studies is in a period of reassessment and upheaval. Concern with historical origins and the development of the biblical materials has in many places been replaced by an emphasis on the reader and the meanings supplied by present contexts and communities. The Studies in Theological Interpretation series will seek to appreciate the constructive theological contribution made by Scripture when it is read in its canonical richness. Of necessity, this includes historical evaluation while remaining open to renewed inquiry into what is meant by history and historical study in relation to Christian Scripture. This also means that the history of the reception of biblical texts—a discipline frequently neglected or rejected altogether—will receive fresh attention and respect. In sum, the series is dedicated to the pursuit of constructive theological interpretation of the church's inheritance of prophets and apostles in a manner that is open to reconnection with the long history of theological reading in the church. The primary emphasis is on the constructive theological contribution of the biblical texts themselves.

New commentary series have sprung up to address these and similar concerns. It is important to complement this development with brief, focused, and closely argued studies that evaluate the hermeneutical, historical, and theological dimensions of scriptural reading and interpretation for our times. In the light of shifting and often divergent methodologies, the series will encourage studies in theological interpretation that model clear and consistent methods in the pursuit of theologically engaging readings.

An earlier day saw the publication of a series of short monographs and compact treatments in the area of biblical theology that went by the name Studies in Biblical Theology. The length and focus of the contributions were salutary features and worthy of emulation. Today, however, we find no consensus regarding the nature of biblical theology, and this is a good reason to explore anew what competent theological reflection on Christian Scripture might look like in our day. To this end, the present series, Studies in Theological Interpretation, is dedicated.

ABBREVIATIONS

AB	Anchor Bible
ABD	*Anchor Bible Dictionary*. Edited by David Noel Freedman. 6 vols. New York: Doubleday, 1992.
AGJU	Arbeiten zur Geschichte des antiken Judentums und des Urchristentums
AS	Advances in Semiotics
ASRS	Ashgate Science and Religion Series
BBR	*Bulletin for Biblical Research*
BChr	Beginnings of Christianity
BECNT	Baker Exegetical Commentary on the New Testament
BETL	Bibliotheca ephemeridum theologicarum lovaniensium
Bib	*Biblica*
BibOr	Biblica et orientalia
BNTC	Black's New Testament Commentaries
BThS	Biblisch-theologische Studien
CBQ	*Catholic Biblical Quarterly*

CIT	Current Issues in Theology
CML	Classics of Medicine Library
CTHP	Cambridge Texts in the History of Philosophy
CurTM	*Currents in Theology and Mission*
DDCT	Distinguished Dissertations in Christian Theology
DJG	*Dictionary of Jesus and the Gospels*. Edited by Joel B. Green and Scot McKnight. Downers Grove, IL: InterVarsity, 1992.
DPL	*Dictionary of Paul and His Letters*. Edited by Gerald F. Hawthorne, Ralph P. Martin, and Daniel G. Reid. Downers Grove, IL: InterVarsity, 1993.
EdF	Erträge der Forschung
ETL	*Ephemerides theologicae lovanienses*
EvQ	*Evangelical Quarterly*
FRLANT	Forschungen zur Religion und Literatur des Alten und Neuen Testaments
GNS	Good News Studies
HTR	*Harvard Theological Review*
Int	*Interpretation*
JJS	*Journal of Jewish Studies*
JPsyT	*Journal of Psychology and Theology*
JPT	*Journal of Pentecostal Theology*
JPTSup	Journal of Pentecostal Theology: Supplement Series
JSNTSup	Journal for the Study of the New Testament: Supplement Series
KEK	Kritisch-exegetischer Kommentar über das Neue Testament
LCL	Loeb Classical Library
MBPS	Mellen Biblical Press Series
MM	Moulton, James Hope, and George Milligan. *The Vocabulary of the Greek Testament*. London, 1930. Reprint, Peabody, MA: Hendrickson, 1997.
MNTS	McMaster New Testament Studies
NDBT	*New Dictionary of Biblical Theology*. Edited by T.D. Alexander and Brian S. Rosner. Downers Grove, IL: InterVarsity, 2000.

NIDOTTE *New International Dictionary of Old Testament Theology and Ethics.* Edited by W.A. VanGemeren. 5 vols. Grand Rapids, MI: Zondervan, 1997.
NIGTC   New International Greek Testament Commentary
NovTSup Supplements to Novum Testamentum
NSBT   New Studies in Biblical Theology
NTS   *New Testament Studies*
NTT   *New Testament Theology*
OBT   Overtures to Biblical Theology
OCD   *Oxford Classical Dictionary.* Edited by Simon Hornblower and Antony Spawforth. 3rd ed. Oxford: Oxford University Press, 1996.
OTL   Old Testament Library
PBM   Paternoster Biblical Monographs
PPQ   *Pacific Philosophical Quarterly*
SBLAB   Society of Biblical Literature Academia Biblica
SBLDS   Society of Biblical Literature Dissertation Series
SBLMS   Society of Biblical Literature Monograph Series
SBT   Studies in Biblical Theology
S&CB   *Science & Christian Belief*
SH ns   Studies in History New Series
SHR   Studies in the History of Religions
SJT   *Scottish Journal of Theology*
SNT   Studien zum Neuen Testament
SNTSMS   Society for New Testament Studies Monograph Series
SNTW   Studies of the New Testament and its World
SP   Sacra pagina
StABH   Studies in American Biblical Hermeneutics
SUNT   Studien zur Umwelt des Neuen Testaments
TDOT   *Theological Dictionary of the Old Testament.* Edited by G. Johannes Botterweck, et al. 15 vols. Grand Rapids, MI: Eerdmans, 1974–2006.
THNTC   Two Horizons New Testament Commentary
TSc   Theology and the Sciences
TynBul   *Tyndale Bulletin*
UBT   Understanding Biblical Themes

WBC	Word Biblical Commentary
WMANT	Wissenschaftliche Monographien zum Alten und Neuen Testament
WUNT	Wissenschaftliche Untersuchungen zum Neuen Testament
WW	*Word and World*

PREFACE

Not long ago, a *New York Times* article reported, "Neuroscientists have given up looking for the seat of the soul, but they are still seeking what may be special about human brains, what it is that provides the basis for a level of self-awareness and complex emotions unlike those of other animals." Noting the now-common view that morality and reason grow out of social emotions and feelings that are themselves linked to brain structures, the article suggests that, maybe, what makes us human is all in the wiring of the brain.[1]

Does our brain account for our essential humanity? What of the long-held and popular view that the sine qua non of genuine humanity is the soul? This is not the stuff of mere curiosity. A host of pressing issues is at stake. What portrait of the human person is capable of casting a canopy of sacred worth over human beings, so that we have what is necessary for discourse concerning morality

---

[1] Sandra Blakeslee, "Humanity? Maybe It's All in the Wiring," *New York Times*, 9 December 2003, F1.

and for ethical practices? If humans, like sheep, can be cloned, will the resulting life form be a "person"? Are we free to do what we want, or is our sense of decision-making a ruse? What happens when we die?

Questions of this sort increasingly find their way into our daily newspapers, internet magazines, and evening news reports. More and more, it is neuroscientists who are setting the agenda for these discussions, some of whom (Antonio Damasio, for example, or Joseph LeDoux) have proven remarkably adept at telling their stories and thinking through the implications of their findings for audiences of non-specialists. Largely missing from the conversation are voices that take seriously what scientists are finding *while at the same time* bringing to bear on the discussion the perspectives and insights of biblical faith. As a result, we find ourselves treated to astonishing claims about how neuroscience has undermined biblical views of the human person, typically by persons who apparently have little exposure to the biblical materials.

My entrée into this conversation came just over a decade ago when Nancey Murphy invited me into a workgroup led by Warren Brown, Newton Malony, and herself. This was an interdisciplinary project on "Portraits of Human Nature," associated with the Lee Edward Travis Institute for Biopsychosocial Research at Fuller Theological Seminary and funded by The Templeton Foundation.[2] This invitation led to another, from Malcolm Jeeves, and to my participation in an interdisciplinary consultation on "Mind, Brain, and Personhood: An Inquiry from Scientific and Theological Perspectives," also funded by The Templeton Foundation.[3] I am grateful to these friends. Each in their own way, they have pressed upon me the critical nature of these issues. Interaction with Malcolm Jeeves in particular – as well as the indefatigable encouragement of another friend, Jim Holsinger, M.D. – led me finally to graduate

---

[2] See Warren S. Brown, Nancey Murphy, and H. Newton Malony, eds., *Whatever Happened to the Soul? Scientific and Theological Portraits of Human Nature* (TSc; Minneapolis: Fortress, 1998).

[3] See Malcolm A. Jeeves, ed., *From Cells to Souls – And Beyond: Changing Portraits of Human Nature* (Grand Rapids, MI: Eerdmans, 2004).

work in neuroscience at the University of Kentucky, which allowed me more fully to engage in the sort of interdisciplinarity requisite to this study. This book, then, is a progress report on where my thinking at the interface of these disciplines has led me.

One of the features of interdisciplinary study is the difference in protocols regarding language-use. My readers will note that the non-inclusive term "man" appears repeatedly in my citations of others' works – not only in writing from earlier historical periods but also among our contemporaries. This is because concerns with inclusive language for human beings usually taken for granted in the church and in theological scholarship have not found their way into the other areas of academic discourse with which I am concerned in this work. I hope it will not prove too much a stumbling-block that I have decided, when citing others, to allow them their own words without emendation.

Throughout the lengthy and involved period of incubation of the perspectives and substance of this book I have given lectures and papers in a number of settings: Southeast Regional Meetings of the Society of Biblical Literature; Society of Biblical Literature Consultation on the Use of Cognitive Linguistics in Biblical Interpretation; Society of Christian Philosophers; Society of John Wesley Scholars; The Society for the Study of Psychology and Wesleyan Theology; Joint Meeting of the American Scientific Affiliation (USA) and Christians in Science (UK); and Pacific Coast Theological Society. I am grateful for opportunities for interaction on these concerns afforded me in those contexts. In preparing this book, I have drawn from a range of earlier publications, including: "'Bodies – That Is, Human Lives': A Re-examination of Human Nature in the Bible," in *Whatever Happened to the Soul? Scientific and Theological Portraits of Human Nature* (ed. Warren S. Brown, Nancey C. Murphy, and H. Newton Malony; TSc; Minneapolis: Fortress, 1998), 149–73; "Restoring the Human Person: New Testament Voices for a Wholistic and Social Anthropology," in *Neuroscience and the Person* (ed. Robert John Russell, Nancey Murphy, Theo Meyering, and Michael A. Arbib; Scientific Perspectives on Divine Action 4; Vatican City State: Vatican

Observatory; Berkeley, CA: Center for Theology and the Natural Sciences, 1999), 3–22; "Eschatology and the Nature of Humans: A Reconsideration of the Pertinent Biblical Evidence," *S&CB* 14 (2002): 33–50; "What Does It Mean to Be Human? Another Chapter in the Ongoing Interaction of Science and Scripture," in *From Cells to Souls – And Beyond: Changing Portraits of Human Nature* (ed. Malcolm A. Jeeves; Grand Rapids, MI: Eerdmans, 2004), 179–98; "Body and Soul? Questions at the Interface of Science and Christian Faith" and "Resurrection of the Body: New Testament Voices concerning Personal Continuity and the Afterlife," in *What about the Soul? Neuroscience and Christian Anthropology* (ed. Joel B. Green; Nashville: Abingdon, 2004), 5–12, 85–100; "Body and Soul, Mind and Brain: Critical Issues," in *In Search of the Soul: Four Views of the Mind-Body Problem* (ed. Joel B. Green and Stuart Palmer; Downers Grove, IL: InterVarsity, 2005), 7–32; and "Humanity – Created, Restored, Transformed, Embodied," in *Rethinking Human Nature: A Multidisciplinary Approach* (ed. Malcolm Jeeves; Grand Rapids, MI: Eerdmans, in press). Although there is no one-to-one relationship between any previous publication and the chapters of this book, overlap is most noticeable with chapter 5; hence, I am grateful to Denis Alexander, editor of *Science & Christian Belief*, for permission to borrow extensively from "Eschatology and the Nature of Humans: A Reconsideration of the Pertinent Biblical Evidence," *S&CB* 14 (2002): 33–50.

1

THE BIBLE, THE NATURAL
SCIENCES, AND THE
HUMAN PERSON

There is a new image of man emerging, an image that will dramatically
contradict almost all traditional images man has made of himself in the
course of his cultural history. (Thomas Metzinger)[1]

The idea that the soul can continue to exist without the body or brain,
strains scientific credibility. ... The dualistic approach is also unattrac-
tive theologically. (Fraser Watts)[2]

But someone has testified somewhere, "What are human beings that
you are mindful of them, or mortals, that you care for them? You have

---

[1] Thomas Metzinger, "Introduction: Consciousness Research at the End of
the Twentieth Century," in *Neural Correlates of Consciousness: Empirical
and Conceptual Questions* (ed. Thomas Metzinger; Cambridge, MA: The
MIT Press, 2000), 1–12 (6).
[2] Fraser Watts, *Theology and Psychology* (ASRS; Aldershot: Ashgate,
2002), 46.

made them for a little while lower than the angels; you have crowned
them with glory and honor, subjecting all things under their feet."
(Heb 2:6–8)[3]

Self-assessment is often needed, but not always welcome. In the
case of an examination of humanity in the Bible, however, temptations may run in a different direction. Rather than avoiding analysis of ourselves as the human family or members of that family, we
risk imagining that the Bible is "about" us. However, as Barth rec-
ognized in his 1916 lecture on "The Strange New World within the
Bible," the "stuff" of the Bible is not fundamentally about human
history, human needs, human potential, human practices.

> The Bible tells us not how we should talk with God but what he says to
> us; not how we find the way to him, but how he has sought and found
> the way to us; not the right relation in which we must place ourselves to
> him, but the covenant which he has made with all who are Abraham's
> spiritual children and which he has sealed once and for all in Jesus
> Christ. It is this which is within the Bible.

Barth concludes, "We have found in the Bible a new world, God,
God's sovereignty, God's glory, God's incomprehensible love."[4]
Recent work in biblical theology has only underscored this insight,
insisting again and again that the unity of the biblical witness
resides in God's self-revelation – not the "idea" or "concept" of
God but God himself.[5] Given the human propensity to regard with
hyperbole our significance in the cosmos, this is an important
opening reminder. On the one hand, we have been reticent to
acknowledge the continuity of humanity with all other animals

---

[3] Unless otherwise indicated, biblical citations are from the NRSV.

[4] Karl Barth, "The Strange New World within the Bible," in *The Word of
God and the Word of Man* (Gloucester: Peter Smith, 1978), 28–50 (43, 45).

[5] E.g., Ferdinand Hahn, *Theologie des Neuen Testaments* (2 vols.;
Tübingen: Mohr Siebeck, 2001–5); Ulrich Wilckens, *Theologie des Neuen
Testaments* (4 vols.; Neukirchener-Vluyn: Neukirchener, 2002–5); Christo-
pher R. Seitz, *Word without End: The Old Testament as Abiding Theological
Witness* (Grand Rapids, MI: Eerdmans, 1998).

and, indeed, the degree to which our lives are bound up with the world we indwell. On the other, we are slow to recognize our creatureliness in relation to God. Consequently, we have found ourselves humbled by scientific discovery – in the modern age, first by Copernicus, who demonstrated that our planet and, thus, we who inhabit the earth, are not the center around which the universe turns; and second, by Darwin and evolutionary biology, which has located *Homo sapiens* within the animal kingdom with a genetic make-up that strongly resembles the creatures around us.[6] Were we to take Barth seriously, we might entertain a further "humbling" – namely, the realization that the Bible is about God, first and foremost, and only derivatively about us.

Study of the human person in the Bible – that is, a biblical-theological anthropology or, more simply, a biblical anthropology – is thus a derivative inquiry. It is secondary. However, insofar as it struggles with the character of humans in relation to God and with respect to the vocation given humanity by God, it is nonetheless crucial. We are concerned, then, with how the Bible portrays the human person, the basis and *telos* of human life, what it means for humanity, in the words of Irenaeus, to be "fully alive" (*Adversus haereses*, 4.20). Unavoidably, this raises questions about relations within the human family, and about the place of humanity in the world.

Humanity and Human Identity in Biblical Theology

By way of setting the stage, a brief review of key voices in the discussion is in order. Although my chief concern is with more recent directions and emphases, it is impossible to consider study of biblical anthropology without first recognizing the towering and stubborn influence of the perspective on

---

[6] Helmut Thielicke lists "three humblings" – Copernicus, Darwin, and Freud (*Being Human . . . Becoming Human: An Essay in Christian Anthropology* [Garden City, NY: Doubleday, 1984], 29–32).

humanity developed in Rudolf Bultmann's *New Testament Theology*, published 60 years ago.[7]

Bultmann's work encompassed some six hundred pages, with almost one-third of the project devoted to humanity; this alone belies the importance of this topic in his rendering of NT theology. Another measure of the importance of anthropology for Bultmann is his location of such theological issues as God's righteousness, grace, the death and resurrection of Christ, and the church as subcategories of a theology of the human person. Although the center of his concern is Paul's anthropology, we quickly discover that Bultmann sees the Pauline perspective as representative of much of the Bible's anthropology and, in any case, as the Bible's determinative witness. Recognizing that Paul provides nothing in the way of a theological treatise on humanity, as one might find among the Greek philosophers, Bultmann turns to the fragmentary and occasional evidence of the seven assuredly Pauline letters with a concern to clarify the peculiarity of human existence.[8] His approach takes the form of extensive, theologically shaped word studies, the primary of which is concerned with σῶμα (*sōma*), often, but for Bultmann problematically, translated as "body." As Bultmann famously remarked, "Man does not *have* a *soma*; he *is soma*."[9] Indeed, "*man, his person as a whole*, can be denoted by *soma*. ... Man is called soma in respect to his being able to make himself the object of his own action or to experience himself as the subject to whom something happens. He can be called *soma*, that is, *as having a relationship to himself* – as being able in a certain sense to distinguish himself from himself."[10] The human person does not consist of two (or three) parts, then, but is a living whole. What is more, human lives are oriented toward a purpose; they live always on a quest, though the human creature can find or lose one's self.

---

[7] Rudolf Bultmann, *Theology of the New Testament* (2 vols.; New York: Charles Scribner's Sons, 1951–55).

[8] For Bultmann, the list of Pauline letters includes Romans, 1–2 Corinthians, Galatians, Philippians, 1 Thessalonians, and Philemon.

[9] Bultmann, *Theology*, 1:194; emphasis original.

[10] Bultmann, *Theology*, 1:195–96; emphasis original.

For Paul, Bultmann observes, "*Man has always already missed the
existence that at heart he seeks,* his intent is basically perverse,
evil."[11] This "missing" of life is sin, which is a power that domi-
nates everyone completely.

If, until the onset of the twentieth century, Pauline anthropology
was understood in dichotomous (body-soul) or even trichotomous
(body-soul-spirit) terms,[12] the same could not be said by mid-
century or subsequently. Credit for this transformation is due especially to the authority of Bultmann, whose reading dominated subsequent discussion.[13] Other scholars might wish to nuance his

---

[11] Bultmann, *Theology,* 1:227; emphasis original.

[12] So, e.g., Graham J. Warne, *Hebrew Perspectives on the Human Person in the
Hellenistic Era: Philo and Paul* (MBPS 35; Lewiston, NY: Mellen, 1995), 157. In
fact, the evidence is mixed, though clearly weighted toward a dichotomous or
trichotomous view of the human person. For example, in the major reference
works edited by James Hastings at the turn of the twentieth century, the human
person is conceived by Jesus and/or the Gospels as having "two parts" according
to E. Wheeler ("Man," in *A Dictionary of Christ and the Gospels* [2 vols.; ed.
James Hastings; New York: Charles Scribner's Sons, 1908], 2:107–10 [110]); a
"clear duality" by F. Meyrick and J.C. Lambert ("Body," in *A Dictionary of
Christ and the Gospels* [2 vols.; ed. James Hastings; New York: Charles
Scribner's Sons, 1908], 1:217–18); as a dichotomy or even trichotomy by J.C.
Lambert ("Soul," in *A Dictionary of Christ and the Gospels* [2 vols.; ed. James
Hastings; New York: Charles Scribner's Sons, 1908], 1:520); and the NT pres-
ents the body in a "clear and constant antithesis to 'soul' and 'spirit'" (J.
Laidlaw, "Body, in *Dictionary of the Bible* [5 vols.; ed. James Hastings; New
York: Charles Scribner's Sons, 1903], 1:309). Yet J.C. Lambert finds no dualism
in Paul ("Body," in *Dictionary of the Apostolic Church* [3 vols.; ed. James
Hastings; New York: Charles Scribner's Sons, 1922], 1:154–56 [155]). The
complexity of the problem is seen in the apparent waffling of H. Wheeler Robinson. In his essay on "Man" in *Dictionary of the Apostolic Church* ([3 vols.; ed.
James Hastings; New York: Charles Scribner's Sons, 1922], 2:3–6), he claims
that Paul inherits the monism of the Hebrew Scriptures and that, while Paul was
influenced by Hellenism, he did not succumb to its dualism. Similarly, in his presentation of *The Christian Doctrine of Man* ([3rd ed.; Edinburgh: T&T Clark,
1926], 104–5), Robinson refers to Paul as "a Hebrew of the Hebrews" who sub-
ordinated and assimilated Hellenistic influences to his "Jewish psychology," but
then refers to the "separation of the 'spirit' from its present body of flesh, an idea
which was not reached in the Old Testament."

[13] See the survey in Robert H. Gundry, *Sōma in Biblical Theology with Emphasis
on Pauline Anthropology* (SNTSMS 29; Cambridge: Cambridge University
Press, 1976), 3–8.

work in one direction or another – for example, by querying the
subject-object relationship by which Bultmann articulated the person's relationship with self or by urging a stronger sense of
relationality in Pauline anthropology – but this emphasis on the
essential unity of human existence seems to have been established.
Paul is "a Hebrew of Hebrews," as John A.T. Robinson put it,
drawing attention to Paul's wholistic understanding of the human
creature.[14] F.F. Bruce echoed this sentiment two decades later,
observing that, in his anthropology, "Paul was a 'Hebrew born
and bred.'"[15] Also writing in the mid-twentieth century, W.G.
Kümmel observed both that, for Paul, we can speak only of the
"complete" person,[16] and that other NT writers share Paul's view
of things as well.

Of particular importance among those who have registered
concern about Bultmann's basic thesis is Robert Gundry, whose
monograph on *Sōma in Biblical Theology* appeared in 1976. His
primary contribution was to counter the loss of any notion of
physicality in Bultmann's understanding of *sōma* – an argument he
grounds in an extensive survey of the use of *sōma* in biblical and
extrabiblical literature, an examination of the use of *sōma* within
the framework of anthropological duality, and a wide-ranging discussion of the ramifications of his study for central aspects of
Christian theology. In the end, Gundry apparently thinks that the
semantic reach of *sōma* is limited to the notion of physicality, with
the result that the terminology he prefers, "duality," connotes not
simply differences of aspect but of essence – that is, some sort of
body-soul dualism.[17] On the other hand, in one of the more

---

[14] John A.T. Robinson, *The Body: A Study in Pauline Theology* (SBT 5; London: SCM, 1952), 11.
[15] F.F. Bruce, "Paul on Immortality," *SJT* 24 (1971): 457–72 (469); Bruce
thus attributes to Paul an OT conception of an animated body over against a
body-soul dualism.
[16] Werner Georg Kümmel, *Man in the New Testament* (London: Epworth,
1963), 47.
[17] In fact, Gundry identifies his position – which segregates the human corporeal from the incorporeal – with a virtual collage of terms; e.g., the human is
made up of "two substances" (*Sōma in Biblical Theology*, 83), and "there is

concentrated treatments of NT anthropology in recent years, Udo Schnelle is able to critique Bultmann on this very point without finding dualism in Paul. Even though "a person has a body and is a body" (a self-evident emendation of Bultmann's dictum, "man does not *have* a *soma*; he *is soma*"), Schnelle writes, Paul nevertheless "uses σῶμα as the comprehensive expression of the human self."[18] And in an extensive examination of *Paul's Anthropological Terms*, published in 1971, Robert Jewett undermined Bultmann's existentialist approach to Paul's anthropology by demonstrating that Paul borrowed and recast the anthropological terms of his antagonists. That is, his anthropology emerges in historical settings wherein anthropology is a means for defending the gospel (*pace* Bultmann, for whom anthropology comprised the core of the kerygma). Jewett finds that the coherence in Paul's view of humanity is found in his usage of καρδία (*kardia*, "heart"), which connotes the human "as an integral, intentional self who stands in relationship before God."[19] For Jewett, Paul *never* uses ψυχή (*psychē*) in the strict sense of "soul," and, while acknowledging occasional references to the observable human body in its physicality, he concludes that Paul uses the term σῶμα (*sōma*) especially to emphasize "the somatic basis of salvation" as a counter to "the gnostic idea of redemption from the body and the libertinistic actions which resulted from such an idea."[20]

Without embracing Bultmann's existentialism or his evacuation of physicality from the concept of *sōma*, a number of more recent,

---

an ontological duality, a functional pluralism, and an overarching unity" (84). Clearly, Gundry is casting about for language appropriate to nuance what he regards as Paul's position. In doing so, though, he employs terms that have a life of their own – and in some cases that stand in mutual opposition. The distinction between dualism and duality is pivotal in subsequent discussion – see, e.g., Malcolm A. Jeeves, "Human Nature: An Integrated Picture," in *What about the Soul? Neuroscience and Christian Anthropology* (ed. Joel B. Green; Nashville: Abingdon, 2004), 171–89.

[18] Udo Schnelle, *The Human Condition: Anthropology in the Teachings of Jesus, Paul, and John* (Minneapolis: Fortress, 1996), 58, 57.

[19] Robert Jewett, *Paul's Anthropological Terms: A Study of Their Use in Conflict Settings* (AGJU 10; Leiden: Brill, 1971), 447.

[20] Jewett, *Paul's Anthropological Terms*, 457.

extensive studies have led to verdicts similarly supportive of Paul's essential wholism. In his study of the Pauline expression "the inner person," for example, Theo Heckel underscores Paul's emphasis on embodied life in this world and the next, while combating body-soul dualism.[21] In his dissertation on "Hebrew Perspectives on the Human Person," Graham Warne argues that "Paul maintains an Hebraic perspective which emphasizes the wholeness of the human person's existence, both in the present life and beyond it." Warne's study is of special interest since it demonstrates how, from within a roughly analogous philosophical and theological milieu, Paul and Philo reach contrasting views of the human person.[22]

With reference to the anthropology of the OT, the consensus has continued to support a unified portrait of the human person. Indeed, that the OT does not think of the human being as made up of or pos-sessing "parts" is often passed over quickly, as if it were an unassail-able truism, in the service of other theological considerations. Thus, having noted that the OT "is familiar neither with the dichotomy of body and soul nor a trichotomy of body, soul, and spirit,"[23] Horst Preuss goes on to survey the anthropology of each of the major voices represented in the OT, concluding that the basic, common frame-work of OT anthropology includes the human's basic dependence on God in community with whom authentic life was possible; the covenantal relationship of humanity and God (i.e., the human's dialogical responsibility before God); an egalitarianism of status among persons; the formation of humans for community; God's con-trol over life and death; the framework of life as purposeful under God's providential guidance; and the residence of a person's charac-ter in his or her practices.[24]

---

[21] Theo K. Heckel, *Der innere Mensch: Die Paulinische Verarbeitung eines Platonischen Motivs* (WUNT 2:53; Tübingen: Mohr Siebeck, 1993); idem, "Body and Soul in Saint Paul," in *Psyche and Soma: Physicians and Meta-physicians on the Mind-Body Problem from Antiquity to Enlightenment* (ed. John P. Wright and Paul Potter; Oxford: Clarendon, 2000), 117–31.

[22] Warne, *Hebrew Perspectives*, 252.

[23] Horst Dietrich Preuss, *Old Testament Theology* (2 vols.; OTL; Louisville: Westminster John Knox, 1992), 2:110.

[24] More fully, see Preuss, *OT Theology*, 2:109–208.

Earlier, Brevard Childs had reminded his readers that, even if the OT views humanity from different wholistic perspectives, the human creature "does not *have* a soul, but *is* a soul" – that is, the human is "a complete entity and not a composite of parts from body, soul and spirit."[25] Moreover, humanity is set within a relational nexus – with God, whose own activity in drawing humanity to himself constitutes the basis of human openness to God; and with other humans, with relationships determined by righteousness. The OT, too, recognizes sin as disruption, alienation, and falsehood among humans and in relation to God. On such points as these, Childs finds basic coherence between the Old and New Testament witnesses to the nature of humanity.[26]

Walter Brueggemann observes that to speak of humanity in the divine image is to speak especially of the human person in relation to God. Indeed, in his description of "The Human Person as Yahweh's Partner," he stakes his claim on a relational, dynamic notion of personhood, eschewing any interest in an essentialist definition of the human creature. As such, the human person is utterly dependent on Yahweh for life, experiences human vitality only in relation to God, is a "living being" that precludes any notion of dualism, and is human only in relation to the human community.[27]

In addition to Gundry's work, and more influential than Gundry in subsequent discussion, a key voice in support of an anthropological dualism in the Bible has come from the philosophical theologian John Cooper. The concerns of his book, *Body, Soul and Life Everlasting*, are, as the title suggests, primarily eschatological. More particularly, he argues that the Bible teaches the existence of an intermediate state and that this intermediate state

[25] Brevard S. Childs, *Old Testament Theology in a Canonical Context* (Philadelphia: Fortress, 1985), 199.
[26] Brevard S. Childs, *Biblical Theology of the Old and New Testaments: Theological Reflection on the Christian Bible* (Minneapolis: Fortress, 1992), 566–94. To be sure, he finds points of tension as well, though not on matters pertaining to the issues I have noted. He admits that NT language occasionally adopts a more Hellenized idiom reflecting "a dualistic flavour" (579).
[27] Walter Brueggemann, *Theology of the Old Testament: Testimony, Dispute, Advocacy* (Minneapolis: Fortress, 1997), 450–54.

requires an ontologically distinct soul that guarantees personal existence between death and resurrection. As he summarizes in the preface to the book's second edition, "The Old Testament notion of ghostly survival in Sheol, eventually augmented with an affirmation of bodily resurrection, is developed by the Holy Spirit into the New Testament revelation of fellowship with Christ between each believer's death and the general resurrection at Christ's return."[28] Cooper articulates his position in terms of a wholistic dualism: though composed of discrete elements, the human person is nonetheless to be identified with the whole, constituting a functional unity. The significance of Cooper's work can be measured by the fact that, not only philosophers like himself,[29] but biblical scholars as well have employed it as a foundation for maintaining a dualistic anthropology of the Bible.[30] Although his perspective on the biblical data seems not to have changed, in his characterization of the human person Cooper more recently has moved away from the language of wholistic dualism in favor of terminology that makes "unity" the more basic term, in support of his developing view that the soul is neither a substance nor an entity.[31]

By way of drawing this survey of the lay of the land in biblical anthropology to a close, let me turn finally to three recent studies that expand somewhat the range of issues under consideration. Adriana Destro and Mauro Pesce have examined issues of "self"

[28] John W. Cooper, *Body, Soul, and Life Everlasting: Biblical Anthropology and the Monism-Dualism Debate* (2nd ed.; Grand Rapids, MI: Eerdmans, 2000), xv.
[29] E.g., William Hasker, *The Emergent Self* (Ithaca: Cornell University Press, 1999).
[30] E.g., Philip F. Esler, *New Testament Theology: Communion and Community* (Minneapolis: Fortress, 2005), 241; Philip S. Johnston, "Humanity," in *NDBT*, 564–65 (565); J. Knox Chamblin, "Psychology," in *DPL*, 765–75 (766–67). See also the combined effort of James Porter Moreland (philosopher) and Scott B. Rae (biblical scholar and ethicist): *Body and Soul: Human Nature and the Crisis in Ethics* (Downers Grove, IL: InterVarsity, 2000), 17–47.
[31] John W. Cooper, "Response to *In Search of the Soul*: 'I Don't Think It's Lost'" (paper presented at the annual meeting of the Society of Christian Philosophers, Philadelphia, 20 November 2005).

and "identity" in John's Gospel and the Pauline letters, emphasizing especially the spatial categories each theologian deploys – in the case of Paul, "inner" and "outer"; in the case of John, "above" and "below."[32] The struggle between these opposing parts constructs a dualism of sorts, but a dialectic rather than an ontological division. To substitute chronological for spatial images, the center of this dialectic is the embodied metamorphosis of the old person into the new, a transformation instigated in "new birth" (John) or "new creation" (Paul) by the work of the Holy Spirit. Destro and Pesce introduce into their analysis a potentially helpful ambiguity when they speak of "the non-bodily parts" of the human, and when they claim that "the Spirit is in contact not only with the mind, but transforms the body, taking over the entire man."[33] They deny that Paul works with "a radical dualism,"[34] but leave open the possibility of other anthropological models; at the very least, they remind us that, for these two early Christian theologians, human capacities cannot be reductively explained by recourse to human physicality. What is more, Destro and Pesce surface issues of personal "identity" by urging that these two NT voices articulate the formation of "self" as a journey from previous self-identity to a new identity arising from the work of the Spirit.

Robert Di Vito has performed an invaluable service by situating OT anthropology, and specifically the construction of personal identity, in relation to contemporary perspectives in the West, the latter most notably sketched by the philosopher Charles Taylor.[35]

[32] Adriana Destro and Mauro Pesce, "Self, Identity, and Body in Paul and John," in *Self, Soul and Body in Religious Experience* (ed. Albert I. Baumgarten, J. Assmann, and G.G. Stroumsa; SHR 78; Leiden: Brill, 1998), 184–97.
[33] Destro and Pesce, "Self, Identity, and Body," 193, 196.
[34] Destro and Pesce, "Self, Identity, and Body," 189 n. 24.
[35] Robert A. Di Vito, "Old Testament Anthropology and the Construction of Personal Identity," *CBQ* 61 (1999): 217–38; see also his essay, "Here One Need Not Be One's Self: The Concept of 'Self' in the Old Testament," in *The Whole and Divided Self: The Bible and Theological Anthropology* (ed. David E. Aune and John McCarthy; New York: Crossroad, 1997), 49–88. For Charles Taylor's construction of the modern self, see his *Sources of the Self: The Making of the Modern Identity* (Cambridge, MA: Harvard University Press, 1989).

Refusing the kind of extreme polarity between "modern" and
"ancient" views of the human person one finds in some attempts to
employ insights from cultural anthropology in biblical studies,[36] Di
Vito nonetheless documents clear points of tension. From Taylor,
he summarizes the modern sense of the human in terms of the location of dignity in self-sufficiency and self-containment, sharply
defined personal boundaries, the highly developed idea of my
"inner person," and the conviction that my full personhood rests
on my exercise of autonomous and self-legislative action. Di Vito
finds in the OT a very different portrait, one in which the person

> 1) is deeply embedded, or engaged, in his or her social identity, 2) is
> comparatively decentered and undefined with respect to personal
> boundaries, 3) is relatively transparent, socialized, and embodied (in
> other words, is altogether lacking in a sense of "inner depths"), and
> 4) is "authentic" precisely in his or her heteronomy, in his or her obedi-
> ence to another and dependence upon another.[37]

One of the benefits of Di Vito's work is its movement beyond the
question of "the essence of the human person" to consideration of
a wider range of issues in the study of human identity. Of course,
one may still inquire, what portrait of the human person (unity,
duality, etc.) best supports this way of conceiving of personal
identity?

Finally, returning again to a more narrow interest in the NT,
Klaus Berger has written an engaging and wide-ranging "biblical
psychology," including discussion of several motifs relevant to our
interests: personal identity, the nature of embodied existence, and
the notion of an "inner" and "outer" person.[38] Of special interest is
Berger's dexterity in drawing out the implications, whether theological or psycho-social, of his observations. Thus, for example,
having asserted that NT texts "know nothing of a bifurcation of

---

[36] E.g., Bruce J. Malina, *The New Testament World: Insights from Cultural
Anthropology* (rev. ed.; Louisville: Westminster John Knox, 1993), 63–89.
[37] Di Vito, "OT Anthropology," 221.
[38] Klaus Berger, *Identity and Experience in the New Testament* (Minneapolis: Fortress, 2003).

the human being into separate categories called 'body' and 'soul,'"[39] he goes on to suggest how many of the contemporary questions we pose have no traffic in the world of the NT. In that world, elements of such polarities as visible and invisible, knowledge and behavior, and faith and works resist unambiguous differentiation, with the one merging into the other. Moreover, if the self is experienced as outer-directed, in terms of one's community, then relationality, freedom, status, suffering, marginality, and even clothing, are cast in a different light. Berger's historical psychology urges reconsideration of all sorts of taken-for-granted categories, including, for example, Gundry's emphasis on physicality. In this case, it is not that Berger wants to deny the flesh and bones of human corporeality, but that this emphasis on body-as-physicality undermines what is for Berger the more basic category of embodied relationality endemic to a theological anthropology of the *sōma*.

Perusing the literature on biblical anthropology, one might be forgiven for imagining that at least one aspect of the discussion on the nature of the human person had been resolved by the turn of the twenty-first century. This is the question whether the human creature is a singular whole, a bio-psycho-spiritual unity, as opposed to either a dichotomous (body-soul) or trichotomous (body-soul-spirit) being. However, even if a threefold division of the human person attracts few champions today,[40] dualism, in its many forms, continues to enjoy widespread popularity. Undoubtedly, this is due in part to the elevated importance of dualism in the theological tradition. So much of Christian anthropology is anchored to a dualist narrative that any other rendering of the human person might seem to shake one of the main pillars of

---

[39] Berger, *Identity and Experience*, 6.

[40] Outside of scholarly discussion, a trichotomous view is more prevalent. In some popular Christian circles, esp. among charismatics, the influence of Watchman Nee has been enormous; see esp. his *The Spiritual Man* (3 vols.; New York: Christian Fellowship, 1968). Among more recent writers, see, e.g., John C. Garrison, *The Psychology of the Spirit: A Contemporary System of Biblical Psychology* (Philadelphia, PA: Xlibris, 2001).

Christian faith itself. It is not for nothing that Francis Crick entitles
the last chapter of his book, *The Astonishing Hypothesis*: "Dr.
Crick's Sunday Morning Service." Having dispensed with the soul
on scientific grounds, Crick goes on to dispense with the worship
of God, substituting in its place a celebration of neurons and the
promise that scientific certainty will rid us of the errors of revealed
religion.[41] And, in fairness to Crick, I doubt that the Sunday morning sermon announcing, "Sorry, but your soul just died" (to borrow the title of novelist Tom Wolfe's lamentation of "the
neuroscientific way of life"),[42] is likely to be heard as "good news."

   What is clear, though, is the pivotal importance allocated by students of biblical anthropology to the witness of the Old and New
Testaments to the *embodied* existence of humans. A second common motif is the understanding of the human person always in
relation to God – a perspective that, since Bultmann, has transformed so as to emphasize relationality within the human community as well. Interestingly, this heightened emphasis on
embodiedness and relationality has not led the discussion far in the
direction of the human relatedness to the cosmos, though this
seems to be an inescapable ramification.[43] Where the status of the
human creature vis-à-vis the non-human creation has thus far
entered the conversation is in relation to debate around the "image
of God" in which humanity is created (see below, ch. 2).

   A third concern that has surfaced is the issue of method – that is,
how best to approach a biblical anthropology. Earlier studies were
more dependent on word studies, later studies less so. This shift is
due in part to the inconclusive nature of the lexical evidence, itself a
demonstration that the Old and New Testaments develop no technical vocabulary to denote human essences, but also to heightened

---

[41] Francis H. Crick, *The Astonishing Hypothesis: The Scientific Search for
the Soul* (New York: Simon & Schuster, 1994), 255–63.
[42] Tom Wolfe, "Sorry, but Your Soul Just Died," in *Hooking Up* (New York:
Farrar, Strauss & Giroux, 2000), 89–109.
[43] See Michael A. Rynkiewich, "What about the Dust? Missiological Musings on Anthropology," in *What about the Soul? Neuroscience and Christian
Anthropology* (ed. Joel B. Green; Nashville: Abingdon, 2004), 133–44.

sophistication in the study of language among biblical scholars portended by James Barr's 1961 shot across the bow of the traditional "word study."[44]

This problem of language is related to the further obstacle that the Bible knows nothing of a speculative or a philosophical interest in definitions of the human person. This means that scholars may struggle with finding the appropriate vocabulary for representing the anthropology of the biblical material. Theologian Ted Peters has complained that, "when philosophers of religion get their intellectual fingers wrapped around an issue such as the human soul, they squeeze out more distinctions than Minute Maid can squeeze out orange juice."[45] The nuance we find in the biblical materials is far less discriminating – hence, the struggle to represent well the character of the evidence.

Apart from this interest in the "essence(s)" of the human person, other issues have begun to surface, primarily in the service of attempts to hear the voices of biblical texts on their own terms and for their potential challenge to contemporary constructions of the human person and the family of humanity. The character of sin (including the theological problem of "original sin"), the nature of human freedom and responsibility, what constitutes personal identity – these and a host of related issues invite renewed attention. Why these interests? First, theologically, I am interested in the potential of a disorientation or destabilization funded by the juxtaposition of alien perspectives with familiar ones, those promoted by Scripture with those taken for granted today, on such staples as freedom, salvation, Christian formation, and the character of the church and its mission. Given the human propensity to find in the biblical materials a mirror for already-held views, including the

---

[44] James Barr, *The Semantics of Biblical Language* (Oxford: Oxford University Press, 1961). Unfortunately, the confusion between *words* and *concepts* continues in more popular circles, where use of the term "soul" in a biblical text (e.g., Mary's words, "My soul magnifies the Lord, and my spirit rejoices in God my Savior" [Lk. 1:46–47]) is taken as proof of dualism (or, in this case, perhaps even a trichotomous anthropology).
[45] Ted Peters, "The Soul of Trans-Humanism," *Dialog* 44 (2005): 381–95 (389–90).

16 BODY, SOUL, AND HUMAN LIFE

contours of theological anthropology, might there yet be probing perspectives and nuance to which we may tune our ears? Second, I am concerned to take seriously the scientific underpinnings of all assessments of the human person – whether those of the biblical writers, those of the tradition of interpretation of the biblical materials, or those of contemporary readers of these materials, including our own. What is the effect of studying biblical anthropology in today's context of scientific inquiry?

Traditional Theological Anthropology and Contemporary Challenges

My interest in biblical anthropology is not a speculative exercise, but grows out of interaction with perspectives on the human person in biology and philosophy. In particular, the emerging discipline of "neurophilosophy"[46] – that is, study at the interface of the neurosciences and more traditional concerns of the philosophy of mind – has surfaced questions of genuine interest to persons who turn to the Bible for religious insight and formation. Well-known in the annals of the relationship between scientific innovation and theology are the revolutionary proposals of Copernicus and Darwin. Today, some theologians have rightly seen that the encounter of long-held theological tenets regarding the human person with principled reflection on neuroscientific innovation is a major storm brewing on the horizon, one with the potential to be just as sweeping (if not more so) in its effects among theologians and within the church. As OT scholar Lawson Stone has rightly predicted, given traditional theological views about the human person

---

[46] For this neologism, see Patricia Smith Churchland, *Neurophilosophy: Toward a Unified Science of the Mind-Brain* (Cambridge, MA: The MIT Press, 1986); and the user-friendly sequel, *Brain-Wise: Studies in Neurophilosophy* (Cambridge: MA: The MIT Press, 2002). For a self-consciously Christian and theological foray into this discussion, see the various publications of Nancey Murphy, esp. now *Bodies and Souls, or Spirited Bodies?* (CIT; Cambridge: Cambridge University Press, 2006).

– for example, regarding body-soul dualism and the immortality of
the soul – ideas that have become the bread and butter of most
strands of neurophilosophy raise serious challenges against the
coherence of the Christian vision of human life.[47]
   Neuroscientists and philosophers conclude similarly. "Bit by
experimental bit," writes Patricia Smith Churchland, "neuroscience is morphing our conception of what we are."[48] Introducing
recent work on the origins and nature of human consciousness,
Thomas Metzinger observes, "There is a new image of man emerging, an image that will dramatically contradict almost all traditional images man has made of himself in the course of his cultural
history." This new image "will be strictly incompatible with the
Christian image of man, as well as with many metaphysical conceptions developed in non-Western religions." Genetics, evolutionary psychology, computational neuroscience – these and other
fields of inquiry are generating "a radically new understanding of
what it *means* to be human," he writes, before going on to index
some of our previously secure beliefs that now teeter on the brink
of obsolescence: free will, for example, or the locus of one's "self"
in an ontologically distinct "soul."[49] Francis Crick, who shared the
1962 Nobel Prize for Physiology or Medicine for discoveries concerning DNA and its significance for information transfer in living
matter, thought that developments in the neurosciences challenged
many widely held views of the human person. This led him to claim
that "the idea that man has a disembodied soul is as unnecessary as
the old idea that there was a Life Force. This is in head-on contra-
diction to the religious beliefs of billions of human beings alive

---

[47] Lawson G. Stone, "The Soul: Possession, Part, or Person? The Genesis of
Human Nature in Genesis 2:7," in *What about the Soul? Neuroscience and
Christian Anthropology* (ed. Joel B. Green; Nashville: Abingdon, 2004), 47–
61 (48). Similarly, see John Taylor, "Humanity as a Species among the Species," in *The Dynamics of Human Life* (ed. Mark Elliott; Carlisle: Paternoster, 2001), 1–33 (2–5); stating that "the soul is under threat from scientific
advance," Taylor adds the corollary of diminished notions of human freedom and, thus, moral responsibility.
[48] Churchland, *Brain-Wise*, 1.
[49] Metzinger, "Consciousness Research," 6.

today." Crick wonders, "How will such a radical change be received?"[50]

Of course, theological reflection on the human person has not been sitting idly by. Jürgen Moltmann, for example, observes that, "from its earliest beginnings, the history of Western anthropology shows a tendency to make the soul paramount over the body, which is thus something from which the person can detach himself, something to be disciplined, and made the instrument of the soul." Indeed, he observes, "This tendency is an essential element in the history of freedom in the Western world."[51] Moltmann goes on to develop an alternative approach, emphasizing human embodiment within the biblical tradition, but he is well aware that, in doing so, he is swimming against the tide. For his part, Wolfhart Pannenberg has observed that advances with regard to the close mutual interrelations of physical and psychological occurrences have robbed of their credibility traditional ideas of a soul distinct from the body that is detached from it in death.[52] Nevertheless, Paul Jewett spoke for many when he insisted that the biblical witness to the essential unity and wholeness of the personal self does not counter a twofold view of human nature that distinguishes body and soul, with the soul an immaterial objective reality.[53]

Theologians ancient and contemporary have found in an anthropology of body-soul dualism either the necessary supposition or corollary of a number of theological loci, including creation in the divine image, a theology of free will and moral responsibility, hope of life-after-death, and Christian ethics. Even if they would debate the precise *origin* of the soul,[54] as early as the second century

---

[50] Crick, *Astonishing Hypothesis*, 261.
[51] Jürgen Moltmann, *God in Creation: A New Theology of Creation and the Spirit of God* (The Gifford Lectures 1984–85; San Francisco: Harper & Row, 1985), 244.
[52] Wolfhart Pannenberg, *Systematic Theology* (3 vols.; Grand Rapids, MI: Eerdmans, 1991–98), 2:181–202.
[53] Paul K. Jewett, *Who We Are: Our Dignity as Human: A Neo-Evangelical Theology* (with Marguerite Shuster; Grand Rapids, MI: Eerdmans, 1996), 36–46.
[54] Are souls created by God *ex nihilo* at the moment of their infusion into the body (Lactantius, Aquinas, Peter Lombard)? Are body and soul formed together (Tertullian, Luther)? Are souls pre-existent (Origen)?

of the Christian era it was nonetheless clear to most theologians, as the *Epistle to Diognetus* (§6) puts it, that "the soul lives in the body, but it does not belong to the body"; indeed, "the soul, which is invisible, is put under guard in the visible body" and "the soul is imprisoned in the body, but it sustains the body."[55] That these statements provide the basis for a parabolic description of the place of Christians in the world speaks to their status as widely held presupposition. "Without the soul, we are nothing," wrote Tertullian, adding, "there is not even the name of a human being – only that of a carcass" (*On the Flesh of Christ* 12). Summarizing in his *Treatise on the Soul*, Tertullian writes, "The soul, then, we define to be sprung from the breath of God, immortal, possessing body, having form, simple in its substance, intelligent in its own nature, developing its power in various ways, free in its determinations, subject to be changes of accident, in its faculties mutable, rational, supreme, endued with an instinct of presentiment, evolved out of one (archetypal soul)" (22). Lactantius observed early in the fourth century that the body, formed from the earth, is solid and mortal – "made up of a ponderous and corruptible element," "is tangible and visible, is corrupted and dies"; but the soul "received its origin from the Spirit of God, which is eternal" (*Divine Institutes* 12). He observes, "The body can do nothing without the soul. But the soul can do many and great things without the body" (*Divine Institutes* 11). Traditionally, the doctrine of humanity develops the uniqueness of humanity with respect to human creation in the divine image and the human possession of a soul. Often these two affirmations are reduced to one, with the soul understood as the particular expression of creation in God's image.

It is true that, for persons of faith – Christians included, but many others besides – the idea of a soul separable from the body

---

[55] ET in Bart D. Ehrman, ed., *The Apostolic Fathers* (2 vols.; LCL 24–25; Cambridge, MA: Harvard University Press, 2003), 2:143. Apart from the documents collected by Ehrman, translations of the church fathers are taken from Alexander Roberts et al., eds., *Ante-Nicene Fathers* (10 vols.; Buffalo, NY: Christian Literature, 1885–87; reprint ed., Peabody, MA: Hendrickson, 1994).

has contributed a great deal. A register of what is at stake in the current discussion is as impressive as it may be troubling. For example:

- Given contemporary experimentation and innovation in the area of Artificial Intelligence, can we imagine anything about humans that our mechanical creations will be unable to duplicate?[56]
- If, like sheep and pigs, humans can be cloned, will the resulting life form be a "person"?
- On what basis might we attribute sacred worth to human beings, so that we have what is necessary for discourse concerning morality and for ethical practices?[57]
- What view of the human person is capable of funding what we want to know about ourselves theologically – about sin, for example, as well as moral responsibility, repentance, and growth in grace?[58]
- Am I free to do what I want, or is my sense of decision-making a ruse?[59]
- How should we understand "salvation"? Does salvation entail a denial of the world and embodied life, focusing instead on my "inner person" and on the life to come? How ought the church to be extending itself in mission? Mission to what? The spiritual or soulish needs of persons? Society-at-large? The cosmos?[60]
- What happens when we die? What view(s) of the human person is consistent with Christian belief in life-after-death?[61]

---

[56] Cf., e.g., Michael Fuller, "A Typology for the Theological Reception of Scientific Innovation," *S&CB* 12 (2000): 115–25; Paul Mullin, "Can the Image of God Ever Be Artificial?" *Research News and Opportunities in Science and Theology* 3, no. 6 (2003): 7, 27; Noreen L. Herzfeld, *In Our Image: Artificial Intelligence and the Human Spirit* (TSc; Minneapolis: Fortress, 2002).

[57] Cf., e.g., Kevin J. Corcoran, *Rethinking Human Nature: A Christian Materialistic Alternative to the Soul* (Grand Rapids, MI: Baker Academic, 2006), 83–117; Moreland and Rae, *Body and Soul*.

[58] See below, chs. 3–4.

[59] See below, ch. 3.

[60] See below, ch. 4

[61] See below, ch. 5.

Juxtaposed with study of the portrait of humanity in the biblical materials in the past 70 years, this list of contemporary questions suggests the degree to which biblical studies and the natural sciences have inhabited different worlds. This is unfortunate, since assumptions about the natural sciences are inescapable for students of the Bible, irrespective of whether those assumptions are acknowledged.

Why Science Matters

As I will document in successive chapters, the neurosciences impinge on many of the classical loci of theological anthropology and, at the least, provide a context within which to struggle with biblical-theological claims regarding the human person. Some may be slow to allow these two claims, dismissing the idea that neuroscience might have a seat at the table of theological method. For example, when, as neurobiology and evolutionary psychology increasingly urge, the attributes and capacities traditionally allocated to the human soul are conditioned in every detail by biological processes, on what basis can belief in a soul be maintained? Some might simply exclaim, So much the worse for science! If science and Christian belief stand at odds on the question of the existence of the soul, then Christian belief must trump science. Presumably, the same response would be forthcoming on other issues too – for example, regarding human freedom and responsibility. But this way of thinking begs an important question – namely, whether science ought to be excluded as a source for Christian theology.

Some may grant the former claim but not the latter, presuming that systematic theologians and ethicists might take notice of neuroscientific discovery, but exegetes have no business allowing twenty-first-century data on fMRI's, dendritic plasticity, and Alien Hand Syndrome to inform our interpretive work. The most simple reply is that science *already* informs exegesis; it is only a question of which science or whose, good science or bad.

At the same time, in terms of a biblical anthropology, it is important to recall that the questions I have identified have for the most part not come as alien intrusions into the discipline of biblical studies. The neurosciences may underscore their importance, but the basic questions are already familiar in biblical scholarship. In fact, as we have seen, in the discipline of biblical studies, impulses toward a reconstruction of our understanding of human nature – away from notions of body-soul dualism, toward some form of monism – cannot be tied to the influence of or familiarity with neurological or psychological explorations. Rather, a constellation of issues and concerns has coalesced in biblical studies over the last century with the result that theories of body-soul dualism are today difficult to ground in the Bible.

Should neuroscience have a voice in theological method? In a biblical hermeneutic? In the last century, Karl Barth's voice was prominent in these matters. For Barth, natural science had little relevance for theology, for science comprises a competing ideology. Since faith comes by means of divine encounter, Barth spoke against the possibility of discovering, discerning, or encountering God through natural science. The revelation of God is not available through natural mediation. Although creation makes possible the covenantal relationship between God and humanity, the chasm between Creator and creation disallows humans from making valid judgments about what we may know concerning the Creator on the basis of creation. For Barth, theology and the natural sciences comprise non-interactive disciplines, with each having its own respective magistrate.[62]

In the history of the interaction of faith and science, however, Barth's is a minority position.[63] Indeed, in concert with the rise of the

---

[62] See Karl Barth, *Church Dogmatics*, vol. 3: *The Doctrine of Creation*, part one (Edinburgh: T&T Clark, 1958).

[63] See, e.g., Denis Alexander, *Rebuilding the Matrix: Science and Faith in the 21st Century* (Grand Rapids, MI: Zondervan, 2003); also Edward Grant, *Science and Religion, 400 BC to AD 1550: From Aristotle to Copernicus* (Baltimore: Johns Hopkins University Press, 2004); Richard G. Olson, *Science and Religion, 1450–1900: From Copernicus to Darwin* (Baltimore: Johns Hopkins University Press, 2004).

New Science in the 1600s, the concept of "two books" became a regular fixture in seventeenth-century English natural theology. Science was nothing more than investigation into God's creation. True, the materialist focus of New Science could marginalize the need for God, but, it was insisted, this was neither a necessary consequence of scientific investigation nor an appropriate use of science. First published in 1642, Thomas Browne's *Religio medici* insisted that the physician was not doomed to atheism, for the physician's work leads to God; Scripture and the natural world formed a dual pathway to God.[64] Similarly, Richard Cumberland's *De legibus naturae* argued that mechanistic physics need not devolve into unorthodoxy in ethical theory nor into atheism; when atheism was the result, not science but impiety was to blame.[65] Perhaps most famous was Robert Boyle's *A Free Inquiry into the Vulgarly Received Notion of Nature,* which opposed the materialist infidels and insisted that the new, mechanistic science was religion's invincible ally.[66] Thomas Willis, who coined the term "neurology," was a key figure in setting the study of the brain and nervous system on its present course. In his preface to *The Anatomy of the Brain* (1681), Willis likened his dissection table to "the most holy Altar of Your Grace" – Gilbert Sheldon, Archbishop of Canterbury – and referred to his work as an examination of "the Pandects of Nature, as into another Table of the Divine Word, and the greater Bible: For indeed, in either Volume there is no high point, which requires not the care, or refuses the industry of an Interpreter; there is no Page certainly which shews not the Author, and his Power, Goodness, Trust, and Wisdom."[67]

---

[64] Andrew Cunningham, "Sir Thomas Browne and his *Religio Medici*: Reason, Nature and Religion," in *Religio Medici: Medicine and Religion in Seventeenth-Century England* (ed. Ole Peter Grell and Andrew Cunningham; Aldershot: Scolar, 1996), 12–61.

[65] Jon Parkin, *Science, Religion and Politics in Restoration England: Richard Cumberland's De legibus naturae* (SH ns; Woodbridge: Boydell, 1999).

[66] Robert Boyle, *A Free Inquiry into the Vulgarly Received Notion of Nature* (ed. Edward B. Davis and Michael Hunter; CTHP; Cambridge: Cambridge University Press, 1996 [1686]).

[67] Thomas Willis, *The Anatomy of the Brain and Nerves* (trans. Samuel Pordage; ed. William Feindel; CML; Birmingham: McGill-Queens University Press, 1978 [1681]), 51–52.

More recently, Alister McGrath has insisted that the Christian
doctrine of creation demands a unitary approach to knowledge. If
God made the world, then it is only to be expected that something
of God's character would be disclosed in creation. Consequently,
for McGrath, there are two modes of knowing God – the natural
order and Scripture – with the second clearer and fuller than the
first.[68] As Augustine had written centuries earlier, "Some people
read books in order to find God. But the very appearance of God's
creation is a great book." He advised, "Ponder heaven and earth
religiously."[69]

Theologically, science must be taken seriously, first, on account
of our doctrine of creation. This means that, for the Christian,
inquiry starts not from "science," but from the Christian tradition
in its understanding of nature in its creatureliness. Of course, until
the modern era, discussion of science-theology relations was
almost unnecessary, since science, philosophy, and religion comprised the same vocation, proceeded from the same intellectual
impulses, and focused on the same subject matter. In fact, Galen
(129–199/216 CE), the celebrated medic whose writings were to
dominate medicine for almost 1400 years, entitled one of his
books, *That the Best Physician Is also a Philosopher.* On account
of the Christian doctrine of creation, theology is an all-
encompassing enterprise, so that the subsequent segregation of
science from theology could not mean that science would fall outside the purview of theology. Moreover, in so far as science is present as one of the sources for the theological enterprise, theology
remains open to the possibility of reformulation in relation to scientific discovery.

Epistemologically, we cannot bypass the reality that, whether
acknowledged or not, natural science is and has always been part

[68] Alister E. McGrath, *A Scientific Theology,* vol. 1: *Nature* (Grand Rapids,
MI: Eerdmans, 2001). Cf. R.J. Berry, *God's Book of Works: The Nature and
Theology of Nature* (Glasgow Gifford Lectures; London: T&T Clark, 2003).
[69] Augustine, *Sermo Mai* 126; ET in Karlfried Froehlich, "'Take up and
Read': Basics of Augustine's Biblical Interpretation," *Int* 58 (2004): 5–16
(12).

of our worldview – recognizing, of course, that "natural science" takes forms and follows protocols today that in many of its particulars would hardly be recognizable to Babylonian, Egyptian, or Greek scientists and natural philosophers. The question is not whether science will influence exegesis (or vice versa) since the two, science and religion, have interacted and continue to interact in a far more organic way than is typically acknowledged. As a consequence, from a historical perspective, it is virtually impossible to extricate the one influence from the other, or chronologically to prioritize one vis-à-vis the other. This is true in regard to the science presumed of the biblical writers. It is also true of the science presumed of biblical interpreters and theologians from the second century onward. We have before us a long history of interpreters of biblical texts who have engaged those texts on the basis of scientific views of the human person pervasive in the worlds of those interpreters (irrespective of their currency in antiquity or today).

A case is easily made, for example, that the New Science that emerged in the 1600s, characterized by a materialist focus that continues to this day, was a byproduct of innovations in biblical hermeneutics. Peter Harrison has argued that the sort of biblical interpretation championed by the Protestant Reformers, with its focus on "literal interpretation," opened up the possibility for new ways of viewing the order of nature.[70] According to the medieval encyclopedia, the universe was "nothing other than an emanative outpouring from the unknowable and unnameable One down to the furthest ramifications of matter," with every being functioning as "a synecdoche or metonymy of the One."[71] If the entire sensible world is a book written by the hand of God, then all of nature serves metaphorically to reveal the Divine Author. Exegesis of the cosmos, then, proceeded along the lines of exegesis of the Bible, in accordance with the traditional theory of the four levels of interpretation: the literal, the allegorical, the moral, and the analogical.

---

[70] Peter Harrison, *The Bible, Protestantism, and the Rise of Natural Science* (Cambridge: Cambridge University Press, 1998).
[71] Umberto Eco, *Semiotics and the Philosophy of Language* (AS; Bloomington: University of Indiana Press, 1984), 103.

When Protestant interpretation countered this fourfold method of exegesis, in favor of the *sensus litteralis*, it followed only naturally that nature, too, would be examined along different lines. "Literalism means that only words refer; the things of nature do not. In this way the study of the natural world was liberated from the specifically religious concern of biblical interpretation, and the sphere of nature was opened up to new ordering principles."[72] In effect, Harrison insists, it is not that the New Science urged new interpretations of the Bible, but that new emphases in hermeneutics, worked out with reference to Holy Scripture, pressed for fresh conceptualizations of the world. Even if Harrison has too easily cast Protestant interpretation into a single mold and exaggerated the innovations of Protestant exegetes vis-à-vis their Catholic counterparts,[73] his study further underscores the significant degree to which biblical interpretation and science have interacted in ways that are mutually forming and informing.

On the other hand, it is worth inquiring whether a substantive view of the soul in Christian thought is a consequence of unadulterated exegesis (i.e., read out of the text) or a philosophical-scientific assumption read into the text (i.e., eisegesis). Representing Pharisaic views, for example, Josephus catered to the Greco-Roman intelligentsia, formulating a body-soul dualism quite at odds with Israel's Scriptures but very much at home in the Platonic tradition. The question remains to what degree Josephus has accurately represented, or exaggerated, Pharisaism on this point. And it almost goes without saying that OT views of the human person, death, and the afterlife underwent metamorphosis in some Second Temple Jewish literature under the influence of Greek and later Roman science/philosophy.

In any case, the path blazed by Josephus was taken by early Christian theologians as well, who articulated the faith in culturally relevant terms – so much so that this articulation would

---

[72] Harrison, *Bible*, 4.
[73] See Kenneth J. Howell, *God's Two Books: Copernican Cosmology and Biblical Interpretation in Early Modern Science* (Notre Dame, IN: University of Notre Dame Press, 2002).

eventually seem to be the core of biblical anthropology itself. Indeed, with the rise of "neurology," the human soul (or, as Thomas Willis labeled it, the "Rational Soul") was a given, the existence of which was unassailable; it stood outside the realm of inquiry and yet was left without any real purpose. That is, in the work of Willis, "soul" was delimited in ways that left the doctrine singularly undeveloped: What role any longer justifies its existence in a conception of the human person? If the capacities constitutive of the human being traditionally allocated to the immaterial soul are identified with neuronal processes, then the need underlying the attribution of an immaterial soul to the human being vanishes. In this case, one might conclude that what makes us singularly human is the complexity of our brain – or, better, the properties and capacities that have this complex brain as their anatomical basis.[74] If human identity is grounded in consistency of memory; if the differentiating marks of the human person are the development of consciousness, individuality within community, self-consciousness, the capacity to make decisions on the basis of self-deliberation, planning and action on the basis of that decision, and taking responsibility for these decisions and actions;[75] and if these have a neural substrate, then the concept of "soul," as traditionally understood in theology as a person's "authentic self," seems redundant. That is, the "Rational Soul" seems to have been relegated to the status of an epiphenomenon, not involved causally in bringing about the actions attributed to it and so without real explanatory force. It would be too much to say that Willis is responsible for all of this. However, given his emerging view that psychological processes are dependent on neural activity – and, more specifically, his location of thought, volition, perception, affect, imagination, and memory in the various structures of the brain – it is easy to see that Willis' work set neurobiology firmly on

---

[74] See Silvia Helena Cordoso and Renato M.E. Sabbatini, "What Makes Us Singularly Humans?" *Brain & Mind* (2000) {http://www.epub.org.br/cm/n10/editorial-n10_i.htm}; accessed 21 January 2002.

[75] See Philip Hefner, *The Human Factor: Evolution, Culture, and Religion* (TSc; Minneapolis: Fortress, 1993), 118–19.

this path. This is true in spite of the facts that Willis himself deflected such metaphysical concerns and that, on so many points in his discussions of cerebral localization, Willis' thoughts were often more speculative than data-based and, as it turned out, simply wrong.[76]

To put the question sharply: If the "truth" about the human person were decisively determined by Scripture, what would happen were contravening evidence to surface from extrabiblical inquiry, particularly from scientific observation? Twenty-first-century hermeneuts will recognize the naiveté of the question itself, since "what the Scriptures teach" about the human person is always found in dialectical relationship to the presumptions brought by the interpreter to the enterprise of interpreting those texts. The better question is, then: Will we allow a particular scientific rendering of the voice of Scripture to masquerade as "timeless truth"?

Hermeneutically, then, my point is that deliberately locating our interpretive work in relation to science does not necessitate our reading contemporary science back into the ancient text in a gross form of anachronism, nor that it subject biblical interpretation to the ebb and flow of scientific discovery. We have no need to imagine that the ancients, even the biblical writers, had it right with respect to the role of cerebral spinal fluid or the ventricular cavities. (They were wrong on both accounts.) Rather, doing exegesis in an age of science increases our awareness of the scientific assumptions of the third or fourth or even eighteenth centuries that have already shaped the history of interpretation – and that have the potential to set artificially the parameters for our own reading of biblical texts. As in other forms of "interested" interpretation (whether those interests are defined socially, theologically, racially, economically, or otherwise), situating our exegetical work in relation to the neurosciences has the potential to liberate us from certain predilections that might guide our work unawares and to

---

[76] See Joel B. Green, "Science, Religion, and the Mind-Brain Problem: The Case of Thomas Willis (1621–1675)," *S&CB* 15 (2003): 165–85; more extensively, Carl Zimmer, *Soul Made Flesh: The Discovery of the Brain – and How It Changed the World* (New York: Free Press, 2004).

allow questions to surface that might otherwise have remained buried. Reading biblical texts through this prism, what do we find in these texts that would otherwise have remained veiled?

Some Definitions

To many Christians, the range of possible ways of giving an account of the human person may be surprising, and the assumptions and vocabulary that characterize the discussion can be bewildering, if not overwhelming. This would come as a surprise to mid-twentieth-century readers of one of the early histories of neurology, in which Walther Riese confidently asserted that the human soul, a stranger to the anatomical structures of the cerebrum, had been eliminated in the 1800s by philosophers, naturalists, and physicians.[77] More recently, biologist Richard Dawkins confidently pronounced over the demise of the idea of a human soul, "Good riddance."[78] Nevertheless, standard textbooks on the philosophy of mind continue to discuss a range of options for articulating the nature of the relationship between mind and brain, just as neurobiologists admit to the persistence of an "explanatory gap" regarding how the physical correlates of a phenomenal state are related to our subjective feelings of that state.[79]

Unrest around these issues, especially among philosophers, has yielded a plethora of options, including, for example, substance dualism, wholistic dualism, emergent dualism, naturalistic dualism, emergent monism, two-aspect monism, dipolar monism, reflexive monism, constitutional materialism, deep physicalism,

---

[77] Walther Riese, *A History of Neurology* (New York: MD Publications, 1959), 19–48.

[78] Richard Dawkins and Steven Pinker, "Is Science Killing the Soul?" *The Guardian-Dillons Debate*, chaired by Tim Radford, London, 10 February 1999 (*Edge* 53 [8 April 1999] {http://www.edge.org/documents/archive/edge53.html}; accessed 2 January 2004.

[79] Cf. Joseph Levine, "Materialism and Qualia: The Explanatory Gap," *PPQ* 64 (1983): 354–61; Susan Greenfield, "Soul, Brain and Mind," in *From Soul to Self* (ed. M. James C. Crabbe; London: Routledge, 1999), 108–25.

nonreductive physicalism, and eliminative materialism. With this renaissance in philosophical attention the debate has come full circle, since, in Western thought, its beginnings can be traced to the dualism of Plato (*ca.* 429–347 BCE), the monism of Aristotle (384–322 BCE), and the range of metaphysical permutations aligned along this continuum.[80] Even as early as the late fifth century BCE, however, the most famous physician of classical antiquity, Hippocrates (and those treatises attributed to him), weighed in on the relation of σῶμα (*sōma*, "body") and ψυχή (*psychē*, "self," "soul," "personality"), and historically the terms of this debate have been correlated with anatomical and physiological factors, especially as these have been related to concerns of a religious sort. That is, the mind-body problem has long been the gathering point for wide-ranging perspectives – philosophy, theology, the natural sciences, and the psychological sciences being among the most prominent.

Some of the language defining the discussion can be off-putting to the non-initiated, so it may be helpful to provide brief linguistic and conceptual orientation. Arranged along a continuum, perspectives championed today can be characterized as more or less materialist, more or less dualist. On the extreme poles are two positions: (reductive or eliminative) materialism and radical dualism, both of which are difficult to square with Christian theological commitments. Dispersed between these two poles are other, generous categories within which the debate among Christians tends to be localized.

Reductive Materialism has it that the human person is a physical (or material) organism, whose emotional, moral, and religious experiences will ultimately and decisively be explained by the natural sciences. People are nothing but the product of organic chemistry. As Francis Crick has famously remarked, "'you,' your joys and

---

[80] For historical perspective, see John P. Wright and Paul Potter, eds., *Psyche and Sōma: Physicians and Metaphysicians on the Mind-Body Problem from Antiquity to Enlightenment* (Oxford: Clarendon, 2000); Paul S. MacDonald, *History of the Concept of Mind: Speculations about Soul, Mind and Spirit from Homer to Hume* (Aldershot: Ashgate, 2003).

your sorrows, your memories and your ambitions, your sense of identity and free will, are in fact no more than the behavior of a vast assembly of nerve cells and their associated molecules."[81]

Radical Dualism advocates the view that the soul (or mind) is separable from the body, having no necessary relation to the body, with the human person identified with the soul. Apart from further qualification or explanation, in this view the soul acts apart from bodily processes and the body is nothing more than a temporary and disposable holding tank (or shell) for the soul.

Wholistic Dualism in its various renditions qualifies as a form of substance dualism, but posits that the human person, though composed of discrete elements, is nonetheless to be identified with the whole which, then, constitutes a functional unity. "The soul and the body are highly interactive, they enter into deep causal relations and functional dependencies with each other, the human person is a unity of both."[82]

Various forms of *monism* defended among Christians require no second, metaphysical entity, such as a soul or spirit, to account for human capacities and distinctives, while insisting that human behavior cannot be explained exhaustively with recourse to genetics or neuroscience. Using various models, the monists with whom I am concerned argue that the phenomenological experiences that we label "soul" are neither reducible to brain activity nor evidence of a substantial, ontological entity such as a "soul," but rather represent essential aspects or capacities of the self.[83]

---

[81] Crick, *Astonishing Hypothesis*, 3.

[82] James Porter Moreland, "Restoring the Substance to the Soul of Psychology," *JPsyT* 26 (1998): 29–43 (35). Among Christian writers who champion views in this category: Cooper, *Body, Soul, and Life Everlasting* (wholistic dualism); Hasker, *Emergent Self* (emergent dualism).

[83] Among Christian writers who champion views in this category: Philip Clayton, *Mind and Emergence: From Quantum to Consciousness* (Oxford: Oxford University Press, 2005) (emergent monism); Corcoran, *Rethinking Human Nature* (constitution); Murphy, *Bodies and Souls* (nonreductive physicalism); and Gregory R. Peterson, *Minding God: Theology and the Cognitive Sciences* (TSc; Minneapolis: Fortress, 2003); idem, "Minding Minding God: A Response to Spezio and Bielfeldt," *Zygon* 39 (2004): 605–14 (open-system emergence or deep physicalism).

Other terms will surface along the way, and will be defined at those points, usually in relation to these four major categories. This is enough, though, to lay the basic groundwork.

In Anticipation

An inductive approach to a biblical-theological anthropology would present its own wide-ranging agenda. This is the path often taken, whether by reference works or in the sort of project undertaken, for example, in Udo Schnelle's "New Testament Anthropology."[84] Without turning a blind eye to the usual register of anthropological issues that might occupy a biblical-theological study, the framework for this examination is somewhat different. I am particularly concerned about the perspectives on and challenges to either biblical interpretation more specifically or the Christian theological tradition more generally from reflection on modern advances in the neurosciences. If, as is often alleged, neuroscientists have discredited a dualist interpretation of the human person, I want to explore the usual corollary that, in doing so, they have also discredited biblical faith. It will become clear that I take the former claim to be true, the latter to be false. Accordingly, my selection of motifs is somewhat more focused.

Chapter 2 is concerned with what it means to be human in Scripture, focusing particular attention on the problem of "identity," the theological significance of the creation of humanity in the divine image, and, then, the importance of embodied relationality in biblical understandings of the human person. I will begin to demonstrate why I am confident that the history of interpretation in the twentieth century is essentially right in gravitating toward a monist interpretation of the human person – even if, in the end, the biblical materials urge that we resist some of the basic parameters of the discussion of portraits of the human as this is carried out by

---

[84] Udo Schnelle, *Neutestamentliche Anthropologie: Jesus, Paulus, Johannes* (BThS 18; Neukirchen-Vluyn: Neukirchener, 1991); translated as *Human Condition*.

neuroscientists and philosophers of the mind alike. My analysis will demonstrate that, at a number of key points, biblical studies and the neurosciences are paths characterized by convergence (in the sense that they reach similar conclusions, though coming at the issues in discrete ways), not competition or contrast.

Chapter 3 takes up potential neurobiological and neurophilosophical challenges to a range of traditional affirmations of sin, original sin, free will, and the nexus between volition and responsibility. For many, in this constellation of motifs we find the chief point of conflict between evolutionary biology and evolutionary psychology on the one hand, biblical faith on the other. Without denying the potential of ongoing tension among these disciplines on these issues, it is nevertheless the unfortunate case that much of the concern from the side of Christian theology is grounded in journalistic hyperbole concerning the scope of biological determinism. If ideas of determinism have been exaggerated, however, so also philosophical and, in some cases, theological perspectives on volition and responsibility have overstepped the biblical materials. My analysis will demonstrate that the neurosciences and biblical studies come at these issues from quite different perspectives but end up making a series of complementary affirmations regarding human formation and what theologians refer to as the human condition. I will also suggest that the Bible has little to say about some current expressions of free will, but what the Bible does have to say nonetheless leaves us with a notion of free will worthy of the name.

Chapter 4, in many ways, comprises the crux of an investigation of this kind, since the issues gathered here demonstrate the cash value of a cross-disciplinary conversation like the one I am promoting. How we understand salvation (and the soteriological journey of the "saved") and the heightened importance of a local community of believers – these are two of the central concerns of this study, and they have far-reaching ramifications for our construal of the mission of the church on behalf of God in the world.

It is here that contemporary philosophical discussion around portraits of the human person comes in for its most thoroughgoing critique. Given the strength of Cartesian categories and the experience of many since the Enlightenment, it is perhaps not surprising to see the degree to which humanity has come to be understood "one person at a time," so to speak. This is not biblical faith, however. Although biblical faith would naturally resist any suggestion that our humanity can be reduced to our physicality, it also challenges those, past and present, who insist that the human person can ever be understood on individual terms. If we would articulate an account of the human person that takes with utmost seriousness the biblical record, we would have far less conversation about the existence or importance of "souls" and far more about the embodied human capacity and vocation for community with God, with the human family, and in relation to the cosmos. These are profoundly ecclesiological, soteriological, and missiological concerns.

Chapter 5 allows me to take up those eschatological questions that have come often to dominate body-soul discussion. The two central problems are interrelated. Given the Christian belief in life-after-death, and given the manifest death and decay of the observable human body, how does the "person" cross the bridge from this life to the next; and how can we be sure that the "person" in the afterlife is in fact the same "person" who lived out his or her years in this life? Here I take up the argument put forward by John Cooper in his influential book, *Body, Soul, and Life Everlasting*, as well as other, related issues, in order to demonstrate why I find his rendering of the biblical evidence unconvincing. More importantly, my analysis will demonstrate how the Bible can portray the human person as a single whole or unified being (some form of monism); allow that death is really death, allowing no prisoners, whether people are parts of persons; and nonetheless affirm resurrection of the body and life-after-death. Though I make no promises that the biblical account I will narrate will be satisfying to contemporary philosophers, I will argue that the coherence of the biblical account of the human person as a unified whole extends to its eschatological vision.

2

WHAT DOES IT MEAN TO BE HUMAN?

[T]he soul clothes itself with a body as a man clothes himself with a garment. For the soul flows into the human mind, and through this into the body, bearing with it the life which it continually receives from the Lord, and transferring it thus indirectly into the body, where, by means of the closest union, it causes the body, as it were, to live. From this, and from a thousand testimonies of experience, it is evident that what is spiritual, united to what is material, as a living force with a dead force, causes a man to speak rationally and to act morally. (Emanuel Swedenborg)[1]

The more that breakthroughs like . . . brain-scanning open up the mind to scientific scrutiny, the more we may be pressed to give up comforting metaphysical ideas like interiority, subjectivity and the soul. Let's enjoy them while we can. (Jim Holt)[2]

---

[1] Emanuel Swedenborg, *The Interaction of the Soul and Body* (London: The Swedenborg Society, 2005 [1769]), 23.
[2] Jim Holt, "Of Two Minds," *The New York Times Magazine*, 8 May 2005, 11–13 (13).

So God created humankind in his image, in the image of God he
created them; male and female he created them. God blessed them,
and God said to them, "Be fruitful and multiply, and fill the earth
and subdue it; and have dominion over the fish of the sea and over
the birds of the air and over every living thing that moves upon the
earth." (Gen 1:27–28)

Over the past two decades, widespread and long-held beliefs
about the nature of the human person have come in for serious
questioning. Notions about what makes humans "human" – that
is, distinctive vis-à-vis non-human creatures – are under almost
continuous negotiation. The slowly accumulating evidence from
natural scientists is rewriting what and how we think about ourselves. And the ramifications of these studies increasingly find
themselves in feature articles in national news magazines, newspapers, and internet reports, from whence they are bound to spark an
increasingly public discussion about these issues.

For a long time and for many, it has been enough to identify the
human person with his or her soul. This marker of humanness
remains popular even in wider culture, though even here the
ground is shifting. In a classic collection of short stories entitled *I,
Robot* (1950), Isaac Asimov portrayed robots with traits that others might have reserved for humans. Robbie the robot, for example, wants to "hear a story," is "faithful and loving and kind," and
is even called "my friend . . . not no machine" by his young companion, Gloria. Gloria's mother, however, is adamant in her assessment: Robbie is "nothing more than a mess of steel and copper in
the form of sheets and wires with electricity." Because "it has no
soul," Robbie should never be confused with a human being.[3]
Almost forty years later, the best-selling novelist Dean Koontz
introduced a genetically engineered golden retriever, Einstein, in
Watchers, his first book (1987). In conversation with Nora,
regarded by the non-initiated as Einstein's owner, the dog com-
plains about the tattoo identification in his ear. It "marked him as

---

[3] Isaac Asimov, *I, Robot* (New York: Doubleday, 1950), 5, 9, 23.

mere property, a condition that was an affront to his dignity and a violation of his rights as an intelligent creature." Nora responds empathetically, "'I do understand. You are a . . . a *person*, and a person with' – this was the first time she had thought of this aspect of the situation – 'a soul.'" She continues, "If you've got a soul – and I know you do – then you were born with free will and the right to self-determination."[4] Apparently, how to draw the line between humans and other animals, humans and machines, or whether there are such lines to be drawn, is on the minds of folks around us.

My aim in this chapter is twofold. First, I want to summarize some evidence from the biological sciences and neuropsychology that, taken together, presses the question: What separates us from non-human creatures? My concern here is not to collapse these categories, human and non-human, but to show the seriousness of the challenge to some more general ways of parsing human distinctiveness. It will be obvious that the evidence I will summarize actually exemplifies the close connection between humans and non-humans as creatures that we might have expected from the Genesis narrative. Second, I want to turn more specifically to the biblical materials in order to reflect on the significance of the theological affirmation of the creation of humanity in the divine image. In this way, I want to stake out a way of talking about human identity and the human construction of the self, grounded not in an ontologically distinctive entity known as the "soul," but rather in our genetically enabled, embodied capacity for ongoing formation as storied, relational beings. I will develop this portrait further in subsequent chapters.

Work in biblical and theological studies, together with insight from the neurosciences, I will demonstrate, encourages a way forward marked by an account of the human person that rejects the necessity of a separate, metaphysical entity such as a soul to account for human capacities and distinctives; that underscores the material location of the human person in relation to the created order; that refuses to reduce personal identity to our neural

---

[4] Dean Koontz, *Watchers* (New York: Berkley, 1987), 434.

equipment, emphasizing instead the personal contribution and relatedness of human beings to the human family and the cosmos; and thus that has as its primary point of beginning and orientation the human in a partnering relationship with God.

Distinctively Human?

Among the range of possible evidences of the collapse of meaningful distinctions between humans and non-human creatures, let me mention three: genetic similarity; evidence I will collect under the loose heading of consciousness; and the more particular phenomenon known as "mind reading." I will discuss a fourth category, moral agency, in Chapter 3.

The human genome

In 2005, the American Association for the Advancement of Science published in its weekly journal, *Science,* a series of short essays entitled "125 Questions: What Don't We Know?" Appearing third in the list was the query, "Why do humans have so few genes?"[5] In actuality, the puzzle is not so much why humans have only about 25,000 genes, but why we anticipated we would have so many – upwards of 100,000, according to earlier conventional wisdom.[6] If common rice has some 50,000 genes and the worm *Caenorhabditis elegans* has about 20,000, must not the infinitely more complex *Homo sapiens* require a more expansive genome? The realization that mammalian genes are far more flexible than previously thought does not mask the impression that surprise over our limited number of genes rests significantly on the mistaken assumption that humans simply must be more complex, genetically unique, in comparison with non-human creatures.

---

[5] Elizabeth Pennisi, "Why Do Humans Have So Few Genes?" *Science* 39, no. 5731 (2005): 80.
[6] Nancey Murphy helpfully discusses historical reasons why the idea of continuity from non-human animals to humans has been an embarrassing problem (*Bodies and Souls,* 49–51).

In fact, chimpanzees share practically all of our DNA, in spite of relative, observable differences like language or tree-climbing abilities. Earlier reports identified the degree of DNA overlap upwards of 98 percent, though more recent analysis has lowered that number by two or three points. More astonishing, perhaps, is that the variation in DNA among members of the human family is actually larger than the variation between humans and chimpanzees.

Consciousness

In discussion of Christian anthropology generally, appeal is often made to a baseline human experience that I am more than my body – that is, to my experience of a subjective inner life, the perceptions, thoughts, feelings, and awareness of my experiences, including what it is like to be a cognitive agent. This subjective, first-hand quality of experience goes by the shorthand "consciousness,"[7] and, for most of us, it is difficult to believe that our first-person experiences of embarrassment or fulfillment, love or hate, and smells or colors are nothing more than brain states. However, in recent years a series of remarkable findings have begun to pull the rug out from under the notion that with consciousness we reach the threshold of human uniqueness. Of course, pet owners have long intuited the presence of human-like consciousness among their cats, dogs, or horses – and woe to the unbeliever who thinks differently. Now, however, scientists have begun to find evidence that fish might have a subjective awareness of pain,[8] and research on mammalian play supports the conclusion that animals are capable of a range of emotional feelings.[9]

---

[7] For the problem of defining consciousness, see David J. Chalmers, *The Conscious Mind: In Search of a Fundamental Theory* (Oxford: Oxford University Press, 1996).

[8] See James Gorman, "Fishing for Clarity in the Waters of Consciousness," *New York Times*, 13 May 2003 {http://query.nytimes.com/gst/fullpage.html?res=9800E0D6133FF930A25756C0A9659C8B63&sec=&spon=&partner=permalink&exprod=permalink}; accessed 6 June 2003.

[9] Jaak Panksepp, "Beyond a Joke: From Animal Laughter to Animal Joy?" *Science* 308, no. 5718 (2005): 62–63.

Of course, how to discern whether – and if so, what – an animal is thinking or feeling is a mystifying problem fraught with difficulties, and skeptics abound. But the line between human and non-human animals has had to be redrawn sufficiently often that denial of surmounting evidence on this point can appear to be little more than special pleading. Sixty years ago, anthropologists segregated humans and apes on the basis of tool-use, but in the 1960s primatologists found that chimpanzees are tool-users. Language was assumed to be a uniquely human characteristic, until the 1970s when primates were found to use symbolic representations for objects. If consciousness is a self-awareness and awareness of others that can be correlated with creativity, language, and empathy, then researchers have increasingly found that animals share this trait with humans. Most recently, this has been shown to be true in the case of problem-solving and future-planning, including the capacity to imagine hypothetical scenarios and their outcomes.[10] For example, an experiment reported in the January 2007 issue of *Psychological Science* utilized a video game to show the ability of monkeys to express their respective levels of confidence in their answers to multiple-choice questions and to request hints for problem-solving. That is, it put on display among monkeys metacognitive abilities – in other words, the ability to think about one's own thinking – long assumed to be exclusively human.[11]

Mind reading

In 2005, neuroscientist V.S. Ramachandran predicted that "mirror neurons will do for psychology what DNA did for biology: they will provide a unifying framework and help explain a host of mental abilities that have hitherto remained mysterious and

---

[10] E.g., Elizabeth Pennisi, "Are Our Primate Cousins 'Conscious'?" *Science* 284, no. 5423 (1999): 2073–76; Thomas Suddendorf, "Foresight and Evolution of the Human Mind," *Science* 312, no. 5776 (2006): 1006–7.
[11] Nate Kornell et al., "Transfer of Metacognitive Skills and Hint Seeking in Monkeys," *Psychological Science* 18 (2007): 64–71.

inaccessible to experiments."[12] These are the nerve cells that fire not only when a person is engaged in a certain activity but also, and remarkably, when that person observes another engaged in the same activity. Such neural activity mirrors the movements of others, as well as their intentions, sensitivities, and emotions. Mirror neurons thus provide the neural correlates for important social capacities and behaviors, like empathy or imitation. They are the basis for what is sometimes called "mind reading" or a "theory of mind."[13]

Although a "theory of mind" (i.e., the cognitive ability to understand others as intentional agents with their own beliefs and desires) may suggest a uniquely human characteristic, mirror neurons were first discovered among monkeys when it was observed, for example, that certain cells fired whether a monkey broke open a peanut or heard someone else break a peanut. Now we know that such tasks as language acquisition and learning the violin have their basis in mirror neurons, just as these specialized nerve cells enable us to predict the actions of others or feel with others their surprise or anger or fear. Even if, on account of our more expansive working memory, humans are capable of more sophisticated imitations, not only primates but also dogs, dolphins, and elephants are capable of mind reading.[14]

Although we have barely scratched the surface with this brief sketch, we have seen enough to realize how unoriginal the human creature is. Cognitive scientist Warren Brown has urged that, even if "nearly every fundamental human mental ability or function exists in some form or to some degree in nonhuman species,"

---

[12] V.S. Ramachandran, "Mirror Neurons and Imitation Learning as the Driving Force behind 'the Great Leap Forward' in Human Evolution," *Edge* 69 (1 June 2000) {http://www.edge.org/documents/archive/edge69.html}; accessed 17 September 2007.

[13] See, e.g., Greg Miller, "Reflecting on Another's Mind," *Science* 308, no. 5724 (2005): 945–47.

[14] See the useful report by Sandra Blakeslee, "Cells that Read Minds," *New York Times*, 10 January 2006 {http://www.nytimes.com/2006/01/10/science/10mirr.html?_r=1&oref=login&pagewanted=all}; accessed 10 January 2006.

humans are endowed "with notably enhanced mental powers."
Those he identifies as critical to the human experience of personal
relatedness – which he names as the sine qua non of human "soul-
fulness" – are:

- *language:* the capacity to communicate a potentially infinite
  number of propositions; to relate regarding complex, abstract
  ideas, as well as about the past and the future
- *a theory of mind:* an ability to consider the most likely thoughts
  and feelings of another person
- *episodic memory:* a conscious historical memory of events,
  persons, times, and places
- *conscious top-down agency:* conscious mental control of
  behavior
- *future orientation:* ability to run mental scenarios of the future
  implications of behaviors and events
- *emotional modulation* by complex social and contextual cognition that serves to guide ongoing behavior and decision-
  making.[15]

What about the soul?

Long ago, Pierre Gassendi (1592–1655) claimed that animals must
have souls since they apparently possess a memory, a capacity for
reason, and other traits typically associated with the soul. But, if
this is true, what distinguishes humanity from "the brutes"? One
important, early contributor to this question was Thomas Willis, a
seventeen-century medic and celebrated founder of neurology. In
his thinking we find recourse to a second soul, the presence of
which allows for a material "soul," characteristic of both humans
and non-human animals, alongside the immaterial and immortal
soul, found alone in humans. Willis thus distinguishes between the

---

[15] Warren S. Brown, "Cognitive Contributions to Soul," in *Whatever Happened to the Soul? Scientific and Theological Portraits of Human Nature* (ed.
Warren S. Brown, Nancey Murphy, and H. Newton Malony; TSc; Minneapolis: Fortress, 1998), 99–125 (103–4).

Corporeal Soul (common to humans and "brutes") and the Rational Soul (superior to the Corporeal Soul, found in humans only). Although Willis claims that "divers Authors both Ancient and Modern and both Philosophers and Theologists" have observed the difference between these souls,[16] in the highly politicized world of the century of Galileo this distinction between two souls served Willis as a ready means for avoiding a clash with ecclesiastical authority. Only rarely in his writings does Willis take up the role of the Rational Soul, and its chief *raison d'être* seems to be to superintend the Corporeal Soul. Instead, having acknowledged an immortal soul, he then devotes himself at length to the function and properties of the "animal soul," enabling him to include psychical issues within the competence of medicine and to present a coherent psycho-physiological approach to human capacities and behaviors. As Paul F. Cranefield summarizes, "The soul of brutes, in the hands of Willis, really seems to be simply a handy name for the assemblage of anatomical and physiological mechanisms which underlie psychological processes."[17]

Our difficulty in grasping what to make of the immaterial, Rational Soul is illustrated in Willis' description of the brain:

> The Brain is accounted the chief seat of the Rational Soul in a man, and of the sensitive [soul] in brute beasts, and indeed as the chief mover in the animal machine, it is the origine and fountain of all motions and conceptions. But some Functions do chiefly and more immediately belong to the substance of this, and others depend as it were mediately and less necessarily upon it. Among these, which of the former sort are accounted the chief, are the Imagination, Memory, and Appetite. ... The rest of the Faculties of this Soul, as Sense and Motion, also the Passions and Instincts merely natural, though

---

[16] Thomas Willis, *Two Discourses concerning the Soul of Brutes, which Is that of the Vital and Sensitive of Man* (Gainesville, FL: Scholars' Facsimiles and Reprints, 1971 [1683]), 38.

[17] Paul F. Cranefield, "A Seventeenth-century View of Mental Deficiency and Schizophrenia: Thomas Willis on 'Stupidity or Foolishness'," *Bulletin of the History of Medicine* 35 (1961): 291–316 (306).

they depend in some measure upon the Brain, yet they are properly performed in the oblong Marrow [i.e., spinal cord] and Cerebel [cerebellum], or proceed from them.[18]

Here, Willis allows that the brain is the origin of all motions and conceptions, apparently of both Rational Soul and Corporeal (i.e., "sensitive") Soul. Moreover, as here, throughout his writings on the central nervous system, Willis locates in the brain or spinal column not only reflexes and sensory and motor centers, but also cognition, imagination, volition, and affect. Thought he assigned to the cerebrum, voluntary movement to the cerebral hemispheres, perception to the corpora striata, imagination to the corpus callosum, memory to the cerebral cortex, instinct to the midbrain, and involuntary regulation to the cerebellum. In effect, Willis adopted a metaphysical solution to the problem of personhood that allowed him to proceed along an empiricist path, with matters of an ethereal sort partitioned off, outside the realm of experimentation or even consideration.

This solution could only be short-lived. Galen was maligned for his ambiguity on the immortality of the soul, yet in the work of Willis "soul" was delimited in ways that left the doctrine shriveled and languishing. Indeed, Willis' heirs typically speak of human life almost exclusively in terms of embodiment as physical persons. Typically, they do this on account of the complex and subtle dependencies of our thought processes on the state and functioning of our brains. They might draw attention to any variety of research reports, including:

- experimental data demonstrating that the psychological pain of social loss, such as the loss of a loved one, has neural correlates in the prefrontal cortex and the anterior cingulate cortex, suggesting a "human sadness system" in the brain;[19]
- the use of functional magnetic resonance imaging (fMRI) to show that the orbital and medial prefrontal cortex and the

---

[18] Willis, *Anatomy of the Brain and Nerves*, 91.
[19] Naomi I. Eisenberger, et al., "Does Rejection Hurt? An fMRI Study of Social Exclusion," *Science* 302, no. 5643 (2003): 290–92.

superior temporal sulcus regions of the brain play a central role
in moral appraisals in humans, demonstrating a neural substrate
for the emotions by which we assign moral values to events,
objects, and actions;[20]
- study establishing that the brain's anterior cingulate cortex is
  implicated in monitoring the consequence of one's actions;[21]
- a celebrated study among cloistered Carmelite nuns demonstrating that mystical experiences are mediated by several brain
  regions and systems otherwise implicated in such functions as
  consciousness, body representation, and emotion;[22] and
- the identification of neural responses in the caudate nucleus
  underlying the human capacity to trust.[23]

Such studies as these demonstrate again and again the thoroughly
embodied character of an increasingly broad variety of human
experiences. If the capacities traditionally allocated to the "soul" –
for example, consistency of memory, consciousness, spiritual
experience, the capacity to make decisions on the basis of self-
deliberation, planning and action on the basis of that decision, and
taking responsibility for these decisions and actions – have a neural
basis, then the concept of "soul," as traditionally understood in
theology as a person's "authentic self," seems redundant.

Given Willis' legacy as the "Father of Localization" (i.e., the science of locating particular capacities in terms of their neural correlates), it is easy to see that his work set neurobiology firmly on this
path. Indeed, in one of the early histories of neurology, Walther
Riese confidently assured his readers that philosophers and natural
scientists had dispensed with the need for recourse to the idea of a

[20] Jorge Moll, et al., "The Neural Correlates of Moral Sensitivity: A Functional Magnetic Resonance Imaging Investigation of Basic and Moral Emotions," *Journal of Neuroscience* 22, no. 7 (2002): 2730–36.
[21] Shigehiko Ito, et al., "Performance Monitoring by the Anterior Cingulate
Cortex during Saccade Countermanding," *Science* 302, no. 5642 (2003):
120–22.
[22] Mario Beauregard and Vincent Paquette, "Neural Correlates of a Mystical
Experience in Carmelite Nuns," *Neuroscience Letters* 405 (2006): 186–90.
[23] Brooks King-Casas, et al., "Getting to Know You: Reputation and Trust in a
Two-Person Economic Exchange," *Science* 308, no. 5718 (2005): 78–82.

human soul.[24] This does not mean that neuroscientists and neurophilosophers are unanimous in their reducing humanity to their brains or bodies; rather, many, in urging that humans are more than their physicality, simply refuse to identify that "something more" with an ontologically distinctive entity such as a "soul" or "spirit."[25]

How does this comport with the biblical materials?

Clearing the Deck

What does it mean to be human? From the standpoint of the biblical materials, addressing this question is less easy than one might expect. The nature of the evidence presses us to address three issues of approach.

Implicit evidence

The first obstacle concerns the nature of the evidence: the books of the OT and NT only very rarely turn to anthropology per se. That the biblical materials have little to say explicitly regarding the nature of humanity does not render the Bible irrelevant to the discussion, however. The biblical writers do engage questions regarding the nature of humanity, but they do so implicitly. At times, they assume a view of the human person; at other times, they counter the views of others; and, at still other times, they project an anthropology in their portraits of renewed humanity.

To draw attention to one example of this sort of phenomenon we may turn to an otherwise unremarkable text in Revelation 18, in which John divulges the contents of the Rome-bound seafaring cargo in order to portray the center of the Roman Empire as a

---

[24] Riese, *History of Neurology*, 19–48.

[25] Cf., e.g., Murphy, *Bodies and Souls* – nonreductive physicalism; Peterson, *Minding God* – open-system emergence or deep physicalism; Clayton, *Mind and Emergence* – emergent monism; Malcolm A. Jeeves, *Human Nature at the Millennium: Reflections on the Integration of Psychology and Christianity* (Grand Rapids, MI: Baker Academic, 1997) – two-aspect monism.

mistress-harlot who maintains a luxurious lifestyle at the expense of her lovers, the conquered peoples of the Roman Empire. The list itself is an abbreviated version of the bills of lading already known to us from Roman trade in the first century; for precedent John also had before him the text of Ezekiel 27:12–24.[26] According to the NRSV, this cargo record consists of "gold, silver, jewels and pearls, fine linen, purple, silk and scarlet, all kinds of scented wood, all articles of ivory, all articles of costly wood, bronze, iron, and marble, cinnamon, spice, incense, myrrh, frankincense, wine, olive oil, choice flour and wheat, cattle and sheep, horses and chariots, slaves – and human lives" (18:12–13). Including this catalogue here, John exposes a network of economic interests – including kings, merchants, and mariners, who have most to gain from Roman economic dominance; as well as common subjects, exploited but bedazzled by Roman opulence and propaganda. For our present purposes, what interest us about this inventory are the occupants of its climactic finale. Where the NRSV reads "slaves – and human lives," the Greek text reads σωμάτων, καὶ ψυχὰς ἀνθρώπων, *sōmatōn, kai psychas anthrōpōn*). Using σῶμα (*sōma*, "body") for "slave" was a commonplace in Roman antiquity.[27] Taking the *kai* as epexegetical, as most commentators and translations do,[28] we depart from the NRSV by reading, "bodies – that is, human lives." This translation highlights the reductionism inherent in the habit of referring to slaves as mere bodies, and recognizes John's criticism of this debasement of human beings – and, indeed, the inhumane travesty on which the whole of Rome's prosperity depended. Even slaves are more than their physicality; they are

[26] See the discussion in Richard Bauckham, *The Bible in Politics: How to Read the Bible Politically* (Louisville: Westminster John Knox, 1989), 94–97.

[27] For evidence, cf. MM 621; David E. Aune, *Revelation* (vol. 3; WBC 52c; Nashville: Thomas Nelson, 1998), 1002.

[28] E.g., Grant R. Osborne, *Revelation* (BECNT; Grand Rapids, MI: Baker Academic, 2002), 650; Stephen S. Smalley, *The Revelation to John: A Commentary on the Greek Text of the Apocalypse* (Downers Grove, IL: InterVarsity, 2005), 455–56; Richard Bauckham, "The Economic Critique of Rome in Revelation 18," in *The Climax of Prophecy: Studies on the Book of Revelation* (Edinburgh: T&T Clark, 1993), 338–83 (370–71).

human beings wrongly catalogued by their materiality, like so
many carcasses, alongside cattle and sheep. Here, then, we find on
display testimony for the presence of body-soul dualism in the
Greco-Roman world together with the distorted human portrait
that might emanate from dualism, as well as evidence of how a NT
author can stand against a distorted anthropology.

Presupposing the human person

A second obstacle is the ease with which our contemporaries have
read a Cartesian interest in "the mind" back into the Bible. This is
an example of the problem of ethnocentrism – the erroneous
assumption that all people everywhere think, believe, and act as we
do – in biblical interpretation. For René Descartes the physician
and philosopher, we may recall, to understand a human phenomenon we must ascertain whether to attribute it to the soul or body
for these are characterized by an essential, a real distinction. Given
the importance of the horizons of our own taken-for-granted
assumptions in acts of reading and interpretation, and given the
pervasive influence of the Cartesian idea of a disembodied mind
even today, it is no surprise that many readers of the Bible have
found body-soul dualism in its pages.

We can illustrate the problem with reference to Western medicine, where the Cartesian mind-body split is pervasive. Only with
slight hyperbole can Trinh Xuan Thuan remark, "To this day, the
brain and mind are regarded as two distinct entities in Western
medicine. When we have a headache, we consult a neurologist;
when we are depressed, we are told to see a psychiatrist."[29] Given
this way of structuring reality, why would we not unreflectively
segregate healing (biomedical) from salvation (spiritual)?[30] In the

---

[29] Trinh Xuan Thuan, *Chaos and Harmony: Perspectives on Scientific Revolutions of the Twentieth Century* (Oxford: Oxford University Press, 2001),
294.
[30] For a prominent example of this bifurcation, see John Wilkinson, *The Bible
and Healing: A Medical and Theological Commentary* (Edinburgh: Handsel;
Grand Rapids, MI: Eerdmans, 1998). For an antidote to this way of thinking,
see Joel B. Green, *Salvation* (UBT; St. Louis, MO: Chalice, 2003).

OT, however, the identity of God as "healer" is preeminently focused on salvation for the people of God; "I, Yahweh, am your healer," God's people are told, following the narration of the incredible lengths to which Yahweh has gone to liberate Israel from Egypt (Exod 15:26; see 2 Kgs 5:7). To cite another example, in Matthew 8–9 miraculous events are lined up, one after the other, depicting Jesus as one who makes available the presence and power of God's dominion to those dwelling on the periphery of Jewish society in Galilee – a leper, the slave of a Gentile army officer, an old woman, the demon-possessed, a paralytic, a collector of tolls, a young girl, and the blind. Intertwined with accounts of restoration to physical health are chronicles of the restoration of persons to status within their families and communities, the faith-full reordering of life around God, and the driving back of demonic forces. Note the mixing of categories whose distinctiveness we tend to take for granted. Cleansing a leper allows him new access to God and to the community of God's people (8:1–4), healing a paralytic is tantamount to forgiving his sins (9:2–8), extending the grace of God to toll collectors and sinners illustrates the work of a physician (9:9–13), and recovery of sight serves as a metaphor for the exercise of the insight of faith (9:27–31). Here we find no room for segregating the human person into discrete, constitutive "parts," whether "bodily" or "spiritual" or "communal."

A further consequence of Descartes' separation of the activity of thinking from the non-thinking body has been a perspective on human nature understood largely in terms of individual human beings, with the proper subject of individual human beings, the "I" or self to which one referred, identified as the ψυχή (psychē, "soul"). This view is alien to Scripture – and is generally acknowledged within biblical studies to be so, as we shall see shortly.

We can press further down this track by observing what portrait of the human person has emerged in the context of the pervasive dualism of the West. In Sources of the Self, Charles Taylor sketches the development of modern identity from Augustine through Descartes, Locke, and Kant, and on into the Romantics. He finds that personal identity has come to be shaped by assumptions such as these: human dignity lies in self-sufficiency and self-determination; identity is grasped in self-referential terms: I am who I am; persons have an inner self, which is the authentic self; and basic to authentic personhood are self-autonomy and self-legislation.[31] Although he does not major on the notion of a metaphysical entity of the "soul," he does (along with others before him) identify the precondition for the modern emphasis on the human sense of the "authentic, inner person" in Plato's concept of the "soul" (*psychē*). However, even though Plato posited a radical distinction between body and soul, he nevertheless thought that "soul" was constructed from elements of the world, with the result that modern views of substance dualism are just that, modern, owing far more to Descartes even than to Hellenistic anthropology.

The point is that constructions of personal identity that pervade the world of the interpreter are easily read back into the texts under scrutiny, and yet, in the case of the human self discerned by Taylor, can stand at odds with biblical anthropology at almost every turn. As Di Vito has documented, an examination of OT anthropology unveils a relatively congruous list of characteristics that contrasts sharply with the "modern self" depicted by Taylor.[32] These include such emphases as the construction of the self as deeply embedded in social relationships and thus the importance of dependence/interdependence for human identity; a premium on the integrity of the community and thus the contribution of individuals to that integrity; the assumption that a person *is* one's behavior – that is, that one's dispositions are on display in one's practices; an emphasis on external authority – that is, the call to holiness is a call to a human vocation drawn from a vision of Yahweh's "difference"; and the reality of dualism vis-à-vis good/evil, resident in and manifest *both* outside *and* inside a person.

---

[31] Taylor, *Sources of the Self.*
[32] Di Vito has analyzed this material for the OT, but many of his observations are equally apropos such NT materials as Matthew, Luke-Acts, or James, to name only a few representatives ("OT Anthropology").

Problems of method

In addition to concerns over interpretive assumptions, three issues of method deserve attention: Hebrew versus Greek thinking, word-study approaches to biblical anthropology, and an emphasis on eschatology.

Hebrew versus Greek thinking

Focusing at the level of presuppositions in method, we now recognize that the longstanding and pervasive view that posited a dichotomy between Hebrew thought (which affirmed some form of monism) and Greek thought (which affirmed some form of dualism) was a gross caricature. On the one hand, we refer to the complex relationship between Hellenism and Judaism that followed in the centuries after the military successes of Alexander the Great in the Near East in the last half of the fourth century BCE – relationships of acculturation, to be sure, but otherwise on a continuum between resistance and integration. On the other, Greek thought itself was more variegated on the nature of the soul than a reading focused on Plato (or on some first-century neo-Platonists) would allow. Consequently, the environment within which the NT was taking shape provided for the presence of a variety of views, both within Roman Hellenism and within Hellenistic Judaism. For both of these reasons, it is erroneous to allege that the NT authors lived in a milieu pervaded by body-soul dualism. Of these two claims, the first is universally acknowledged in biblical studies, even if scholars continue to assess how best to interpret Jewish responses to Hellenism;[33] whereas the second is less widely understood, thus requiring a few summary comments.

Others have sketched the history of ancient philosophical views of the human person, noting that, by and large, the Greeks never took the path Descartes would take – namely, juxtaposing

---

[33] Compare, e.g., Martin Hengel, *Judaism and Hellenism: Studies in Their Encounter in Palestine during the Early Hellenistic Period* (2 vols. in 1; Philadelphia: Fortress, 1974); and Louis Feldman, *Jew and Gentile in the Ancient World* (Princeton, NJ: Princeton University Press, 1993).

corporeal and incorporeal as if this were the same thing as juxtaposing material and immaterial (or physical/spiritual).[34] Although
belief in a form of body/soul duality was widespread in philosophical circles, most philosophers regarded the soul as composed of
"stuff." Aristotle, for example, considered the soul, the basis of
animate life, as part of nature, so that psychology and physics
("nature") could not be segregated. For him, "soul" was not
immaterial; even if "soul" is not the same thing as body, neither is
it not "nonmatter" but can still occupy "space." Even Plato
thought that the soul was constructed from elements of the world,
though he argued for a radical distinction between body and soul.
Within Epicureanism, mind and spirit were understood to be corporeal because they act on the body, and all entities that act or are
acted upon are bodies. Borrowing in part from Aristotle, Stoicism
taught that everything that exists is corporeal; accordingly, only
non-existent "somethings" (like imagined things) could be
incorporeal.

Following the demise of the Platonic academy as an institution,
neo-Platonism took many forms, especially as influenced by Stoicism. As Martin notes, "When we analyze the Platonism – or perhaps we should say the Platonisms – that were around [in the first
century CE], we encounter self-styled Platonists whose ideas of
body and soul look to us remarkably like the monisms of Aristotle
and the Stoics."[35] When one departs the work of these philosophers
and examines the views of ancient medical writers (who were,
themselves, philosophers of a sort), one finds a keen emphasis on

---

[34] See esp. the opening chapters of John P. Wright and Paul Potter, eds., *Psyche
and Soma*: "Soma and Psyche in Hippocratic Medicine," 13–35 (Beate
Gundert); "The Defining Features of Mind-Body Dualism in the Writings of
Plato," 37–55 (T.M. Robinson); "Aristotle's Psycho-physiological Account of
the Soul-Body Relationship," 57–77 (Philip J. van der Eijk); a cluster of Helle-
nistic philosophers and physicians, from Epicurus to Galen (Heinrich von
Staden), and Paul (Theo K. Heckel); in addition, e.g., Dale B. Martin, *The
Corinthian Body* (New Haven: Yale University Press, 1995), 3–37; MacDon-
ald, *History of the Concept of Mind*; Richard Sorabji, "Soul and Self in
Ancient Philosophy," in *From Soul to Self* (ed. M. James C. Crabbe; London:
Routledge, 1999), 8–32.
[35] Martin, *Corinthian Body*, 12.

the inseparability of the internal processes of the body ("psychology," in modern parlance) and its external aspects ("physiology"). This is not because of tendencies to think in terms of "psychosomatic conditions" (to use concepts that are quite anachronistic), but because any differentiation between inner and outer was fluid and permeable.

In short, although some may find it useful to speak of a body-soul duality in the Greco-Roman world as a lowest common denominator in educated circles, this hardly relates the whole story. The Hellenism that would have occupied a prominent place on the horizon of early Christians and the NT writers cannot be reduced so easily to a common denominator on questions of body and soul. This means that one cannot solve the problem of the relationship between body and soul in earliest Christianity merely by referring to parallels of thought or cultural settings. Such parallels and settings are themselves too complex for such decisions, and the ingredients available to those early Christian writers were more diverse than usually thought.[36]

Sharply put, there was no singular conception of the soul among the Greeks, and the body-soul relationship was variously assessed among philosophers and physicians in the Hellenistic period. Thus, Heinrich von Staden summarizes "the belief cluster" shared by philosophers and physicians of the Hellenistic period by noting, among other things, that the "soul" is corporeal; and that the "soul" is generated with the "body" and neither exists before the body nor is separable from it after the body's demise. That is, "the soul does not exist independently of the body in which it exists."[37] What happens after we die? It may be useful to refer to Cicero, who summarizes the two primary, competing views: either the body and soul are annihilated at death or the soul separates from the body.[38]

---

[36] The ease with which decisions of this sort have been made in the twentieth century derives in part from our failure to perceive the depth of Descartes' innovations. The Cartesian view of humanity was understood to have embraced ancient ways of thinking, with the result that few seemed to notice when Plato (for example) was conscripted to support Cartesian categories.
[37] Heinrich von Staden, "Body, Soul, and Nerves: Epicurus, Herophilus, Erasistratus, the Stoics, and Galen," in *Psyche and Soma*, 79–116 (79).
[38] Cicero *Tusculan Disputations* 1.11.23–24.

This is hardly the dualism widely assumed of "the Greeks" in the Hellenistic and Roman periods.

A word-study approach

We must also account for advances in linguistics, following the work of Ferdinand de Saussure in the early twentieth century, that (should) disallow the confusion between words and concepts, and thus that, say, the Greek term ψυχή (*psychē*) *means* "soul" and therefore refers to (something like) an ontological entity separate from the σῶμα (*sōma*, "body"). Until recently, one of the mainstays in the conversation about biblical anthropology has been the contribution of Hebrew and Greek lexicography.[39] Certain words, vested with particular meanings, have been said to point to certain conclusions regarding the make-up of the human person. As in statistics, however, so in linguistics: the same evidence base, in different hands, can lead to sometimes opposing results. This is the case in the discussion of the human person, in which Hebrew terms (such as *nephes̆, bāśār, lēb,* and *rûah*) and Greek terms (such as *sōma, psychē, pneuma,* and *sarx*) are investigated for their meaning. Unfortunately for this debate, these words are each polysemous, and are capable of a range of translations into English. Thus, depending on context, *nephes̆,* though often identified with the idea of a "soul," might be translated into English as "life," "person," "breath," "inner person," "self," "desire," or even "throat." *Bāśār* might be translated with the English terms "flesh," "body," "meat," "skin," "humankind," or "(the) animal (kingdom)." Translations of *lēb* might include "heart," "mind," "conscience," and "inner life." Finally, *rûah* might be taken as a reference to "wind," "breath," "seat of cognition and/or volition," "disposition," "spirit," or "point on a compass."

In Israel's Scriptures, the Hebrew term *nephes̆* is used with reference to the whole person as the seat of desires and emotions, not to the "inner soul" as though this were something separate from one's being. *Nephes̆* can be translated in many places as "person," or

---

[39] For the continued appearance of such data in recent study, see, e.g., Cooper, *Body, Soul, and Life Everlasting,* 42–49; Jewett, *Who We Are,* 35–46.

even by the personal pronoun (e.g., Lev 2:1; 4:2; 7:20). It denotes the entire human being, but can also be used with reference to animals (e.g., Gen 1:12, 24; 2:7; 9:10). From time to time, the Hebrew term *bāśār* stands in parallel with, but not in contrast to, *nepheš* – the one referring to the external being of the person, the other to the internal (e.g., Isa 10:18). Indeed, although *bāśār* frequently refers to the fleshly aspect of a person (e.g., Ps 119:73; Isa 45:11–12), this term is also prominent as an expression of the spiritual. *Bāśār* and *nepheš* "are to be understood as different aspects of man's existence as a twofold unity."[40] The related term, *gewiyya*, refers to the human being in her wholeness, though usually in a weakened condition; typically, it is used to denote the body of a human only in its state as a corpse or cadaver.[41] The Scriptures of Israel employ other terms, too, to speak of humans from the perspective of their varying functions – for example, *lēb*, with reference to human existence, sometimes in its totality (e.g., Gen 18:5; Ezek 13:22), sometimes with reference to the center of human affect (e.g., Prov 14:30) or perception (Prov 16:9);[42] and *rûah*, used with reference to the human from the perspective of his being imbued with life (e.g., Gen 2:7; Job 12:10; Isa 42:5).

Similar polysemy is found among the relevant Greek terms: *sōma* is capable of translation into English as "body," "physical being," "church," "slave," and even "reality"; *psychē* as "inner self," "life," and "person"; *pneuma* as "spirit," "ghost," "inner self," "way of thinking," "wind," and "breath"; and *sarx* as "flesh," "body," "people," "human," "nation," "human nature," and, simply, "life."

Thus, although *psychē* could refer to "soul," understood within the framework of a body-soul dualism, this cannot be presumed on lexical grounds. Aristotle, for example, devotes an entire treatise to "the soul" (ΠΕΡΙ ΨΥΧΗΣ, "On the Soul"), and defines *psychē* in terms of what we today would designate a physicalist account of human nature, just as the Septuagint, a Greek translation of Israel's

---

[40] N.P. Bratsiotis, "בשר‎," *TDOT* 2:313–32 (326).
[41] See H.-J. Fabry, "גויה‎," *TDOT* 2:433–38 (esp. 435–36).
[42] See H.-J. Fabry, "לב‎," *TDOT* 7:399–437.

Scriptures dating from the Hellenistic period, typically translates the Hebrew *nephes* ("vitality") with *psychē*, without thereby introducing anthropological dualism into the OT.

Actually, Aristotle presents us with an interesting test case, since his position is often misrepresented. To this day, neuroscientists can write, erroneously, of Aristotle's views of the nonmateriality of the soul and its location in the heart.[43] It is true that Aristotle privileged heart over head as the primary sense organ, and relegated the brain to service as a kind of radiator for the blood, but he was no dualist and any attempt to specify on Aristotle's behalf the "seat of the soul" is misguided. Having devoted an entire treatise to the subject, he sketches a view of "soul" (*psychē*) as that in virtue of which an organism is alive (*On the Soul* 2.1 §§412a–413a10), the form or essence of the living body that a plant or animal or human being is. Accordingly, "soul" is no "it" with an independent existence, nor a quality characteristic of humankind in contradistinction to other forms of life. Plants are alive and are therefore "soulish" because they have and perform certain vital functions (such as grow and reproduce), yet they perform no functions that we might call cognitive or psychological. Not only is Aristotle a monist, then, but his position disallows reductionism of a living organism to the matter out of which it is made. Moreover, on the positive side of the ledger, Aristotle's conception urges a unified view of the human person, highlights the importance of human capacities, underscores the essential relatedness of humanity with other living beings, and emphasizes, in the case of the human, especially social activity. For this reason, philosophers and psychologists at the turn of the twenty-first century might find themselves drawn to Aristotle's psychology for its potential in shaping present-day accounts of the human person. But for many moderns, Aristotle's position has been transformed, by Descartes, from

---

[43] E.g., Andrew Peacock, "The Relationship between the Soul and the Brain," in *Historical Aspects of the Neurosciences: A Festschrift for Macdonald Critchley* (ed. F. Clifford Rose and W.F. Bynum; New York: Raven, 1982), 83–98 (83); Bryan Kolb and Ian Q. Whishaw, *An Introduction to Brain and Behavior* (New York: Worth, 2001), 8.

theoretical psychology into epistemology, and thus from talk of "soul" to the category of "mind,"[44] and it is often through Cartesian categories that Aristotle has been accessed.

As for the Hebrew Bible, *nepheš* occurs almost 800 times, with the primary meaning of "throat" or "gullet" (very much a physical referent!), and with the extended sense of "vitality" or "the impulse of life over against death." When used anthropologically, its typical reference is to the entire human being, and not to some portion of the person. Persons in the OT "do not think of themselves in a subject-object relationship (spirit and soul); the subject in particular is not thematic. On the basis of being alive, of individuation within life, of perceiving life as an in-and-out rhythm (breathing?), they find themselves to be living quanta with respect to *ayyîm*, life."[45]

Given this polysemy, we would be mistaken to assume that the word *psychē*, which someone might wish to translate as "soul," actually *means* "soul" (or requires an identification with the concept of "soul"), defined as the spiritual part of a human distinct from the physical or as an ontologically separate entity constitutive of the human "self." Nor should we imagine that in any given utterance *psychē* refers to "inner life," "life," *and* "person" – or to even one of these possible referents. (In the same way, we would not expect native speakers of English to confuse a "light blue" with a "blue mood" or a "light switch.") In the end, studies of the human person oriented toward the semantics of biblical Hebrew or Greek are capable of only limited and primarily negative results. We can show, for example, that words like *nepheš* or *psychē* do not necessarily refer to ontologically separate (or separable) parts of

---

[44] For discussion, see Stephen Everson, "Psychology," in *The Cambridge Companion to Aristotle* (ed. Jonathan Barnes; Cambridge: Cambridge University Press, 1995), 168–94; Michael Frede, "On Aristotle's Conception of the Soul," in *Essays on Aristotle's De anima* (ed. Martha C. Nussbaum and Amélie Oksenberg Rorty; Oxford: Clarendon, 1992), 93–107; K.V. Wilkes, "*Psuche* versus the Mind," in *Essays on Aristotle's De anima* (ed. Martha C. Nussbaum and Amélie Oksenberg Rorty; Oxford: Clarendon, 1992), 109–27.

[45] H. Seebass, "נפשׁ," *TDOT* 9:497–519 (503–4); see Seebass' excursus, "The Translation 'Soul'" (508–10).

the human person. On the other hand, neither can such study show that, in individual texts, the opposite is necessarily the case.[46]

By way of more specific illustration, let us examine the anthropological language of 1 Peter – a suitable test case precisely because its terminology might invite a dualist reading.[47] By the time of the writing of 1 Peter, three hundred years of admixture of Greco-Roman and Hebrew perspectives on the nature of humanity had yielded a range of positions. Some would be more clearly dualistic (e.g., the writings of Josephus and Philo), others monist, though with most Jewish writers rejecting body-soul dualism in favor of a more "integrated" anthropology.[48] The question before us is how Peter portrayed the human person, and the significance this has for his theology. Did he lean in a more dualist perspective, or did he situate himself more fully in continuity with the monism of the Scriptures and of parts of the Greco-Roman tradition?

Peter deploys the expected range of terms associated with the nature of the human person. He uses *sōma* ("body") only once, in 2:24, with reference to Christ's having borne "our sins in his body on the tree." Since this is the very Christ who was present in times past to inspire the prophets (1:11) and who will be revealed in glory (e.g., 1:13; 4:13) – that is, since Christ is also portrayed as a transcendent figure who shares in the identity of God – then this is

---

[46] This précis is enough to suggest with what lack of precision the anthropological vocabulary of the Scriptures of Israel is utilized. Some scholars go further, to suggest that, although the Scriptures of Israel provide no particularly "scriptural" vocabulary for anthropological analysis, they do draw on the common terminology of the ancient Near East in order to depict the human person as an integrated whole. See, e.g., Fabry, "לב," 412–13; Childs, *Biblical Theology,* 566, 571–72; Eduard Schweizer, "Body," *ABD* 1:767–72 (esp. 768).

[47] Indeed, see Reinhard Feldmeier, "Seelenheil: Überlegungen zur Soteriologie und Anthropologie des 1. Petrusbriefes," in *The Catholic Epistles and the Tradition* (ed. J. Schlosser; BETL 176; Leuven: Leuven University Press, 2004), 291–306. I am borrowing this analysis from Joel B. Green, *1 Peter* (THNTC; Grand Rapids, MI: Eerdmans, 2007), 27.

[48] So, e.g., N.T. Wright, *The New Testament and the People of God* (vol. 1 of Christian Origins and the Question of God; Minneapolis: Fortress, 1992), 254–55; more fully, see Warne, *Hebrew Perspectives.*

a profound affirmation of bodily existence and of the significance of embodied, human suffering. *Sarx* ("flesh, body") refers to "humanity" in 1:24, and otherwise refers to life as a human in 3:18, 21; 4:1 (2x), 2, 6. *Psychē* ("life, vitality," sometimes translated as "soul") appears in 1:9, 22; 2:11, 25; 3:20; 4:19. In 2:11, *psychē* is set in contrast to σαρκικός (*sarkikos*, "belonging to this world"), but it never appears in relation to *sarx*. (*Sarx* is juxtaposed with *pneuma* ["spirit"] in 3:18; 4:6, however.) Christ is the guardian of the Christian's *psychē* in 2:25, just as God is guarding "you" for a salvation ready to be revealed at the last time. Those who suffer entrust their *psychai* (plural) to God (4:19). In 3:20, *psychē* refers to "persons," Noah and his kin, rescued through the flood. For Peter, *sarx* concerns "life as it reflects and/or pertains to this world" and *psychē* connotes "life as it reflects and/or pertains to the world to come." The dualism with which Peter operates, then, is eschatological and not anthropological.

In this way, Peter proves himself to be more the heir of the Scriptures of Israel than of Plato in his understanding of the human person. This allows him to take with the utmost seriousness the dire situation in which his audience finds itself; after all, it is not the case for him that they could retreat from physical pain into their genuine selves, their souls, untouched by calamity suffering, as though their suffering were purely physical. Nor does he offer the related "hope" that, even though they are suffering in their bodies, this does not matter since God is really concerned with and will rescue their souls. His emphasis on embodied existence provides life in this world its fullest significance and it serves as the basis for his emphasis on a faithful "manner of living" in the material world. Human physicality also ties Peter's audience to the rest of creation, thus pressing the question how their suffering participates in the situation of the cosmos and, perhaps more to the point, how their liberation is tied to the fate of the cosmos. Importantly, the work of Christ in death and exaltation has repercussions for humans and for the cosmos.

Consequently, the idea that one could simply pile up all of the references in Scripture to "body" or "soul," and from this deduce "the biblical understanding of the human person" is misguided on linguistic grounds. We must face the reality that neither the Old nor the New Testament writers developed a specialized or technical, denotative vocabulary for theoretical discussion of the human person. And if this is so, then contemporary interpreters ought to exercise care when reading the biblical materials in light of specialized language that has developed subsequently.

Eschatology

In the absence of word-study approaches, some studies have focused primarily on the question, What happens when we die? That is, eschatology has determined semantics and anthropology. This is particularly the case among those who have correlated Christian dogmas like "general resurrection" or "eternal life" with the need for a personal "essence" that outlives the decaying corpse. This approach is problematic on three grounds. First, anxiety regarding "what happens when we die" was not rampant in Greco-Roman antiquity, and viewpoints ranged from skepticism or agnosticism about any form of afterlife to suggestions of continuing embodied existence, to a belief in the soul's immortality.[49] Second, within contemporary Judaism one finds a diversity of expectations about what might follow death – for example, some Jewish texts speak of the immortality of the soul, others fail to speak of any afterlife or reject outright such an existence, while still others anticipate some form of embodied or re-embodied resurrection.[50] Third, evidence of this nature is necessarily analogical and speculative, since discussion of the afterlife in our texts is carried on by those who have no firsthand knowledge on which to draw.

---

[49] See Ramsey MacMullen, *Paganism in the Roman Empire* (New Haven: Yale University Press, 1981), 53–57; Martin, *Corinthian Body*, 108–17.

[50] See Kevin L. Anderson, *'But God Raised Him from the Dead': The Theology of Jesus Resurrection in Luke-Acts* (PBM; Carlisle: Paternoster, 2006), 48–91; N.T. Wright, *The Resurrection of the Son of God* (vol. 3 of Christian Origins and the Question of God, Minneapolis: Fortress, 2003), 85–206; C.D. Elledge, *Life after Death in Early Judaism: The Evidence of Josephus* (WUNT 2:208; Tübingen: Mohr Siebeck, 2006), 5–44.

Hence, for our purposes here it is better to ask, Given the biblical evidence regarding the nature of the human person on this side of the eschaton, what can we say about human nature on the other? than to ask, Given our theories about eschatology, what must we say about the nature of the human person in the present? Of course, this does not mean that we can escape altogether the questions posed by eschatology since it is incumbent on any biblical anthropology to address the question of continuity between present life and the promise of eschatological existence. It does raise questions against our looking to eschatology as our point of departure, however.[51]

"In the Image of God He Created Them" (Gen 1:27)

Not least on account of its prominent location at the beginning of the biblical canon, the Genesis creation account is a critical point of departure for constructing a biblical portrait of humanity. Two immediate affirmations derive from the perspective on humanity provided in Genesis 1:27–31 and 2:4–25 – namely, continuity and difference: the continuity of humanity with all other animals and, indeed, with the rest of creation; and the difference between humanity and other animals.

Humans are like other living things in their being created by God and thus in their relation to God. Moreover, like them, humanity is formed from the stuff of the earth. "Humans are wholly embedded in creation," LeRon Shults rightly observes, "and no special part of humanity, not even the mind, escapes this creaturely continuity."[52] Vegetation is for both humans and animals (Gen 1:30). Animals share with humans the command to reproduce, increase, and fill the seas and the earth (Gen 1:22). The additional vocation given humanity, "to subdue" and "to have dominion" over the earth (Gen 1:26, 28), does not call for the

---

[51] See further below, ch. 5.
[52] F. LeRon Shults, *Reforming Theological Anthropology: After the Philosophical Turn to Relationality* (Grand Rapids, MI: Eerdmans, 2003), 164.

human exploitation of nature, but must be understood in the context of the order set forth in the creation account. True, the creation account imbues humanity with royal identity and task, but this is a nobility granted without conquest; its essence is realized in coexistence with all of life in the land, and in the cultivation of life. Similarly, Psalm 8:7 portrays humanity in a stance of dominion over creation, as though standing over its defeated enemies, but with no hint of military action. Stewardship of creation, management and care without conquest or domination – the human family has this responsibility in relation to God's creation because this is how God has made us.

Humans are unlike other creatures in that only humanity is created after God's own likeness, in God's own image (*imago Dei*). Only to humanity does God speak directly. Humanity alone receives from God this divine vocation. The *imago Dei* tradition has been the focus of diverse interpretations among Jews and Christians – ranging widely from some physical characteristic of humans (such as standing upright) to a way of knowing (especially the human capacity to know God), and so on. What is obvious is that humanity is thus defined in relation to God in terms of both similarity and difference: humanity is in some sense "like" God, but is itself not divine. Humanity thus stands in an ambivalent position – living in solidarity with the rest of the created order and yet distinct from it on account of humankind's unique role as the bearer of the divine image, called to a particular and crucial relationship with Yahweh and yet not divine.[53]

Taken within its immediate setting in Genesis 1, "the image of God" in which humanity is made is set in relation to the exercise of

---

[53] See McGrath, *A Scientific Theology*, 197. On the interpretation of the *imago Dei* in Gen 1, see esp. J. Richard Middleton, *The Liberating Image: The* Imago Dei *in Genesis 1* (Grand Rapids, MI: Brazos, 2005); for a complementary perspective, see W. Sibley Towner, "Clones of God: Genesis 1:26–28 and the Image of God in the Hebrew Bible," *Int* 59 (2005): 341–56. For further, theological assessment, see Stanley J. Grenz, *The Social God and the Relational Self: A Trinitarian Theology of the Imago Dei* (The Matrix of Christian Theology; Louisville: Westminster John Knox, 2001).

dominion over the earth on God's behalf. This observation does not take us far, however, since we must then ascertain what it means to exercise dominion in this way – that is, in a way that reflects God's own ways of interaction with his creatures. Additionally, this way of putting the issue does not grapple with the profound word spoken over humanity and about humanity, that human beings in themselves (and not merely in what they do) reflect the divine image. What is this quality that distinguishes humanity? God's words affirm the creation of the human family in its relation to himself, as his counterpart, so that the nature of humanity derives from the human family's relatedness to God. The concept of the *imago Dei*, then, is fundamentally relational, or covenantal, and takes as its ground and focus the graciousness of God's own covenantal relations with humanity and the rest of creation. The distinguishing mark of *human* existence when compared with other creatures is thus the whole of human existence (and not some "part" of the individual). As the Genesis story unfolds, the vocation given humanity entails individuality within community and the human capacity for self-transcendence and morality – that is, the capacity to make decisions on the basis of self-deliberation, planning and action on the basis of that decision, and responsibility for those decisions and actions. The skeleton of what evolutionary biologist Francisco Ayala refers to as "ethical consciousness" (that is, the capacity to judge human actions as right or wrong),[54] is filled out in Scripture with reference to God's own character, God's "difference" (or holiness) in relation to the cosmos. In a signal text, for example, Leviticus 19 indices holy behavior in terms of family and community respect (vv. 3, 32), religious loyalty (vv. 3b, 4–8, 12, 26–31), economic relationships (vv. 9–10), workers' rights (v. 13), social compassion (v. 14), judicial integrity (v. 15), neighborly attitudes and conduct (vv. 11, 16–18), distinctiveness (v. 19), sexual integrity (vv. 20–22, 29), exclusion of the idolatrous and occult (vv. 4, 26–31), racial

---

[54] Francisco J. Ayala, "Biological Evolution and Human Nature," in *Human Nature* (ed. Malcolm Jeeves; Edinburgh: The Royal Society of Edinburgh, 2006), 46–64.

equality (vv. 33–34), and commercial honesty (vv. 35–36).[55] Echoing Leviticus 19, Peter writes, "As he who called you is holy, be holy yourselves *in all your conduct*; for it is written, 'You shall be holy, for I am holy'" (1:15–16).

Genesis 1–2 does not locate the singularity of humanity in the human possession of a "soul," but rather in the human capacity to relate to Yahweh as covenant partner, and to join in companionship within the human family and in relation to the whole cosmos in ways that reflect the covenant love of God. Indeed, as noted above, within the OT, "soul" (*nepheš*) refers to life and vitality – not life in general, but as instantiated in human persons and animals; not a thing to have but a way to be.[56] To speak of loving God with all of one's "soul" (e.g., Deut 6:5), then, is to elevate the intensity of involvement of the entirety of one's being. What, then, of Genesis 2:7 ("the Lord God formed the human being of the dust of the ground, breathed into his nostrils the breath of life, and the human being became a living soul [*nepheš*]" [my translation])? The term in question, *nepheš*, is used only a few verses earlier with reference to "every beast of the earth," "every bird of the air," and "everything that creeps on the earth" – that is, to everything "in which there is life (*nepheš*)" (1:30 [my translation]). This demonstrates that "soul" is not for the Genesis story a unique characteristic of the human person; humans are not distinctively *human* on account of their purported possession of a "soul." Indeed, one might better translate Genesis 2:7 with reference to the divine gift of *life*: "the human being became fully alive" (my translation). Thus, we find here a witness to the nature of human life that is at once naive and profound. It is naive not in the sense of gullibility or primitiveness, but because it has not worked out in what we may regard as a philosophically satisfying way the nature of physical existence in life, death, and afterlife. It is profound in its presentation of the human person fundamentally in relational terms, and its

---

[55] This way of construing holiness is borrowed from Christopher J.H. Wright, "Old Testament Ethics: A Missiological Perspective," *Catalyst* 26, no. 2 (2000): 5–8.

[56] For extended discussion, see Stone, "The Soul."

assessment of the human being as genuinely human and alive only within the family of humans brought into being by Yahweh and in relation to the God who gives life-giving breath. That is, Genesis does not define humanity in essentialist terms but in relational, as Yahweh's partner, and with emphasis on the communal, intersexual character of personhood, the quality of care the human family is to exercise with regard to creation as God's representative, the importance of the human modeling of the personal character of God, and the unassailable vocation of humans to reflect among themselves God's own character.[57]

"To the Measure of the Full Stature of Christ" (Eph 4:13)

Outside of Genesis 1–2 the phrase "image of God" plays little role in the OT, though it is found in Jewish literature from the Second Temple period (e.g., Wis 2:23–24; Sir 17:1–13), including the letters of Paul. By way of preparing for a brief consideration of that evidence, however, it will be instructive to review those related texts where the question is raised, What is a human being? There are four such texts, and they have been helpfully explored by Patrick Miller.[58]

The first, Psalm 8, extols human dignity in the context of divine glory:

You have made them a little lower than God,[59] and crowned them with glory and honor.

---

[57] See Brueggemann, *Theology of the Old Testament*, 451–52; Colin E. Gunton, "Trinity, Ontology and Anthropology: Towards a Renewal of the Doctrine of the *Imago Dei*," in *Persons Divine and Human: King's College Essays on Theological Anthropology* (ed. Christoph Schwöbel and Colin E. Gunton; Edinburgh: T&T Clark, 1991), 47–61.

[58] Patrick D. Miller, "What Is a Human Being? The Anthropology of Scripture," in *What about the Soul? Neuroscience and Christian Anthropology* (ed. Joel B. Green; Nashville: Abingdon, 2004), 63–73.

[59] Some English translations read "a little lower than the angels," on account of how the early versions (Greek, Latin, Aramaic) interpreted the Hebrew ʿlōhîm (literally, "God, gods"). Other early versions translated the Hebrew term as "God," however, and this rendering is favored by the context.

You have given them dominion over the works of your hands;
you have put all things under their feet, all sheep and oxen, and also
    the beasts of the field,
    the birds of the air, and the fish of the sea, whatever passes along
    the paths of the seas.
O Lord, our Sovereign, how majestic is your name in all the earth!
    (vv. 5–9)

On the one hand, this psalm, which functions within the Scriptures
as a kind of commentary on Genesis 1, sharply contrasts God's
majesty with human insignificance. The psalmist appears baffled
that Yahweh's splendor does not completely overshadow the possibility of his attending to mere earthlings: "What are human
beings that you are mindful of them?" (v. 4). On the other hand,
the psalmist recognizes that the human family finds its true identity
only in relation to God. Moreover, in a world that marked differences between royalty and common folk on the basis of family lin-
eage (the accidents of birth, so to speak), Psalm 8 disallows any
concern with inherited status. Instead, it attributes nobility to
every person. Here the prominent place of humankind in relation
to the rest of creation is accentuated, at the same time that human
beings are positioned clearly in relation to God and the heavenly
counsel. Even the nobility of humanity is cause for glorifying God.

In the second, Psalm 144, the psalmist as king addresses God,
"O Lord, what are human beings that you regard them, or mortals
that you think of them?" (v. 3). The reply in this instance is not a
celebration of human dignity but a recognition of human transience: "They are like a breath; their days are like a passing
shadow" (v. 4). After this comes a plea for liberation and blessing.
Psalms 8 and 144 both recognize human insignificance, but here,
as Miller notes, emphasis falls on human limitation, mortality,
impermanence. Human limitations do not diminish God's atten-
tiveness, however, and the psalmist ends by pronouncing a state of
blessedness on those for whom "God is the Lord" (v. 15).

The presence of the God who attends to humanity is underscored in a third OT text, Job 7: "What are human beings, that you

make so much of them, that you set your mind on them, visit them every morning, test them every moment? Will you not look away from me for a while, let me alone until I swallow my spittle?" (vv. 17–19). Unlike the perspective of Psalm 144, though, Job's experience identifies this aspect of human reality as unwanted: "Will you not look away from me for a while?" As Miller puts it, "The one who is crowned with glory in Psalm 8 is also a creature of suffering; the one who is *astonished* by God's attention as making us kings and queens is also one who is *undone* by God's attention, an attention experienced as testing and undoing."[60] Either way, the human reality is finitude, transience, and suffering, and the significance of human life is tied to dependence upon God.

We turn finally to Hebrews 2:6–9, with its citation of Psalm 8:

> But someone has testified somewhere, "What are human beings that you are mindful of them, or mortals, that you care for them? You have made them for a little while lower than the angels; you have crowned them with glory and honor, subjecting all things under their feet." Now in subjecting all things to them, God left nothing outside their control. As it is, we do not yet see everything in subjection to them, but we do see Jesus, who for a little while was made lower than the angels, now crowned with glory and honor because of the suffering of death, so that by the grace of God he might taste death for everyone.

Among Miller's observations, the most telling is how the Hebrew text, *ben 'adam* (Greek: υἱός ἄνθρωπου, *huios anthrōpou*), traditionally translated as "son of man" but in the NRSV as "mortal," has led naturally to a christological, and not simply an anthropological, reading of this text. Miller also draws attention to the phrase, "who for a little while was made lower than the angels," which signifies the earthly sojourn of Christ. This highlights in titular terms the incarnational reality of the status of Jesus Christ as truly human and representatively human. Anthropology

---

[60] Miller, "What Is a Human Being?" 71.

is thus christologically understood, since the human under whom all things have been made subject (Ps 8) is the one born in human likeness (Heb 2). "The writer to the Hebrews hears in the Psalms the word that whatever we say about the human reality must take into account the face of Jesus Christ."[61]

This final emphasis on the incarnation provides a useful point of re-entry into the image of God tradition as this is developed by Paul. In 2 Corinthians 4:4, Paul refers to "the glory of Christ, who is the image of God," and in Colossians 1:15 he says of Christ, "He is the image of the invisible God, the firstborn of all creation." This christology lies at the confluence of two streams of thought: 1) portraits of humanity in Genesis 1:26–27 as created in God's image and in Psalm 8:5 as "crowned . . . with glory and honor"; and 2) Jewish speculation regarding Wisdom, described in Wisdom 7:25–26 as "a pure emanation of the glory of the Almighty . . . a reflection of eternal light, a spotless mirror of the working of God, and an image of his goodness." The apostle's thought in both contexts is similar, for in 2 Corinthians 4 the gospel unveils the very thing that Satan would hide from unbelievers – namely, "the knowledge of the glory of God in the face of Jesus Christ" (4:6); whereas in Colossians the work of Christ is manifest in the renewal of humanity in the image of the creator (3:10).

Not surprisingly, then, the terms "image" and "glory" figure importantly, too, in Paul's depiction of humanity in its need of transformation. In the exodus journey, God's people "exchanged the glory of God for the image of an ox that eats grass. They forgot God, their Savior, who had done great things in Egypt, wondrous works in the land of Ham, and awesome deeds by the Red Sea" (Ps 106:20–22). Expanding this portrait, Paul writes of the whole of humankind, "Claiming to be wise, they became fools; and they exchanged the glory of the immortal God for images resembling a mortal human being or birds or four-footed animals or reptiles" (Rom 1:22–23). What is more, the psalmist observes, human beings become like the object of their worship: "Their idols are

---

[61] Miller, "What Is a Human Being?" 72.

silver and gold, the work of human hands. They have mouths, but
do not speak; eyes, but do not see. They have ears, but do not hear;
noses, but do not smell. They have hands, but do not feel; feet, but
do not walk; they make no sound in their throats. *Those who make
them are like them; so are all who trust in them*" (Ps 115:4–8;
emphasis added). So, too, for Paul, humanity has profaned God's
glory – indeed, "all have sinned and fall short of the glory of God"
(Rom 3:23).

What, then, does it mean to speak of Christ as the image of
God? Colin Gunton aptly summarized: "First, that Jesus represents God to the creation in the way that the first human beings
were called, but failed, to do; and second that he enables other
human beings to achieve the directedness to God of which their
fallenness had deprived them."[62] Not surprisingly, then, Paul can
elsewhere develop this affirmation of Christ as God's image in
terms of its corollary, the conformation of human beings into the
"image of Christ" (Rom 8:29; 1 Cor 15:49; 2 Cor 3:18).

The renewal of the human being in the divine image is profoundly personal, and embraces the human person in his or her
totality. This means that (trans)formation is fully embodied within
a nest of relationships, a community. From Scripture we receive an
all-encompassing perspective on human health in the cosmos and
in relation to God, but also well-developed ways of identifying the
sickness that spreads like a cancer throughout the human family,
even eating away at the world that humans call home. The term
generally given this sickness in the Christian tradition is "sin," a
multivalent term that points to the myriad ways in which humans –
individually, collectively, and systemically – neglect, deny, and
refuse simply to be human – that is, to embrace and live out their
vocation as creatures made in the image of God. Accordingly, a
Christian conception of human transformation does not allow the
categorization of either the person or his or her salvation into
"parts," as though inner and outer life could be separated. Angst

---

[62] Colin Gunton, *Christ and Creation* (Grand Rapids, MI: Eerdmans, 1992),
100.

among Christians in recent decades over how to prioritize minis-
tries of "evangelism" and "social witness" is simply wrongheaded,
therefore, since the gospel, the "evangel" of "evangelism," cannot
but concern itself with *human need in all its aspects.* Only an erroneous body-soul dualism could allow – indeed, require – "ministry" to become segregated by its relative concern for "spiritual"
versus "material" matters. Nor does a Christian conception of
human transformation allow us to think of the restoration of individuals, as it were, one at a time, but pushes our categories always
to account for the human community and, beyond humanity, the
cosmos. Persons are not saved in isolation from the world around
them. Restoration to the likeness of God is the work of the Spirit
within the community of God's people, the fellowship of Christ-
followers set on maturation in Christ. From this vantage point,
"image of God" points ultimately to the transformation of believers in resurrection, a transformation already at work in the creation of a new humanity through the dissolution of barriers
dividing human beings from one another along gender, social, or
ethnic lines (Col 3:10–11; 1 Cor 12:12–13; Gal 3:28).

Conclusion

Some might regard the natural sciences as a challenge to biblical
theology on account of two of its conclusions – namely, the high
degree of their identification of humanity with non-human animals and their questioning of body-soul dualism as a necessary or
defensible portrait of the human. In fact, except in their more
reductionistic forms (humans are "nothing but . . ."), these conclusions are not at all antagonist nor even alien to a biblical account of
humanity. Indeed, a close reading of the Genesis narrative ought to
lead us toward an affirmation of the close connection between
humans and non-human animals. Moreover, the Genesis account
of human creation provides no basis for the human possession of
an ontologically distinctive entity known as the "soul," much less
for the identification of a person's true "self" with such an entity.

This is not necessarily to suggest, however, that the biblical materials and the natural sciences paint entirely with the same brush in their portraits of the human person. Both highlight the character of humans in their embodiedness and relationality. The biblical materials push further, however. First, in presenting the physical embeddedness of the human family, they highlight the vocation of humanity in relation to the created order — not only in relation to other humans but also in relation to the cosmos. Second, the biblical materials urge the view that a biblical theology of humanity must have as its primary point of beginning and orientation the human in a partnering relationship with God.

3

SIN AND FREEDOM

We tend to suppose, without giving it too much thought, that we are the ultimate authors of our actions. This supposition is threatened by the scientific picture of our actions as events, just like others, in an unbroken chain of causes and effects. (Adam Zeman)[1]

I was a free man until they brought the dessert menu around. (Dennis Overbye)[2]

I call heaven and earth to witness against you today that I have set before you life and death, blessings and curses. Choose life so that you and your descendants may live, loving the LORD your God, obeying him, and holding fast to him. (Deut 30:19–20)

---

[1] Adam Zeman, *Consciousness: A User's Guide* (New Haven: Yale University Press, 2002), 342.
[2] Dennis Overbye, "Free Will: Now You Have It, Now You Don't," *The New York Times*, 2 January 2007; {http://select.nytimes.com/search/restricted/article?res=F10616F73D540C718CDDA80894DF404482#}; accessed 2 January 2007.

In 2003, neurologists from the Virginia Health System reported on a forty-year-old male schoolteacher who, throughout the year 2000, collected pornographic magazines and increasingly frequented pornographic web sites emphasizing images of children and adolescents. He also solicited prostitution at "massage parlors." He later noted that he regarded these activities as unacceptable, and that he had gone to great lengths to conceal them, but found that he was unable to stop himself from acting repeatedly on his sexual impulses. "The pleasure principle overrode" his urge restraint, he explained.

When his stepdaughter reported his subtle advances toward her to his wife, his wife discovered his growing preoccupation with child pornography and called the police. He was legally removed from the home, diagnosed as a pedophile, found guilty of child molestation, and sentenced either to an in-patient rehabilitation program for sexual addiction or to prison. Despite his strong desire to avoid jail, he was unable to restrain himself from soliciting sexual favors from women at the rehabilitation center, both staff and other clients, with the result that he was to be imprisoned.

On the eve of his sentencing, complaining of a headache, he went to the emergency room of a local hospital; admitting to suicidal ideation and a fear that he would rape his landlady, he was admitted for neurological observation. The medical staff reported that, during examination, he solicited female members of the neurological team for sexual favors. A magnetic resonance image (MRI) scan found an egg-sized tumor displacing the right orbitofrontal lobe, an area of the brain commonly implicated in moral-knowledge acquisition and social integration. Upon removal of the tumor, his sexually lewd behavior receded to the point that he was believed no longer to pose a threat to his stepdaughter and he returned home. Within a year, he developed a persistent headache and began collecting pornographic materials. Magnetic resonance imaging disclosed tumor regrowth, resulting in further surgery to remove the regrowth, after which his symptoms subsided.[3]

---

[3] Jeffrey M. Burns and Russell H. Swerdlow, "Right Orbitofrontal Tumor with Pedophilia Symptom and Constructional Apraxia Sign," *Archives of Neurology* 60, no. 3 (2003): 437–40.

Was this schoolteacher responsible for his actions? Was he capable of free will? However philosophers parse the term "free will," it seems clear enough that, in this case, the capacity to choose was lacking. As the attending neurologists Burns and Swerdlow comment, that his symptoms resolved with the tumor resection, twice, established a causal relationship from this man's tumor to his sociopathic behavior. What is more, the narrative of his medical and behavioral history demonstrated that his sociopathy was the product of his loss of impulse control rather than a loss of moral knowledge or moral compass.

Reports like this one are deeply disconcerting, harboring as they do the prospect of a loss of our sense of willful agency. We have a great deal invested in our intuitions regarding free will, ranging across our formal judicial systems, our instinctual parental practices, our assumptions about moral formation, and, indeed, our experiences and definitions of mental health.

One of the most enduring and cherished elements of our experience of being human is our presumed capacity to decide. As I move through the lexicon of my mind to determine the precise words I want to place next on this page, as much as when I chose years ago to use one of my undergraduate electives on a first course in Classical Greek, this sense of self-determination – and with it, self-responsibility – is irrepressible. So definitive is our belief in conscious free will that philosopher Thomas Metzinger wonders whether we can give it up and preserve our mental health, and the winner of the 2000 Nobel Prize in Physiology or Medicine, Columbia University's Eric R. Kandel, refers to its loss as "a dangerous idea." This is true even though recent neurological findings have led to the twofold conclusion that my choice at any given moment is restricted by my particular brain-state within a particular set of environmental conditions and that decision-making processes generally occur at a level beneath personal awareness.[4]

[4] Thomas Metzinger, "The Forbidden Fruit Intuition," *Edge* 176 (12 January 2006) {http://www.edge.org/q2006/q06_7.html#metzinger}; accessed 26 January 2006; Eric R. Kandel, "Free Will Is Exercised Unconsciously, without Awareness," *Edge* 176 (12 January 2006) {http://www.edge.org/q2006/q06_5.html}; accessed 26 January 2006.

For many, a distinguishing characteristic of humanity is the capacity to decide. Earthworms, goldfish, and jaguars do not leaf through a register of options before acting; they simply do what they are genetically programmed and neurobiologically hardwired to do. They act on instinct. They are possessed by "animal desires." Humans, on the other hand, possess the capacity to step back from the precipice of innate desires or inborn patterns of behavior in order to elect for or against them, so that even when human action follows the path of instinct this is nonetheless the product of a decidedly human reasonableness. Those who prove incapable of controlling their animal desires are beastly, brutish, somehow subhuman, irrational.

However popular or pervasive this portrait of the human person might be, it is deeply flawed. Its assumptions about human uniqueness lack foundation, and its dependence on notions of conscious rationality or even conscious volition cannot be sustained. This, at least, is the inescapable conclusion of a large and growing body of neurobiological experimentation. The result is a range of contested beliefs around traditional theological affirmations about sin, free will, and the nexus between volition and responsibility. At least potentially, here is one of the chief points of conflict between evolutionary psychology and biblical faith.

My plan is, first, to take up the challenge to "free will" from the natural sciences. This will surface important questions about Christian views of human freedom and sin, and allow me to explore briefly three perspectives on sin and freedom in the NT. This, in turn, will lead to my conclusion that "free will," at least as usually comprehended, is, according to both scientific and biblical-theological perspectives, overrated, yet not in a way that undermines theological affirmations of human responsibility. My analysis will demonstrate that evolutionary psychology and biblical studies come at these issues from quite different perspectives but end up making complementary affirmations regarding human formation and what theologians refer to as the human condition.

Challenges from the Natural Sciences

It may be useful to dismiss at the outset any interest in the question: Did my genes make me do it? In behavioral genetics, studies of identical twins, whether raised separately or in the same nurturing environment, have been attractive for their capacity to trace to what degree all sorts of behaviors – for example, religiosity, violence, sexual – are genetically induced. This is because each twin starts life with the same genetic arrays of potential subject to the influence of responses to diverse situations. From such studies, geneticists have shown that, whereas eye color and height are highly heritable, with the expression of either still subject to such environmental factors as nutrition and disease, behaviors are less so. If the heritability of height is roughly 90 percent, the heritability of "personal interests," as measured by a standard instrument like the Strong Campbell Interest Inventory, falls to 40 percent, and the heritability of such variables as church attendance, sexual permissiveness, and economic and political preferences are measured in the 40–60 percentiles. These data demonstrate the significant contribution of genetic factors but fall well short of genetic determinism. In fact, there is no one-to-one relationship between any gene and a particular behavior. This is not surprising, given the long road from DNA mapping to behavioral expression – from gene sequence to protein structure to cellular functions to the whole organism to the observable and measurable activity of the organism in its environment – with each step along the way subject to environmental interference. Genes, then, are a necessary but insufficient contributor to human behavior. They provide the lines on the page, so to speak, but do not determine what will be written.[5]

If not from genetic determinism, from whence does the challenge from the natural sciences to our treasured notions of free will

[5] See Lindon Eaves, "Genetic and Social Influences on Religion and Values," in *From Cells to Souls*, 102–22; V. Elving Anderson, "A Genetic View of Human Nature," in *Whatever Happened to the Soul? Scientific and Theological Portraits of Human Nature* (ed. Warren S. Brown et al.; TSc; Minneapolis: Fortress, 1998), 49–72.

derive? The story dates back at least as far as the 1874 publication of Thomas Huxley's essay, "On the Hypothesis that Animals Are Automata, and its History." With reference to a frog, he writes,

> The consciousness of brutes would appear to be related to the mechanism of their body simply as a collateral product of its working, and to be as completely without any power of modifying that working as the steam-whistle which accompanies the work of a locomotive engine is without influence upon its machinery. Their volition, if they have any, is an emotion indicative of physical changes, not a cause of such changes.[6]

Turning his reflections to the case of a wounded French sergeant, Huxley illustrates the similarities between the human creature and the beast, concluding that both are "automata creatures" and that consciousness of human volition is only an epiphenomenon – that is, they resemble the steam whistle that contributes nothing to the work of the locomotive. With regard to the experience of the self as a causal agent, in the last decade or two attention has focused on four kinds of evidence: 1) examples from comparative psychology of human-like ethical behavior among non-human species; 2) two widely acclaimed and much-discussed experiments that apparently undermine our basic belief that our conscious selves cause our own voluntary acts; 3) study of persons suffering from what may be classified as "disorders of volition"; and 4) growing evidence of the neural correlates of decision-making. Let me review each of these briefly.

1) Animals acting ethically

Impetus for affirming free will among humans has often come from those concerned to distinguish humans from the rest of the animal world. However, Francis de Waal has famously documented

---

[6] Thomas H. Huxley, "On the Hypothesis that Animals Are Automata, and its History," in *Methods and Results: Essays* (New York: D. Appleton, 1894), 199–250 (240).

among non-human primates dispositions regarded as laudable among humans, including such community-building or -maintaining concerns as altruism, reconciliation, consolation, and care.[7] Social behavior among animals has proven to be far more sophisticated than was earlier imagined. The twentieth-century discovery of tool-making among animals led to rethinking their capacities for planning ahead, for thinking through the consequences of their actions, and for cooperation. The recent discovery of mirror neurons in non-human primates (and in other species, including some elephants) provides clear biological evidence that these animals are, like humans, characterized by a "theory of mind" – that is, by the ability to understand that others have beliefs and intentions – which serves as the basis for social relatedness. That ethical behavior might mark the dividing line between humans and non-human creatures is thus an increasingly arguable assumption.

Before giving way to biological reductionism, however, more needs to be said. Writing of the biological basis of ethical behavior, Francisco Ayala helpfully distinguishes between the *capacity for ethics* and adherence to a particular set of *moral norms,* just as one might distinguish between the capacity for language and one's fluency in a particular language (say, English or Mandarin).[8] This distinction raises two immediate possibilities for our thinking. First, although we find that, under attack, a herd of zebras will protect their young, or that, having sighted a coyote, a prairie dog will issue an alarm to the rest of the colony, these forms of behavior may cohere with a human moral norm we call altruism quite apart from any moral stratagem or self-conscious reflection on the part of the prairie dog or the zebra herd. The appearance in different species of self-sacrificing behavior does not disclose for us the basis of those behaviors. Second, whereas we can see the obvious evolutionary advantage of behavior that puts one's own life at risk for

---

[7] E.g., Francis de Waal, *Good Natured: The Origins of Right and Wrong in Humans and Other Animals* (Cambridge, MA: Harvard University Press, 1996); idem, *Peacemaking among Primates* (Cambridge, MA: Harvard University Press, 1989).

[8] Ayala, "Biological Evolution." See further, Holmes Rolston III, "Kenosis and Nature," in *The Work of Love: Creation as Kenosis* (ed. John Polkinghorne; Grand Rapids, MI: Eerdmans, 2001), 43–65.

the sake of the colony or herd, we cannot escape the observation that humans have proven capable of embracing moral norms that supplant such considerations. This might include placing one's self-interest before that of the community, for example, or taking a stand for the sake of principle, or engaging in behaviors championed by Jesus which seem to defy natural selection as much as cultural conventions (e.g., behaviors that refuse the norms of reciprocity [Luke 14:12–14], enemy-love [Luke 6:35–36], or neighborly compassion to the stranger [Luke 10:30–37]).[9]

2) Mind time and false causes

Of the two widely discussed laboratory experiments designed to test the intuitive sense that our voluntary acts are the effects of the exercise of our own conscious volition, the first was performed by Benjamin Libet. He devised a means for recording the electroencephalograph (EEG) event-related potential that precedes a voluntary finger movement, comparing this to the onset of the subjects' conscious awareness of their intention to cause that movement. Astonishingly, Libet found that conscious awareness occurred temporally *after* the onset of brain activity setting in motion the voluntary movement though *before* the movement itself. This led Libet to argue against "free will" in favor of "free won't" – that is, that even though we do not consciously cause an action like a voluntary finger movement, we are capable of stopping it before it happens.[10]

---

[9] The view that biblical ethics in general, and the ethics of Jesus in particular, promote a life that minimizes our evolutionary drives has been proposed in Patricia A. Williams, *Doing without Adam and Eve: Sociobiology and Original Sin* (TSc; Minneapolis: Fortress, 2001); and Daryl P. Domning and Monika K. Hellwig, *Original Selfishness: Original Sin and Evil in the Light of Evolution* (Aldershot: Ashgate, 2006), esp. 117–35.

[10] Benjamin Libet et al., "Time of Conscious Intention to Acts in Relation to Onset of Cerebral Activity (Readiness-Potential)," *Brain* 106 (1983): 623–42; Libet, "Do We Have Free Will?" in *The Volitional Brain: Towards a Neuroscience of Free Will* (ed. Benjamin Libet et al.; Thorverton: Imprint Academic, 1999), 47–57; idem, *Mind Time: The Temporal Factor in Consciousness* (Cambridge, MA: Harvard University Press, 2004).

The second is a pair of experiments conducted by Daniel Wegner. In the first, a subject was directed to move a cursor randomly around a computer monitor and, approximately every 30 seconds, to stop the cursor over an object depicted on the screen. With each event, subjects were asked to provide an "intentionality rating" across a continuum from feeling completely sure that they had caused the cursor to stop (100%) to feeling completely sure that the experimenter had caused the cursor to stop (0%). The results were again astonishing. When the stops were actually initiated by the subject, the intentionality rating was only 56 percent. When the stops were initiated by the experimenter, the intentionality rating was 56 percent if the subjects heard the name of the object through their headphones either five seconds or one second before the forced stop. The intentionality rating was 52 percent if the subjects heard the name of the object 30 second before or one second after the forced stop. This led to the conclusion that, if we think about the event just before it happens, we tend to imagine that our conscious thoughts are causally related to the event. In the second experiment, subjects viewed other people's gloved hands in the position where their own hands would normally appear. These hands performed a series of actions, with the subjects asked to rate on a scale from 1 ("not at all") to 7 ("very much") whether they had controlled those actions. An average score of 2.05 ± 1.61 (SD) demonstrated that subjects were not entirely sure that they had not controlled the hand movements. Interestingly, though, when the owner of the gloved hands received instructions that were also heard by the subject, subjects rated their control over the hands higher by a significant margin, to 3.00 ± 1.09. This led to the conclusion that, if our thoughts about an entity are consistent with what happens to it, we tend to believe that we caused it to happen.

These and related observations led Wegner to conclude that actions and conscious thoughts about those actions are generated along parallel paths by a single force – namely, unconscious neural events.[11] Wegner speaks frankly of "the illusion of conscious will,"

---

[11] Daniel M. Wegner and Thalia Wheatley, "Apparent Mental Causation: Sources of the Experience of Will," *American Psychologist* 54 (1999): 480–92; Wegner, *The Illusion of Conscious Will* (Cambridge, MA: The MIT Press,

insisting that, "although the experience of conscious will is not evidence of mental causation, it does signal personal authorship of action to the individual and so influences both the sense of achievement and the acceptance of moral responsibility."[12]

Not unexpectedly, the ramifications Libet and Wegner (and others) have drawn from these experiments have fueled ongoing debate, not least among philosophers set on preserving the role of conscious decision-making in the initiation of intentional action.[13] The net effect of the conversation thus far has been either a decision in favor of the neurobiological determination of all choices and behavior or agreement to push for greater fine-tuning around what is meant by conscious awareness and intentional agency.[14]

2002); Wegner et al., "Vicarious Agency: Experiencing Control over the Movements of Others," *Journal of Personality and Social Psychology* 86 (2004): 838–48.

[12] Wegner, *Illusion of Conscious Will,* 318.

[13] See, e.g., Sukhvinder S. Obhi and Patrick Haggard, "Free Will and Free Won't," *American Scientist* 92 (2004): 358–65; Dirk Hartmann, "Neurophysiology and Freedom of the Will," *Poiesis & Praxis* 2 (2004): 275–84; Tillmann Vierkant, "Owning Intentions and Moral Responsibility," *Ethical Theory & Moral Practice* 8 (2005): 507–34; Garry Young, "Preserving the Role of Conscious Decision Making in the Initiation of Intentional Action," *Journal of Consciousness Studies* 13 (2006): 51–68; Sean A. Spence, "The Cycle of Action: A Commentary on Garry Young (2006)," *Journal of Consciousness Studies* 13 (2006): 69–72; Jing Zhu, "Reclaiming Volition: An Alternative Interpretation of Libet's Experiment," *Journal of Consciousness Studies* 10 (2003): 61–77; Susan Pockett et al., eds., *Does Consciousness Cause Behavior?* (Cambridge, MA: The MIT Press, 2006); Mark Hallett, "Volitional Control of Movement: The Physiology of Free Will," *Clinical Neurophysiology* 118 (2007): 117–92.

[14] Other monographs include Paul W. Glimcher, *Decisions, Uncertainty, and the Brain: The Science of Neuroeconomics* (Cambridge, MA: The MIT Press, 2003); Henrik Walter, *Neurophilosophy of Free Will: From Libertarian Illusions to a Concept of Natural Autonomy* (Cambridge, MA: The MIT Press, 2001). Coming at the issue from the perspective of game theory, Glimcher urges that our experiences and ideas about free will are the consequence of longstanding cultural explanations, and that these are in need of re-examination. For his part, Walter argues that a "moderate version of free will" is compatible with what we are learning from neuroscience.

82   BODY, SOUL, AND HUMAN LIFE

3) *Disorders of volition*

Significant advances in neuroscience have often come when things
have gone terribly wrong with human brains. This is because ethical commitments prevent intrusion into or purposeful damaging of
the brain for experimental purposes, though such advances as pos-
itron emission tomography (PET) scanning and magnetic resonance imaging (MRI), for example, have allowed researchers a
fresh kind of window into brain activity.

The most famous story is that of Phineas Gage, a twenty-five-
year-old railroad worker who, in 1848, experienced the piercing
blast of a thirteen-pound iron rod that entered below his left cheek-
bone, penetrated his skull, traversed the front part of his brain, and
exited through the top of his head. Although he survived the accident, his personality underwent a dramatic change. Known
previously as a responsible, efficient, energetic, and capable
person, he was described afterward as irresponsible and careless,
given to raucous profanity, socially backward, and emotionally
stagnant. Simply put, "Gage was no longer Gage." Though largely
intact physically (the accident left him blind in one eye), he suffered
a significantly diminished capacity with regard to social behavior,
ethical comportment, and decision-making oriented toward his
own flourishing or even survival.[15]

Gage's may be the most famous story, but it is hardly unique.[16]
Lesions to the orbitofrontal cortex in childhood have been shown
to lead to analogous, lifelong social and moral behavioral problems resistant to corrective interventions.[17] Pathological lying has

---

[15] Gage's case is the centerpiece for Antonio R. Damasio's book, *Descartes'
Error: Emotion, Reason, and the Human Brain* (New York: Avon, 1994), esp.
3–33. For details and interpretation, see Malcolm Macmillan, "Restoring
Phineas Gage: A 150th Retrospective," *Journal of the History of the
Neurosciences* 9 (2000): 46–66.
[16] See James L. Stone, "Transcranial Brain Injuries Caused by Metal Rods or
Pipes over the Past 150 Years," *Journal of the History of the Neurosciences* 8
(1999): 227–34.
[17] E.g., Steven W. Anderson et al., "Impairment of Social and Moral Behavior
Related to Early Damage in Human Prefrontal Cortex," *Nature Neuroscience*

been tied to abnormality within the prefrontal cortex, giving rise to images of "the lying brain."[18] Patients with focal bilateral damage to the ventromedial prefrontal cortex, an area of the brain implicated in the generation of social emotions, display an abnormally utilitarian pattern of moral judgment, expressing a heightened willingness to kill or harm someone if doing so would save the lives of others.[19] In a collection of studies published under the title *The Volitional Brain: Towards a Neuroscience of Free Will*, scholars representing diverse fields reported on persons who evidenced a "sick will" (e.g., inactivity, lack of ambition, autistic behavior, depressive motor skills, and behavioral inhibition), correlating those symptoms with subnormal activity in the prefrontal cortex.[20] Persons with schizophrenia lack the feeling of personal authorship of some of their own thoughts or actions, attributing them to an agency beyond themselves – hence, the sense of "hearing voices" and more general confabulation of unreal persons and forces. Persons with certain brain lesions have a condition known as Alien Hand Syndrome – that is, they have a hand that acts beyond the subject's conscious, voluntary control. One hand seems to function on its own accord, answering the phone, for example, choosing a shirt from the closet, or attempting to strangle the subject during sleep.[21] Disorders of volition also appear among persons suffering from depression, a condition in which the inability of patients to initiate new goal-oriented activity is correlated with

2 (1999): 1032–37; see the commentary by Raymond J. Dolan, "On the Neurology of Morals," *Nature Neuroscience* 2 (1999): 927–29.

[18] Yaling Yang et al., "Prefrontal White Matter in Pathological Liars," *British Journal of Psychiatry* 187 (2005): 320–25; see the commentary by Sean A. Spence, "Prefrontal White Matter – the Tissue of Lies?" *British Journal of Psychiatry* 187 (2005): 326–27.

[19] Michael Koenig et al., "Damage to the Prefrontal Cortex Increases Utilitarian Moral Judgements," *Nature* (21 March 2007) {http://www.nature.com/nature/journal/vaop/ncurrent/abs/nature05631.html}; accessed 22 March 2007.

[20] Libet et al., eds., *Volitional Brain*; cf. also Elkhonon Goldberg, *The Executive Brain: Frontal Lobes and the Civilized Mind* (Oxford: Oxford University Press, 2001).

[21] See the discussion in Todd E. Feinberg, *Altered Egos: How the Brain Creates the Self* (Oxford: Oxford University Press, 2001), 93–99.

inhibition in the brain's frontal lobe and in the anterior cingulate cortex, parts of the brain implicated in executive functioning. Volitional impairment arises in instances of addiction and substance abuse as regions of the brain related to signaling immediate pain or pleasure override those regions related to future prospects. And virtually everyone has had the experience of acting unselfconsciously – say, walking or driving or doodling – when the action is repetitive or habitual.[22]

4) Hardwired behavior

A host of laboratory studies in the past decade have demonstrated the tight link between neuronal processes and moral decision-making – including, but not limited to, reviewing past decisions and their consequences, weighing options and potential rewards, and envisioning the future.[23] Indeed, the most basic and significant contribution of cognitive science is its irreducible emphasis on the somatic basis of human existence, including the exercise of the mind.[24] Some background on two aspects of human formation will orient us here.

First, as neuroscientist Joseph LeDoux colloquially puts it, "People don't come preassembled, but are glued together by life."[25]

---

[22] For discussion, see Natalie Sebanz and Wolfgang Prinz, eds., *Disorders of Volition* (Cambridge, MA: The MIT Press, 2006); Daniel M. Wegner and Betsy Sparrow, "Authorship Processing," in *The Cognitive Neurosciences* (3rd ed.; ed. Michael S. Gazzaniga; Cambridge, MA: The MIT Press, 2004), 1201–9. On substance abuse, see the recent report, Jeffrey W. Dalley et al., "Nucleus Accumbens D2/3 Receptors Predict Trait Impulsivity and Cocaine Reinforcement," *Science* 315, no. 5816 (2007): 1267–70.

[23] For a readable introduction, see Laurence Tancredi, *Hardwired Behavior: What Neuroscience Reveals about Morality* (Cambridge: Cambridge University Press, 2005).

[24] See, e.g., George Lakoff, "How the Body Shapes Thought: Thinking with an All-Too-Human Brain" and "How to Live with an Embodied Mind: When Causation, Mathematics, Morality, the Soul, and God are Essentially Metaphorical Ideas," in *The Nature and Limits of Human Understanding* (ed. Anthony J. Sanford; The 2001 Gifford Lectures; London: T&T Clark, 2003), 49–73, 75–108.

[25] Joseph LeDoux, *Synaptic Self: How Our Brains Become Who We Are* (New York: Viking Penguin, 2002), 3.

LeDoux thus highlights the effects of environment on human development, drawing attention to how formative influences are encoded in the synapses of the central nervous system, those points of communication among the cells of the brains, or neurons. Even if the organization of the brain is hardwired genetically, genes shape only the broad outline of our mental and behavioral functions; the rest is sculpted through our life experiences. Hence, although our genes bias the way we think, feel, believe, and behave, the systems responsible for much of what we do and how we do it are shaped by learning. What is more, "learning" (or "training") is the product especially of interpersonal experiences, which directly shape the ongoing development of the brain's structure and function.[26] In short, from birth, we are in the process of becoming, and this "becoming" is encoded in our brains by means of synaptic activity as both nature and nurture yield the same effect – namely, sculpting the brain (and thus shaping the mind) in ways that form and reform the developing self. If the neurobiological systems that shape how we think, feel, believe, and behave are forever being sculpted in the context of our social experiences, then it follows that we can speak of personal (trans)formation only in relational terms. Our autobiographical selves are formed within a nest of relationships, a community. As Jim Grigsby and David Stevens summarize, "Personality is shaped by the interaction of constitutional processes and the experiences of individuals in unique environments. In other words, we are, at least in part, who we learn to be."[27]

Second, because of our interest in decision-making and ethical behavior, let me comment on the impossibility of "pure reason," or, more generally, of the error made by Descartes and those who would follow him of imagining that we might engage in "thinking" or "rationality" or "cognition" apart from the influence of our emotions, as if our decisions might be made on the basis of "cool

---

[26] So Daniel J. Siegel, *The Developing Mind: How Relationships and the Brain Interact to Shape Who We Are* (New York: Guilford, 1999).
[27] Jim Grigsby and David Stevens, *Neurodynamics of Personality* (New York: Guilford, 2000), 39.

reason." On the one hand, the work of Joseph LeDoux and others, discussed in *The Emotional Brain*, has demonstrated that the amygdala, that structure of the brain implicated in emotion, is networked with the brain's decision-making center such that, in normal brains, "thinking" is inescapably emotion-laden.[28] On the other hand, in his celebrated work *Descartes' Error*, Antonio Damasio both proposes the illogic of "cool reason" in decision-making, since so many options are available at any point in time that it is simply impossible to analyze each of them, and demonstrates in cases of brain injury that damage to the emotion-processing center of the brain impedes real-life rationality and decision-making.[29] Even when capacities for memory and abstract reasoning are intact, robbed of the biasing function of emotional responses (a somatic marker expressed, usually unconsciously, as a "gut feeling" of attraction or repulsion in the face of a given choice), persons prove to be incompetent decision-makers. Subsequent empirical study has only proven further the role of emotion in decision-making.[30]

---

[28] Joseph LeDoux, *The Emotional Brain: The Mysterious Underpinnings of Emotional Life* (London: Weidenfeld & Nicolson, 1998).

[29] Damasio, *Descartes' Error*. For further discussion of Damasio's "somatic marker hypothesis," which seeks to account for the influence of emotion on decision-making, see Antoine Bechara et al., "Emotion, Decision Making and the Orbitofrontal Cortex," *Cerebral Cortex* 10 (2000): 295–307; for related work, see George Loewenstein, "The Pleasures and Pain of Information," *Science* 312 (2006): 704–6. For an application of this kind of approach to Jewish and Christian moral systems, see Heather Looy, "Embodied and Embedded Morality: Divinity, Identity, and Disgust," *Zygon* 39 (2004): 219–35.

[30] For research reviews, see Morten L. Kringelbach, "The Human Orbitofrontal Cortex: Linking Reward to Hedonic Experience," *Nature Reviews Neuroscience* 6 (2005): 691–702; Jorge Moll et al., "The Neural Basis of Human Moral Cognition," *Nature Reviews Neuroscience* 6 (2005): 799–809. Recent studies include, e.g., Allison N. McCoy and Michael L. Platt, "Risk-sensitive Neurons in Macaque Posterior Cingulate Cortex," *Nature Neuroscience* 8 (2005): 1220–27; Giorgio Coricelli et al., "Regret and Its Avoidance: A Neuroimaging Study of Choice Behavior," *Nature Neuroscience* 8 (2005): 1255–62; Joshua D. Greene et al., "The Neural Bases of Cognitive Conflict and Control in Moral Judgement," *Neuron* 44 (2004): 389–400.

Among the implications of these data, two are of special interest to us in this chapter. The first is simply the embodied nature of decision-making, its manifestly somatic basis, involving predispositions and emotion alongside logical weighing of considerations. Second, decision-making cannot be characterized by the laws of neurobiology in simple bottom-up terms, since our neurobiological profile is itself in a state of ongoing formation and reformation on account of environmental, and especially relational, influences and through self-reflexive evaluation of the bases and futures of past and prospective behaviors.

Freedom and Sin: Three New Testament Coordinates

What is the nature of the challenge of contemporary neuro-scientific findings and ruminations for our understanding of the human situation in biblical terms? Simply put, our traditional understanding of responsibility for sin is collocated with affirmations of free will. Conscious intent and personal culpability are typically conjoined. If, as cognitive science urges, thought and intent are embodied, most of our thought occurs at a subconscious level, and our behavior is generated preconsciously, do the findings of the cognitive sciences not stand in tension with traditional views of freedom and sin?[31] Of course, one easy – and, for some, attractive – response would be to opt for a dualist account of the human person. Paul Jewett, for example, urged that "the choices we make are really free because the will, as a faculty of the spirit, transcends brain functions and therefore is not causally

---

[31] Hence, in addition to important issues in ethical theory, we are being confronted by profound challenges regarding the applicability of the law among persons whose brains lack the physiological capacity for reasoning, judgment, and impulse control expected of adults in cases involving genetic predispositions or brain lesions, for example, but also among normally developing adolescents whose neural capabilities are simply pre-adult. See, e.g., Michael S. Gazzaniga, *The Ethical Brain* (New York: Dana, 2005), 87–142; Mary Beckman, "Crime, Culpability, and the Adolescent Brain," *Science* 305 (2004): 596–98.

determined."[32] By way of response, on the one hand, given the neurobiological evidence regarding decision-making I must admit that it is unclear to me what role a second ontological entity like a soul or spirit would have other than an epiphenomenal one. On the other, it is worth asking how a biblical theology of sin might look in relation to the neurobiological considerations already outlined. By way of initiating that discussion, I will focus on three representative voices: Peter, James, and Paul. Beginning with 1 Peter will allow me briefly to reflect more broadly on biblical perspectives on the character of sin.

1) Sin as sculptor in 1 Peter

Peter's vocabulary of sin is as imaginative as his theology of sin is insightful.[33] Words like "stumble," "transgress," "to offend," "wrongdoing," "hard-hearted," "falling short," or "overstepping" are missing from 1 Peter. Instead we find:

- *References to the former lives of Peter's Christian audience*: "no longer being shaped by the desires that marked your former time of ignorance" (1:14); "you were liberated from the emptiness of your inherited way of life" (1:18); "having set aside every evil and every deceit, and pretenses and jealousies and all slander" (2:1); "enough time has been lost discharging the will of the Gentiles, conducting yourselves in acts of unrestraint, lust, drunkenness, carousing, bawdy partying, and unseemly idolatry" (4:3); and "flood of unrestrained immorality" (4:4);
- *References to behaviors currently to be avoided by Peter's Christian audience*: "to avoid worldly cravings that wage war against life" (2:11); "live your remaining time as a human no longer in accordance with human desires but in accordance with the will of God" (4:2); and "let none of you suffer as a murderer or a thief or an evildoer, or as a mischief-maker" (4:15); and

---

[32] Paul K. Jewett with Marguerite Shuster, *Who We Are*, 74.
[33] I refer to the author of 1 Peter as "Peter" without bias as to the identity of the actual author of the letter. For this section, I am adapting material from Green, *1 Peter*.

- *Labels for the antagonists of Peter's Christian audience*: "disbelievers" (2:8; 3:1; 4:17) and "blasphemers" (4:4).[34]

Additionally, Peter refers once to the "unrighteous" for whom the "Righteous One" suffered (3:18).

According to Peter's diagnosis, the past was marked by the work of an artist who sculpted human life according to the conventions, values, and dispositions of ignorance. Ignorance thus functions like a master determining the thoughts and movements of its slave, or like an artisan creating human life in its own image. Clearly, in such a context, "ignorance" cannot be equated with "lack of data" or "lack of knowledge," in the narrow sense; rather, ignorance is potent as "a faulty pattern of thinking," influential as a mistaken life-world. Ignorance is less "not understanding," more "misunderstanding" – that is, a failure at the deepest level to grasp adequately and thus to participate fully in God's aims. It provides the impetus and muscle for behaviors that Peter catalogues as vices – that is, as outside the boundaries of those whose deepest allegiance is to God. "Sin," then, is inhabiting the muck and executing the ways of a religious and moral climate set against God; it is present as an ethos of unrestrained immorality and craving that cannot but shape persons in its own likeness.

In broader biblical terms, this is simply the way of sin. Sin begets sin, one sin after the other. Sin in Genesis 3 is like a contagion, transmuting from shame and vulnerability to heightened alienation, even to the point where Yahweh's own voice is no longer invitation but threat. Cain's murderous act results in his exile (Gen 4:1–16); a restless, godless society emerges (Gen 4:17–24; 5:28–29); global violence leads to global destruction (Gen 6:1–9:18); sin within Noah's family leads to the enslavement of one people by another (Gen 9:17–27); and, finally, the imperialism of conquest leads to the confusion of languages (Gen 11). In all of this, we are not far from 1 Peter. Using different language, this letter depicts sin as a power, as "worldly cravings that wage war against life," even against the reborn (2:11). It is not for nothing that Peter portrays

---

[34] These citations from 1 Peter follow my own translation.

followers of Christ as slaves to God (2:16), who therefore cannot be enslaved to the empty, ancestral ways that shape society-at-large.

Indeed, it is because of the work of Christ that his followers can be done with sin. In 2:21, Peter portrays the suffering of Jesus as programmatic for Christian life. He reprises this emphasis in a more subtle way when in 4:1 he directs his audience to "ready" themselves "with the same pattern of thought." The analogy between Christ and his followers is not exact, since Christ's behavior provides not only the blueprint for his followers but also its basis. Hence, whereas the saying in 4:1, "the one who has suffered as a human has finished with sin," is general enough to apply both to Christ and his followers, it does so in different ways. Having resolved the problem of sin through his suffering, Christ is "finished with sin." Having departed their former lives of lust, lewdness, and idolatry (4:2–3), a withdrawal that has won for them suffering at the hands of those who continue thus to live, those of Peter's audience have "finished with sin." Thus, they may live their "remaining time as a human no longer in accordance with human desires but in accordance with the will of God" (4:2).

Leaving no doubt but that the capacity for transformation is divine gift, Peter nonetheless addresses his audience as persons capable of choice and responsible for their behavior. Responsibility is not a consequence of intentionality, however. Choices contrary to the will of God in the past were made by those enslaved to ignorance, but this did not make those choices any less sinful. Even for those called to holiness, sin remains a road that need not be taken. But for those who have yet to embrace the empowering grace of God, what sort of choice is this? If the values and practices honored in the universe of day-to-day existence, the ideals and modes of conduct sanctioned by its systems and institutions, are set in opposition to the ways of God, then the pull of sin's gravity is difficult to escape indeed. Genuine choice can come only in the context of authentic options, and this highlights both the profundity of Peter's diagnosis of sin-as-power and the importance for him of the work of the Spirit in hearing the good news and of a community set on following the pattern of Christ and embodying the character of God. Another vision of the world is needed; the ancestral ways may be common heritage but they are not necessarily defining influence. Renewed patterns of thinking must animate the new community oriented toward resisting evil and sin.

Recognition of the oppressive power of the attitudes and practices, the embodied narratives of evil, that pervade the world, does not excuse sin. Peter never countenances a response like, "I was raised in this world; what did you expect?" any more than he might say, "Satan made me do it." The idolatry of life apart from Christ is a sobering recognition of human limits and proclivity to expressions of evil, socially and personally. Yet there is no escaping the reality that human patterns of thinking, feeling, believing, and behaving are cultivated socially. This perspective does not spell the loss of freedom to choose, but it does suggest the degree to which choices are circumscribed already by communities of formation, even formation along evil lines. For this reason Peter urges his audience no longer to be "shaped by the desires that marked your former time of ignorance" (1:14) and claims for them that "you were liberated from the emptiness of your inherited way of life" (1:18).

Contrary to the claims of the serpent in the Garden, the concepts of good and evil do not exist in a vacuum. These are not "objective" realities, but must be understood in relation to some instrument of measuring. Living in a world that measures "the good" always in relation to the interests of "my group" or of "people like me" presses upon us choices that perpetuate disobedience, estrangement, disharmony, alienation. In an agonistic society like that of Peter's world, the canons by which "the good" is measured beckon all the more, since failure to line up behind Roman conventions led to serious and immediate ramifications. What of "the good" as defined by God's own words spoken over creation? Like those who live with life-long disease, humans easily adjust their lives to account for their maladies. The human family can scarcely imagine what the freedom to choose God's "good" would be, so much has humanity adapted itself to estrangement and alienation.

According to this diagnosis, the human family stands in need of the medicine of liberation – and this is precisely what God administers, according to Peter: through Christ's defeat of the powers arrayed against God, through his sacrificial death by which the stain of sin was cleansed, through the power of the Spirit in new birth and sanctification, through the community of believers whose mutuality of love provides a new home and family, and through the new identity that comes as believers are written into the eternal narrative of God's merciful agenda.

For Peter, the basic sin appears to be idolatry. Not only does he refer to the idolatrous past of his audience; he also refers to the blasphemy of those who oppose the faith. (Blasphemy, it is true, is included within but also can extend beyond idolatry.) In this context, Peter's apposition of "becoming holy" and "no longer being shaped by the desires that marked your former time of ignorance" is all the more significant, for it marks holiness as a potent sculptor of life just as we earlier found "ignorance" to be. "As obedient children, no longer being shaped by the desires that marked your former time of ignorance, you yourselves must rather become holy in every aspect of life, just as the one who called you is holy, for it is written, 'You shall be holy, because I am holy'" (1:14–16). This directive on Peter's part reaches back into the past of new birth, claiming that holiness is not only divine declaration but also human vocation. The soteriological journey on which he envisions his audience traveling is a rehabilitation of human relatedness to God and God's creation as this is envisioned in Israel's Scriptures. The existential beginning point of this journey is entry into the new reality to which Peter refers as God's having "given us new birth" (1:3), a dramatic metaphor for the decisive transformation of life that has come in accordance with God's mercy and by means of the resurrection of Jesus. Eschatological salvation has broken into the mundane world, so that nothing can be the same. What Peter announces is nothing less than a conversion to a new way of thinking, feeling, believing, and behaving. Peter acknowledges that a tendency to sin remains; thus, he reminds his audience not to suffer as "a murderer or a thief or an evildoer, or as a mischief-maker"

(4:15). However, if it remains, it no longer reigns. For 1 Peter, sanctifying agents come in various forms, especially the formative influences of suffering (the testing of faith as purgation, 1:6–7) and of the unmitigated love practiced within the household of faith (1:22; 2:17; 3:8; 4:8; 5:14). How is this related to the problem of idolatry? Peter's admonition clarifies the choices: be "shaped by the desires that marked your former time of ignorance" or "become holy in every aspect of life." Speaking more broadly, Robert Jenson urges that idolatry, the primary sin, counters the first command, "You shall have no other gods before me" (Exod 20:3). "One can serve the Lord, or one can plunge into the religious world's welter of possibilities and quests, but one cannot do both at once."[35]

Jenson names a further sin with which Peter is very much concerned even if he never voices it in quite this way. This is the sin of despair: "acting as if I were not delivered over to the future, as if in what I already am I were my proper self."[36] Two possibilities come to mind. The first is life lived under the horrific illusion that *this* is the object of our hope, that *this* is the destination for which the journey of faith was begun, and thus that *this* is our genuine home. The second is abandonment of hope in the face of wrongful suffering. The first forgets that this is Babylon, while the second assumes that Babylon has the last word. The first assumes that courageous resistance in the world is unnecessary, while the second assumes that courageous resistance in the world is useless. The effect is the same – capitulation in the face of that temptation so integral to the experience of exile: defection, apostasy. It is no wonder that Peter urges joyful and hopeful responses even in the midst of suffering (e.g., 1:8; 4:13). And it is no wonder that he anticipates the sin of despair with his sharpest imperatives: "Remain vigilant! Stay alert! Your adversary, the devil, like a roaring lion is on the prowl, seeking someone to devour. Resist him, standing firm in the faith,

[35] Robert W. Jenson, *Systematic Theology* (2 vols.; Oxford: Oxford University Press, 1997–99), 2:134.
[36] Jenson, *Systematic Theology*, 2:145.

recognizing that the same kind of sufferings are being accomplished in the case of your family of believers throughout the world" (5:8–9).

For 1 Peter, then, human life is life on the potter's wheel, so to speak – being shaped one way or the other, by the ancestral ways expressed in taken-for-granted social conventions, or by the sanctifying work of the Holy Spirit and the formative influence of the people of God. Humans act out of their formation, so the primary questions must be, Formed according to what pattern? Formed within what community?

2) *Sin, the child of desire, in James*

In addition to providing a catalogue of sinful behaviors and dispositions (e.g., partiality, faith that does not express itself in works), James has a keen diagnosis of the problem of sin. One pathway into his thought is provided in James 4:4: "Adulterers! Do you not know that friendship with the world is enmity with God? Therefore whoever wishes to be a friend of the world becomes an enemy of God." According to Luke Timothy Johnson, this text, with its apposition of friendship with God and friendship with the world, provides the theological center of the letter's moral exhortation.[37] Its importance derives in large part from the notion of "friendship" which, from the classical period on, signified unity of heart and mind. Indeed, Cicero had described friendship as "nothing other than the agreement over all things divine and human along with good will and affection" (*De amic.* 6.20).[38] Given the unrelentingly negative portrait of the "world" in James (1:27; 2:5; 3:6; 4:4), his polarized rhetoric at this juncture is hardly surprising. And given

---

[37] Luke Timothy Johnson, *The Letter of James: A New Translation with Introduction and Commentary* (AB 37A; New York: Doubleday, 1995), 80–88; also, idem, "Friendship with the World and Friendship with God: A Study of Discipleship in James," in *Brother of Jesus, Friend of God: Studies in the Letter of James* (Grand Rapids, MI: Eerdmans, 2004), 202–20.

[38] See, e.g., David Konstan, *Friendship in the Classical World* (Cambridge: Cambridge University Press, 1997).

the starkness of the choices confronting believers, we may not be surprised to find James' invective unleashed against the "double-minded," another word that helps us to understand the character of sin for James (1:7; 4:8; cf. Ps 119:113). Lacking a pure heart, the "double-minded" (δίψυχος, *dipsychos*) deceive themselves; though regarding themselves as religious, they fail to put into play in their lives the ways of God (see 1:26–27). Similarly, labeling his audience as "adulterers" (4:4), James recalls the biblical tradition of Israel as God's unfaithful wife – that is, as those having (or claiming) a covenant relationship with Yahweh while engaging in idolatry. Insight into what comprises "friendship with the world" can be found in a number of texts in this letter, but perhaps none more clear than his depiction of "earthly" wisdom in terms of "bitter envy and selfish ambition in your hearts," which gives rise to "disorder and wickedness of every kind" (3:14–16). This is the antithesis of the wisdom God gives, which "is first pure, then peaceable, gentle, willing to yield, full of mercy and good fruits, without a trace of partiality or hypocrisy" (3:17; see 1:5). Given what we have found in 1 Peter, it is not surprising to find in James the correlation of personal and relational emphases. The very epitome of the sinful life is not an act but an allegiance, relationally delimited: "friendship with the world."

Another pathway into James' perspective on sin appears in the opening chapter of the letter, in his treatment of his audience's experience of πειρασμός (*peirasmos*, "trial" or "temptation"). First, James sketches a progression from trials to maturity: "My brothers and sisters, whenever you face trials of any kind, consider it nothing but joy, because you know that the testing of your faith produces endurance; and let endurance have its full effect, so that you may be mature and complete, lacking in nothing" (1:2–4). Then, he sketches a parallel progress from trials, now read as "temptations," to death: "But one is tempted by one's own desire, being lured and enticed by it; then, when that desire has conceived, it gives birth to sin, and that sin, when it is fully grown, gives birth to death" (1:14–15). Between these two chains of effects lies a pronouncement of blessing for all who endure πειρασμός, as well as

James' reply to the all-important question he anticipates, What is the source of πειρασμός? Having denied that πειρασμός (the verbal form, πειράζω, *peirazō*, appears in vv. 13–14) has its origins in God, who is rather the source of "every generous act of giving, with every perfect gift" (1:17), James traces the source of πειρασμός back to desire (ἐπιθυμία, *epithymia*). Here we find James' dexterity with the ambiguity resident in the term πειρασμός. As exilic sojourners, those to whom James has addressed this letter are surely facing situations of affliction or conflict. What determines whether πειρασμός is "testing" or "temptation" is one's own desire. As John Wesley concluded, "We are therefore to look for the cause of every sin, *in*, not *out of*, ourselves."[39] This does not mean that James regards the human person as inherently evil – or perhaps, it is better simply to let stand the paradox in James' dual claims that humans are characterized by an inclination toward evil, a predisposition toward sin, and that humans continue in at least some sense to bear the image of God in which they were made (3:9).[40]

In James' calculus of sin, two semantic fields are associated with "desire," both viewed as an almost irrepressible force: a fisherman with a tackle box of tricks to snag a fish, and an irresistible seductress.[41] With his reference to "desire," then, James identifies the source of his audience's real difficulties not in terms of external pressures and certainly not as manifestations of the divine will, but as internal inclinations. 'Επιθυμία, used

---

[39] John Wesley, *Explanatory Notes upon the New Testament* (1754; London: Epworth, 1976), 857.

[40] See Andrew Chester, "The Theology of James," in *The Theology of the Letters of James, Peter, and Jude* (Andrew Chester and Ralph P. Martin; NTT; Cambridge: Cambridge University Press, 1994), 39–41; Walter T. Wilson, "Sin as Sex and Sex with Sin: The Anthropology of James 1:12–15," *HTR* 95 (2002): 147–68 (160–61).

[41] See Timothy B. Cargal, *Restoring the Diaspora: Discursive Structure and Purpose in the Epistle of James* (SBLDS 144; Atlanta: Scholars Press, 1993), 81–82.

in 1:14, 15 (compare ἡδονή [*hēdonē*, "pleasure"] in 4:1, 3; ἐπιθυμέω [*epithymeō*, "I desire"] in 4:2; and ἐπιποθέω [*epipotheō*, "I long for"] in 1:5), can be taken in the neutral sense of "desire," but in moral discourse typically has the negative sense of "evil desire" or "lust." Its generative role with respect to sin and death in this context unmistakably qualifies it as negative, and associates it with the wider Jewish tradition of the evil inclination. Indeed, the evil inclination gives rise to the double-mindedness by which James characterizes sin.[42] Individual responsibility is further highlighted by the addition of ἴδιος (*idios*, "one's own").

In the verses that follow, ἐπιθυμία stands in contrast to God's own desire, and thus to the "word of truth," the "implanted word" (1:18, 21):

God's desire (βούλομαι, *boulomai*)	Human desire (ἐπιθυμία)
by means of the "word of truth," the "implanted word"	
gives us birth (ἀποκυέω, *apokueō*)	gives birth (τίκτω, *tiktō*) to sin
"so that we would become a kind of first fruits of his creatures."	and sin gives birth (ἀποκυέω, *apokueō*) to death.

---

[42] See the recent discussion of relevant texts in Luke L. Cheung, *The Genre, Composition and Hermeneutics of James* (PBM; Carlisle: Paternoster, 2003), 206–13; he demonstrates the appropriateness of locating James' perspective within this tradition.

Accordingly, over against the potency of human desire stands the antidote, the gospel,[43] which when internalized is powerful to save.[44]

Although complex in its presentation, James' argument is easy to follow. The challenges of exilic life provide an arena for the unbridled exercise of human passion, the result of which is sin and death. Although one might be tempted to fault exilic life itself, or to lay the blame for unbearable temptations at the feet of God or the devil, this is a wrong-headed analysis. The problem is internal, not external, to the human person. Similarly, then, the solution must be internalized. Required is a transformation of human nature by means of divine wisdom, the divine word that must be received and fully embodied so that it imbues who one is and what one does. Theologically, this is nothing less than a conversion of the imagination, those patterns of thinking, feeling, believing, and behavior that animate our lives.

3) The dominion of sin in Paul

Among the letters written by or attributed to Paul in the NT, ἁμαρτία (hamartia, "sin") appears 64 times, congregating above

---

[43] Matt A. Jackson-McCabe has argued that James' use of the phrase "the implanted word" derives from a Stoic theory of human reason, with "word" understood not as "kerygma" but as Torah, with the result that the letter stands as testimony to a form of the Christian movement in which soteriology was tied not to rebirth through the kerygma but to Torah-observance (Logos and Law in the Letter of James: The Law of Nature, the Law of Moses, and the Law of Freedom [NovTSup 100; Leiden: Brill, 2001]). Unfortunately, however, Jackson-McCabe's investigation does not take seriously the manifestly soteriological role of "the implanted word"; does not address fully the parallel "word of truth" in 1:18 (cf. Eph 1:13: "word of truth, the gospel of your salvation"; Col 1:5–6: "word of the truth, the gospel that has come to you"; 2 Tim 2:15: "word of truth"); and does not account for James' image of "receiving" (δέχομαι, dechomai) the word, rather than its being a property or faculty of the human family. These considerations stand behind my identification of "the word" with "the gospel."

[44] See the extensive discussion in Matthias Konradt, Christliche Existenz nach dem Jakobusbrief: Eine Studie zu seiner soteriologischen und ethischen Konzeption (SUNT 22; Göttingen: Vandenhoeck & Ruprecht, 1998), 42–100.

all in his letter to the Romans. Even more intriguing, of the 39 appearances of ἁμαρτία in Romans, 30 are found in Romans 5–7. Forms of the verb ἁμαρτάνω (*harmartanō*, "I sin") appear in the Pauline corpus 14 times, six of these in Romans, and four of these in Romans 5–7. And the related adjectival ἁμαρτωλός (*hamartōlos*, "sinful," "sinner") appears eight times in the Pauline letters – four times in Romans, and three in Romans 5–7. Although Paul's vocabulary of sin is not limited to the appearance of this one word-group, this aggregation of the term "sin" does call attention to the importance of this section of Romans for understanding Paul's perspective on sin. Even more interesting is the agency allotted to sin: sin "entered the world" (5:12), where it exercised power reminiscent of a master-slave or king-subject relationship. For example, "death exercised dominion from Adam to Moses" (5:14), we were "enslaved to sin" (6:6), the aim of sin is to "exercise dominion in your mortal bodies, to make you obey their passions" (6:12), people presented their "members to sin as instruments of wickedness" (6:13), and people have presented themselves as slaves to sin (6:16). The baptized were formerly enslaved to sin, but they have been liberated from its dominion (6:17–18, 20, 22).

Indeed, the theme of Romans 6 is the inevitability of human slavery, with the only question being the identity of the master to whom one's life is presented: "to sin as instruments of wickedness" or "to God as instruments of righteousness" (v. 13). As Paul reasons, "For just as you once presented your members as slaves to impurity and to greater and greater iniquity, so now present your members as slaves to righteousness for sanctification" (v. 19). Again: "Do you not know that if you present yourselves to anyone as obedient slaves, you are slaves of the one whom you obey, either of sin, which leads to death, or of obedience, which leads to righteousness?" (v. 16). Earlier, Paul had sketched why this is so, contrasting the deeds of Adam and Jesus Christ (5:12–21). Through Adam's disobedience, many were made sinners. This is not because Paul holds to a doctrine of original sin (i.e., that sin is inherent to human nature and is the inheritance one generation passes on to the next), a view that owes itself far more to Augustine's reading of Romans 5:12 than to the apostle himself.[45] Paul's understanding of the universality of sin derives from the phenomenological observation: "because all sinned" (and not, as in the Latin translation used by Augustine, "in whom all have sinned"). That is, Paul's affirmation of the universality of sin derives from his understanding that Adam's sin set in motion a chain of effects, one sin leading to the next, not because sin was an essential constituent of the human condition but because all humanity followed Adam in his sinfulness. Paradoxically, then, human sinfulness is a sign of both human helplessness and culpability. As the apostle will go on to affirm in Romans 7, sin is an active agent at work in human transgression, performing as an alien intruder at work in the person of the sinner (vv. 17, 20); the potency of sin as the author of human behavior is not a manifestation of human perversity, then, but of human frailty.[46]

What is more, Paul goes on to aver, the Law itself was impotent in the face of sin's power and death's dominion. Consequently, the Law provided neither a prophylactic nor an antidote against the spread of sin and death. Whereas the deed of Adam spelled sin and death, however, the deed of Christ brings righteousness and life. This was available only through the grace that exercised "dominion through justification leading to eternal life through Jesus Christ our Lord" (5:21). Thus, "if, because of the one man's trespass, death exercised dominion through that one, much more surely will those who receive the abundance of grace and the free

---

[45] See the helpful discussion in Mark E. Biddle, *Missing the Mark: Sin and Its Consequences in Biblical Theology* (Nashville: Abingdon, 2005), 33–44. Williams urges that the biblical witness more broadly is bereft of a theology of original sin (*Doing without Adam and Eve*). Henri Blocher, on the other hand, defends the notion of original sin in terms of its universality, its belonging to the nature of human beings, its inheritedness, and its having stemmed from Adam – in Rom 5 and elsewhere – in *Original Sin: Illuminating the Riddle* (NSBT; Grand Rapids, MI: Eerdmans, 1997).
[46] Cf. Schnelle, *Human Condition*, 63–66; Berger, *Identity and Experience*, 207–9.

gift of righteousness exercise dominion in life through the one man, Jesus Christ" (5:17).

For Paul, the power and effect of sin are multidimensional, but for our purposes his portrait of the human condition in 1:18–32 is of special interest. Here, sin (in the broad sense; the language Paul uses in 1:18 is "ungodliness" and "unrighteousness") is identified not with individual acts of wickedness but with a general disposition on the part of the human family to refuse to honor God as God and to render him thanks. Sin is the proclivity to act as though things created, including humanity, were the Creator. It is idolatry, that primary sin, a counter to the first command, "You shall have no other gods before me" (Exod 20:3).[47]

Note, first, that Paul is not giving the autobiography of individual persons; he does not concern himself with following the life of a single person so as to demonstrate how he or she came to be implicated in sin. Rather, his perspective is cosmological, a diagnosis of the condition of the human family taken as a whole (cf. 3:9, 22b–23).

Second, the acts of wickedness that Paul goes on to enumerate by way of illustration are not themselves the problem. Gossip, envy, deceit, same-sex relations, rebelliousness toward parents, and the rest – these are expressions of sin.

Third, within the fabric of Paul's argument, these activities evidence the moral integrity of a God who takes sin seriously. Paul thus defends God's character by showing the progression from the human refusal to honor God, with its consequent denial of the human vocation to live in relation to God, to God's giving humanity over to its own desires – giving humanity, as it were, the life it sought apart from God; and from this to human acts of wickedness. To crib the language of Wisdom, for Paul, God "torments" those who live unrighteously by allowing them their own atrocities (Wis 12:23).

Fourth, in the threefold act of "handing over" humanity attributed by Paul to God, the first is significant for the way it identifies

---

[47] See Jenson, *Systematic Theology*, 2:134.

the human condition of slavery to sin: "Therefore God gave them up in the lusts of their hearts to impurity" (1:24). The term translated by the NRSV as "lust," ἐπιθυμία (*epithymia*), can be used in a neutral or even positive way (e.g., Phil 1:23), but more typically, both in Paul and in wider Greek usage, it refers to unbridled craving. Sin, Paul observes, provokes or cultivates just this sort of desire, which humans stand ready to obey (7:7–8; 6:12). "The implication is of a life lived habitually in terms of satisfying natural or animal appetites as the be-all and end-all."[48]

Fifth, for Paul, sin marks a rupture in the divine-human relationship, but it also manifests itself in human relations and in relations between humanity and the material creation. Sin in this broad sense can never be understood as something private or individualistic, for it always manifests itself in relation to others and to the cosmos (see 1:26–32).

Finally, Paul recognizes that ungodliness and unrighteousness have as their object their own self-legitimation: humanity embraces a lie (1:25) and receives a corrupt mind (1:28), with the consequence that it defines its unjust ways as just. In other words, the conceptual patterns by which humanity perceives the world and orders its behavior is out of touch with the way things really are. This itself is perhaps the most damning indictment, since it renders as an utter failure from the outset any attempts on the part of humans to think, feel, believe, and behave in ways that honor God.

One of the pivotal implications of this diagnosis of the human situation is its explanatory value for the virtual absence in Paul of the language of "forgiveness of sins."[49] Sin needs to be addressed, but, given Paul's perspective on "sin" as less "act" and more "disposition" or "compulsion," mere forgiveness or absolution is insufficient. Nor does Paul develop much the notion of

---

[48] James D.G. Dunn, *The Theology of Paul the Apostle* (Grand Rapids, MI: Eerdmans, 1998), 120.

[49] Among the letters attributed to Paul, the phrase is found in Eph 1:7; Col 1:14. On this point, see Richard B. Hays, "Made New by One Man's Obedience," in *Proclaiming the Scandal of the Cross: Contemporary Images of the Atonement* (ed. Mark D. Baker; Grand Rapids, MI: Baker Academic, 2006), 96–102.

"repentance";[50] after all, the condition of enslavement is not miti-gated by repentance on the part of the slave. Required, rather, is human change, a theological transformation – a deep-seated con-version in one's conception of God and, thus, in one's commit-ments, attitudes, and everyday practices. Not surprisingly, then, what Paul promises in Romans 5–6 is not "remission of sin" but liberation from our enslavement to sin and decay and participation in a new humanity whose home is the new life ushered in by means of the faithfulness of Jesus Christ whose death on the cross com-prises one of the most profound visual representations of the char-acter of God.

Conclusion

In the end, it appears that the distance between evolutionary psy-chology and biblical faith on the question of free will is less than traditional theological views might have allowed.[51] By traditional theological views, I refer to those views that insist on an abstract notion of "choice" (i.e., no matter what I have chosen to do, I might equally have chosen to do the opposite) and on tying respon-sibility to self-conscious agency. In part, this is because theological use of biblical texts has sometimes exaggerated the perspectives on freedom proposed by those texts, which, for example, take seri-ously the importance of freedom from service to sin but cast that freedom in terms of service to God; or which underscore the degree to which we are shaped in our character and limited in our choices by the company we keep.[52] It is also true, though, that any affirma-tion of the relative coherence of biblical faith and evolutionary psy-chology derives from a more nuanced understanding of cognitive

---

[50] Though see Rom 2:4; 2 Cor 7:9–10.
[51] For a different approach, one that is concerned with data from the natural sciences and that helpfully engages traditional definitions of free will philo-sophically, see Murphy, *Bodies and Souls*, 71–110.
[52] In addition to the perspectives developed earlier in this chapter, see, e.g., Matt 16:6, 11–12; Mark 8:15; Luke 12:1; 1 Cor 5:9; 15:33; 2 Cor 6:14–7:1.

science, one that allows for the top-down influence on
neurobiological processes from environmental factors and ongoing reflection on behavior. Other considerations, not developed in
the present discussion, have bearing as well, including the relative
indeterminacy of human behavior that arises from the sheer complexity of neuronal processes and the concomitant reality that
brain states are not entirely predictable,[53] as well as the often-
overlooked but common-sense observation that, if I am constrained in my choices by my biology, this is nothing more or less
than my being constrained by myself. "I," after all, do not stand
over against my body or exist in a potentially agonistic relationship
with my body, as though I could say that it is not me but my brain
that has performed in a certain way.[54]

Among the affirmations that might be drawn from the data we
have reviewed in this chapter, the following three are significant for
their coherence with both neurobiological and NT perspectives:

1) We do what we are. That is, our behaviors are generated out of,
    and so reflect, our character and dispositions.
2) Who we are is both formed and continually being formed socio-
    culturally, and especially relationally.
3) "Choice" is contextually determined, especially vis-à-vis ongo-
    ing relational influence and self-reflexive contemplation on the
    bases and futures of past and prospective decisions.

Biblical faith, as represented by these voices, pushes further, of
course, not with regard to the mechanism of choice per se, but in its
specification of 1) particular moral norms by which some behavior
is condemned and other behavior counseled and celebrated, and 2)
the communities of formation within which we locate ourselves.
What is more, whereas evolutionary psychology might counte-
nance behaviors conducive to one's success in one's social group

---

[53] Cf. Jeffrey D. Schall, "Neural Basis of Deciding, Choosing and Acting,"
Nature Reviews Neuroscience 2 (2001): 33–42.
[54] This is helpfully discussed in Gregory R. Peterson, "Do Split Brains Listen to
Prozac?" *Zygon* 39 (2004): 555–76.

together with the flourishing of that community, biblical faith pushes further, pressing, if you will, for human development understood in terms of what we might call a cultural evolution that outstrips, even contravenes, those developmental patterns recommended to us through our genetic heritage. To illustrate: whereas our brains are hard-wired to favor people that look like us – from our patterns of facial recognition to our intuitive responses of fight or flight – the gospel prescribes a multiethnic instantiation of the people of God.[55] Happily, in a prime example of the human capacity for choice, the laws of neurobiology actually provide for our re-formation – that is, the reformation of our selves – along these biblical-theological lines.

---

[55] Joshua D. Greene notes the evolutionary psychological basis of human dispositions for altruism for neighbors but not strangers ("From Neural 'Is' to Moral 'Ought': What Are the Moral Implications of Neuroscientific Moral Psychology?" *Nature Reviews Neuroscience* 4 [2003]: 847–50 [848–49]).

4

BEING HUMAN, BEING SAVED

The evolution of humanity does not seem to represent any linear progress towards salvation. Rather, it seems that each stage of human development is ambiguous as far as humanity's relationship with God is concerned. At each moment, there are both opportunities to be taken and dangers to be avoided. (Fraser Watts)[1]

Simply stated, becoming a Christian is the process of "naturalization" into a narrative tradition which has been (and is being) shaped by the story of Jesus. (Paul Markham)[2]

Do not be conformed to this world, but be transformed by the renewing of your minds, so that you may discern what is the will of God – what is good and acceptable and perfect. (Rom 12:2)

---

[1] Watts, *Theology and Psychology,* 114.
[2] Paul N. Markham, *Rewired: Exploring Religious Conversion* (DDCT; Eugene, OR: Pickwick, 2007), 163.

R ecent work in cognitive science has underscored the fallacy of
Descartes' notion of the mind, free to engage in its own opera-
tions (quite apart from one's own body and from other minds),
countering with its nonnegotiable emphasis on embodiment – that
is, "the role of an agent's own body in its everyday, situated cognition."[3] Language, dispositions, beliefs, behavior, feelings, experience – these do not belong to the world of the ethereal but are
embodied. This raises important questions regarding the nature of
the Christian experiences of conversion, salvation, and sanctification, and of such Christian practices as prayer, which have long
been associated with the human soul or spirit and not particularly
related to the body.

With the turn of the new millennium an area of study known
variously as "neurotheology" or "spiritual neuroscience" has
emerged in the interstices between psychology, spirituality, and
neuroscience.[4] From the scientific side, the primary focus of investigation is the neural correlates of religious, spiritual, and/or mystical experiences. Extravagant claims notwithstanding, these
experiments explore only the embodied quality of those experiences, and neither impinge in any way on their significance to the
persons and communities who report or enjoy those experiences
nor speak for or against the external reality of God.[5] Examples are
increasingly available. Andrew Newberg and his colleagues have
conducted several related studies:

- a single photon emission computed tomography (SPECT) study
  demonstrated changes in cerebral activity (particularly, the frontal lobes, parietal lobes, and left caudate) during glossolalia;[6]

---

[3] Raymond W. Gibbs Jr., *Embodiment and Cognitive Science* (Cambridge:
Cambridge University Press, 2006), 1.

[4] See Andrew B. Newberg and Bruce Y. Lee, "The Neuroscientific Study of
Religious and Spiritual Phenomena: Or Why God Doesn't Use Biostatistics,"
Zygon 40 (2005): 469–89.

[5] Cf. Eugene G. d'Aquili and Andrew B. Newberg, "The Neuropsychological
Basis of Religions, or Why God Won't Go Away," *Zygon* 33 (1998): 187–201.

[6] Andrew B. Newberg et al., "The Measurement of Regional Cerebral Blood
Flow during Glossolalia: A Preliminary SPECT Study," *Psychiatry Research:
Neuroimaging* 148 (2006): 67–71.

- a SPECT brain imaging of accomplished Tibetan Buddhist meditators yielded results compatible with deafferentation of (or blocking neural input to) the posterior superior parietal lobe and parts of the inferior parietal lobe during profound unitary states – that is, the seemingly timeless and spaceless loss of a differentiated sense of self that, among Christians, would be experienced as a sense of mystical union with God, but among Buddhists would be experienced nonpersonally as Nirvana;[7] and

- a SPECT study measuring cerebral blood flow in Franciscan nuns in meditative prayer which displayed increased activity in the prefrontal cortex, and the inferior frontal and inferior parietal lobes, with changes in the prefrontal cortex reflecting an altered sense of body consciousness during the prayer state.[8]

Similarly, in 2006, Mario Beauregard and Vincent Paquette reported on their functional magnetic resonance imaging (fMRI) study of the brain activity of 15 cloistered Carmelite nuns while they were subjectively in a state of union with God.[9] Belying speculation concerning a "God spot" or "God region" in the brain, these researchers observed the activation of a dozen different brain regions during the mystical experience.

Whatever else such studies indicate, they point clearly to the biological substrate of spiritual experience. Scholars increasingly speak of the innateness of human spirituality, though leaving plenty of room for spiritual development throughout one's life.[10] Although various, related phenomena could attract our attention in this chapter, my focus will be on conversion, particularly on how conversion is represented in the two-volume work, Luke-Acts. I

---

[7] Andrew B. Newberg et al., "The Measurement of Regional Cerebral Blood Flow during the Complex Cognitive Task of Meditation: A Preliminary SPECT Study," *Psychiatry Research: Neuroimaging* 106 (2001): 113–22.

[8] Andrew B. Newberg et al., "Cerebral Blood Flow during Meditative Prayer: Preliminary Findings and Methodological Issues," *Perceptual and Motor Skills* 97 (2003): 625–30.

[9] Beauregard and Paquette, "Neural Correlates of a Mystical Experience."

[10] See Julia C. Keller, "Sacred Minds," *Science and Theology News* 6, no. 4 (2005): 18.

want, first, to set the context for this discussion by reviewing recent work on conversion in Luke-Acts since this will suggest the importance of an approach to the subject that is informed by cognitive science. I then turn to sketch the neural correlates of change as prerequisite to a discussion of a perspective on the Lukan material that takes seriously the idea of *embodied conversion*. I hope to show that a cognitive perspective is not at all alien to the evidence we find in the Lukan narrative – and, indeed, that Luke's theology invites such an approach.

Questioning Conversion in Luke-Acts

Before turning more pointedly to the narrative of Luke-Acts to see how perspectives from cognitive science might be of relevance in an exploration of conversion, some stage-setting is necessary. A brief sketch of recent study of Luke's theology of conversion will give us the lay of the land for our own examination.

Even though the concept of "conversion" has become associated especially with the Christian faith, it is not a particularly biblical term, nor in the ancient world is this concept peculiar to early Christian proclamation and literature.[11] As in Greek literature more widely, so in the NT, the concept is typically lexicalized with the terms μετάνοια (*metanoia*, "repentance") and its verbal form, μετανοέω (*metanoeō*, "to change one's course"), or ἐπιστροφή (*epistrophē*, "a turning [toward]") and its verbal form ἐπιστρέφω (*epistrephō*, "to turn around"). On the basis of word usage alone, however, a whole range of issues important to the interpreter remains ambiguous. Is "conversion" an event, a process, or both?

---

[11] See, e.g., Thomas M. Finn, *From Death to Rebirth: Ritual and Conversion in Antiquity* (New York: Paulist, 1997); Philip Rousseau, "Conversion," in *OCD*, 386–87. The difficulties inherent in defining terms in a study of "conversion" in the NT are often acknowledged – e.g., Beverly Roberts Gaventa, *From Darkness to Light: Aspects of Conversion in the New Testament* (OBT 20; Philadelphia: Fortress, 1986), 1–16; Richard V. Peace, *Conversion in the New Testament: Paul and the Twelve* (Grand Rapids, MI: Eerdmans, 1999), 1–14.

Is conversion a cognitive or a moral category, or both?[12] What is
the relationship between "rejection of one way of life for another"
and "embracing more fully the life one has chosen" – both easily
illustrated connotations of *metanoia?* Is conversion a crossing of
religious boundaries? Moreover, the concept of conversion is often
present where no such terms are used.

Two recent studies surface such issues as these. In 2002, Guy
Nave published his dissertation on *The Role and Function of
Repentance in Luke-Acts.*[13] Nave's focus is narrative-critical, but
his analysis is heavily supplemented by a lengthy survey of the
usage of *metanoeō* and *metanoia* among Luke's literary precursors
and peers – that is, in Classical and Hellenistic Greek literature, in
Hellenistic Jewish literature, and in NT and other early Christian
literature apart from Luke-Acts. This allows him both to undermine the claims of earlier scholars regarding the unprecedented
character of Jewish or Christian views of the meaning of repentance, and to document contextual influences on how Luke and his
audience might have understood the motif. In the end, Nave notes,
he will be able to suggest the dialectical relationship between
Luke's use of the concept of repentance and its usage in the sociohistorical situation within which the Lukan narrative was written.

With respect to the historical matrix within which we might
read Luke-Acts, Nave finds several significant trajectories. Practically from the coining of the terminology of *metanoeō* and
metanoia, the primary sense of these words centered on a "change
in thinking," though, he says, this sense expands to "a change of
mind, heart, view, opinion or purpose," often in tandem with

---

[12] Jacques Dupont ("Conversion in the Acts of the Apostles," in *The Salvation
of the Gentiles: Essays on the Acts of the Apostles* [New York: Paulist, 1979],
61–84) claims that conversion in Acts is moral rather than cognitive. Charles
H. Talbert ("Conversion in the Acts of the Apostles: Ancient Auditors' Perceptions," in *Literary Studies in Luke-Acts: Essays in Honor of Joseph B.
Tyson* [ed. Richard O. Thompson and Thomas E. Phillips; Macon, GA: Mercer University Press, 1998], 141–53) counters that both moral and cognitive
conversion are found in Acts.
[13] Guy D. Nave Jr., *The Role and Function of Repentance in Luke-Acts*
(SBLAB 4; Atlanta: Society of Biblical Literature, 2002).

feelings of remorse due to the perception of having acted or thought wrongly, inappropriately, or disadvantageously. *Metanoia,* if it were genuine, would be accompanied further by a will to make right the wrong committed or to change the situation that eventuated in the wrongdoing, and a concomitant alteration of future behavior. Sometimes *metanoia* was the result of divine and/or human chiding. Ultimately, *metanoia* would lead to forgiveness and reconciliation. With these insights, Nave closes his discussion of Classical and Hellenistic Greek literature, but the picture is not substantively altered by his further exploration of Jewish and early Christian literature.

Indeed, this outline can be traced in its basics through the Lukan narrative, according to Nave. Accordingly, "that which may be considered unique is not the meaning of repentance in Luke-Acts, but rather the role and function of repentance within the author's narrative."[14] Nave emphasizes the importance of this pattern of changed thinking and living for Luke, concluding that "repentance in Luke-Acts represents a fundamental change in thinking that enables diverse individuals to receive the salvation of God and to live together as a community of God's people."[15] Three of his conclusions regarding the motif of repentance in Luke-Acts are central. First, from the standpoint of the overarching theme of soteriology, human response, which includes *metanoia,* is necessary for individuals to appropriate for themselves God's offer of salvation. Second, both *metanoeō* and *metanoia* refer to a change of thinking tied to a related change in behavior – that is, what John labels as "fruits worthy of repentance" (Luke 3:8); these behavioral changes, which include welcoming into the community those whom God has accepted, are necessary for and instrumental in the establishment of the Christian community as this is recounted in Acts. Third, Nave distinguishes sharply between "repentance" and "conversion." Repentance, he argues, has to do with a change of thinking with regard to Jesus, so this is the appropriate response category for the Jewish people in Acts. Conversion, on the other

---

[14] Nave, *Role and Function of Repentance,* 145.
[15] Nave, *Role and Function of Repentance,* 146.

hand, refers to a change of religion, so is descriptive of the Gentile response.

Two years later, but apparently without the benefit of interaction with Nave's study, Fernando Méndez-Moratalla published his dissertation on *The Paradigm of Conversion in Luke*.[16] Méndez-Moratalla recognizes that most of the work on the Lukan perspective on conversion has centered on the second of Luke's two volumes, the Acts of the Apostles. Consequently, employing primarily a redaction-critical methodology, he seeks "to establish a consistent, though not exhaustive, account of conversion in the Third Gospel," demonstrating "a coherent theological pattern of conversion particular to Luke."[17]

By way of setting the Lukan narrative within a larger sociohistorical context, Méndez-Moratalla first examines accounts of conversion in Jewish literature and the writings of selected Greco-Roman philosophical schools. His project is not significantly advanced by this spadework, however, since 1) the literature he surveys is devoted above all to movement among different expressions of Judaism (e.g., movement into the Essene movement), and 2) he finds little by way of evidence for explicating the demands placed on newcomers to those philosophical schools he studies: the Epicureans, Platonists, Stoics, and Cynics. Nevertheless, at least in the case of Gentile conversion to Judaism, Méndez-Moratalla is able to highlight the radical character of a departure from the Gentile world into the Jewish community in terms of a far-reaching transformation of socio-political life, as well as the non-negotiable priority placed on converts as to their allegiance to the God of Israel.

The heart of his study is an exegetical examination of accounts of conversion in the Gospel of Luke. Among these, he includes several obvious choices, such as the conversion of Levi (5:27–32); a text in which the demands of repentance are highlighted (3:1–17); and some accounts that are less obviously conversionist (e.g., 7:36–50; 19:1–10; 23:39–43). Methodologically, his pattern is to

---

[16] Fernando Méndez-Moratalla, *The Paradigm of Conversion in Luke* (JSNTSup 252; London: T&T Clark, 2004).
[17] Méndez-Moratalla, *Paradigm of Conversion*, 2.

gather his observations around key elements of the paradigm he summarizes in his final chapter: divine initiative especially among the marginal, conflict or polarized responses to God's plan, the universal need for a response of repentance, the expression of repentance in the proper use of possessions, the offer of forgiveness (sometimes expressed in joy and table fellowship), and a climactic statement regarding the nature of Jesus' ministry. Additionally, Méndez-Moratalla draws attention to three key, related theological motifs: the orientation of Jesus' ministry toward "sinners," the reversal experienced by the converted in terms of status, and the identification of Jesus as savior.

Although Méndez-Moratalla promised to demonstrate a paradigm that was "particular to Luke," he provides nothing by way of comparison with other possible paradigms – in early Christian literature, for example – so the most that could be said is that he has identified what is characteristic of Luke. What is more, his apparent need to treat as conversion stories some pericopae in which repentance is not recounted suggests that a more nuanced approach is necessary – a possibility that is underscored by his decision not to explore the paradigm once one moves from the Gospel into the narrative of Acts. At various points, too, his overall methodology seems to be deductive to the extent that we might wonder whether his exegetical work assumed rather than supported the presence of a paradigm. In fact, other studies have found a series of formal characteristics of the conversion experience while at the same time denying an identifiably Lukan technique or pattern of conversion.[18]

What issues have surfaced? Collating the issues raised by these two recent studies with the work of other scholars,[19] an outline of the controverted issues would include the following:

---

[18] This point is underscored in Gaventa, *From Darkness to Light*, 52–129. Cf. also Robert F. O'Toole, *The Unity of Luke's Theology: An Analysis of Luke-Acts* (GNS 9; Wilmington, DE: Michael Glazier, 1984), 191–224. See, however, Ulrich Wilckens, *Die Missionsreden der Apostelgeschichte: Form- und traditionsgeschichtliche Untersuchungen* (3rd ed.; WMANT 5; Neukirchener-Vluyn: Neukirchener, 1974), 180–82.

[19] In addition to the work of Nave and Méndez-Moratalla, in what follows I refer to the studies of François Bovon, *L'œuvre de Luc: Études d'exégèse et de*

- Is conversion a cognitive category (Taeger), a moral category (Dupont), or both (Stenschke, Talbert)?
- Are repentance and conversion discrete (Nave) or convergent (Méndez-Moratalla) categories?
- Should we seek the background to Luke's conception of repentance/conversion especially in the Greco-Roman world (Nave) or in Israel's Scriptures and history (Pao, Ravens)?
- Is Luke's (and the early Christian) conception of conversion unique in its world (*passim*) or almost entirely congruent with it (Nave)?
- Is conversion a crossing of religious boundaries and rejection of one manner of life, embracing more fully the life one has chosen, or both (see the semantic nuance in Gaventa)?
- What is the relationship between conversion as a "change of mind" and behavioral transformation (emphasized in Nave and Méndez-Moratalla, both of whom urge that the relationship is one of logical consequence)?
- Is conversion an event or a process (Nave, Méndez-Moratalla, and many others portray conversion in event-oriented, static terms, even when parsing its logical consequences in terms of behavioral change)?
- Is conversion a matter of human self-correction (Taeger), or is it the consequence of divine initiative (Bovon, Stenschke, Wenk)?

This is not an exhaustive list, but it does provide us with something of the horizons within which contemporary issues related to conversion in the Lukan narrative have been discussed.

---

théologie (Paris: Cerf, 1987), 165–79; Dupont, "Conversion in the Acts of the Apostles"; Gaventa, *From Darkness to Light*; David W. Pao, *Acts and the Isaianic New Exodus* (WUNT 2:130; Tübingen: Mohr Siebeck, 2000); David Ravens, *Luke and the Restoration of Israel* (JSNTSup 119; Sheffield: Sheffield Academic Press, 1995); Christoph W. Stenschke, *Luke's Portrait of Gentiles Prior to Their Coming to Faith* (WUNT 2:108; Tübingen: Mohr Siebeck, 1999); J.W. Taeger, *Der Mensch und sein Heil: Studien zum Bild des Menschen und zur Sicht der Bekehrung bei Lukas* (SNT 14; Gütersloh: Gerd Mohn, 1982); Talbert, "Conversion in the Acts of the Apostles"; Matthias Wenk, "Conversion and Initiation: A Pentecostal View of Biblical and Patristic Perspectives," *JPT* 17 (2000): 56–80.

The Neural Correlates of Change

Without reducing conversion to neurobiology, we can none-theless recognize that conversion involves neurobiological transformation.

Neural plasticity

Although early development of the cerebral cortex is largely geneti-cally determined, environmental factors are key in the newborn and continue their influence throughout an individual's life. This is partially due to neurogenesis, which persists even in adults, but is especially realized in the generation and pruning of synapses, those points of communication among the cells of the brain. In this way, formative influences are encoded in the synapses of the central ner-vous system. Hence, although our genes bias our dispositions and character, the neuronal systems and pathways responsible for much of what we think, feel, believe, and do are shaped by learn-ing. Simply put, in our first two years (and beyond), far more syn-apses are generated than are needed. Those neural connections that are used are maintained and remodeled, while those that fall into disuse are eliminated. And fresh connections are generated in response to our experiences, even into adulthood, until the very moment of death. The longstanding nature-nurture argument (Are we products of our genes or of our upbringing?) proves to be wrongheaded, since nature and nurture are both necessary and both end up having the same effect – namely, sculpting the brain in ways that form and reform the developing self.[20]

This means that, to speak of "conversion" or, more basically, of "religious or moral formation," is always to speak of persons and not parts of persons. Transformation of "my inner person" can be nothing more or less than transformation of "me," understood wholistically. For our purposes, this "learning" is particularly

---

[20] See further, Peter R. Huttenlocher, *Neural Plasticity: The Effects of Envi-ronment on the Development of the Cerebral Cortex* (Perspectives in Cogni-tive Neuroscience; Cambridge, MA: Harvard University Press, 2002).

focused on the practices that shape our lives and on interpersonal experiences, which directly shape the ongoing development of the brain's structure and function.[21] If the neurobiological systems that shape how we think, feel, believe, and behave are forever being sculpted in the context of our social experiences, then in a profound sense we must speak of personal (trans)formation in relational terms. Our autobiographical selves are formed within a nest of relationships, a community.[22] The ecclesial context of "conversion" could scarcely be more sharply emphasized.[23]

Illustrations of neural transformation in response to environmental factors abound. In 2000, Eleanor A. Maguire and her colleagues reported on a fascinating study of London taxi drivers.[24] Their work capitalized on two known facts – 1) that one important role of the hippocampus is to facilitate spatial memory in the form of navigation (i.e., the storage and use of mental maps of our environments) and 2) that licensed London taxi drivers are renowned for their extensive and detailed navigation experience. Using structural MRIs, these researchers compared the brains of a select group of taxi drivers with those of matched control subjects who did not drive taxis. They found that the posterior hippocampi of the taxi drivers were significantly larger relative to those of control subjects. Moreover, hippocampi volume also correlated with the amount of time spent as a taxi driver. This led to the conclusion that day-to-day activities induce changes in the morphology of the brain.

Similar conclusions have been reached with reference to psychotherapy. In order to examine whether psychological therapies modulate brain activity, Veena Kumari surveyed recent psychiatric research that utilized neuroimaging techniques to investigate neural events associated with both therapeutic and psychopharmacological interventions in a number of psychiatric

---

[21] See Siegel, *The Developing Mind.*
[22] Cf. Feinberg, *Altered Egos.*
[23] This is a central emphasis of Markham, *Rewired.*
[24] E.A. Maguire et al., "Navigation-related Structural Change in the Hippocampi of Taxi Drivers," *Proceedings of the National Academy of Sciences* 97 (2000): 4398–403.

disorders.[25] These included depression, panic disorder, phobia, obsessive compulsive disorder (OCD), and schizophrenia. According to the empirical research surveyed, clinical improvements were correlated with regional and/or system changes in the brain, leading to the conclusion that these interventions did indeed cultivate changes at the brain level. Similarly, in a series of publications, Jeffrey M. Schwartz has documented the effectiveness of behavioral therapy in the treatment of patients with OCD, with the transformation on display both in a reduction in obsessive tendencies and in a relative deficit of metabolic activity in these brain areas implicated in the disorder as observed in before-and-after neuroimaging.[26]

Believing is seeing

In his introduction to "the machinery of the cerebral cortex," Christof Koch observes the general deficit of incoming sensory data necessary for an unambiguous interpretation of the object of our perception. This is true from the seemingly more mundane activity of our visual systems to larger-scale hermeneutical concerns, our reflection on and the practices of human understanding. Our limitations notwithstanding, our "cortical networks *fill in*. They make their best guess, given the incomplete information. ... This general principle, expressed colloquially as 'jumping to conclusions,' guides much of human behavior."[27] Through "filling in," we find a human face in the full moon, recognize Beethoven playing his piano in a cloud formation, see words rather than individual letters when we read, generally apply old paradigms in new contexts, or prejudicially categorize people by any number of criteria (e.g., accent, gender, race, or the condition or color of their

---

[25] Veena Kumari, "Do Psychotherapies Produce Neurobiological Effects?" *Acta Neuropsychiatrica* 18 (2006): 61–70.

[26] E.g., Jeffrey M. Schwartz and Sharon Begley, *The Mind and the Brain: Neuroplasticity and the Power of Mental Force* (New York: HarperCollins, 2002).

[27] Christof Koch, *The Quest for Consciousness: A Neurobiological Approach* (Englewood, CO: Roberts, 2004), 23.

teeth). Various terms name the structures by which we "fill in" –
"imagination" ("a basic image-schematic capacity for ordering
our experience"[28] or "the power of taking something as something
by means of meaningful forms, which are rooted in our history and
have the power to disclose truths about life in the world"[29]), for
example, or "conceptual schemes" (which are at once *conceptual*
[a way of seeing things], *conative* [a set of beliefs and values to
which a group and its members are deeply attached], and *action-
guiding* [we seek to live according to its terms]).[30] To put it
differently, in order to make life-events meaningful, we must con-
ceptualize them and we do so in terms of well-worn paths in our
brains – that is, imaginative structures or conceptual schemes that
we implicitly take to be true, normal, and good.[31]

Our hermeneutical equipment, then, is formed at the synaptic
level, is capable of reformation, and is even now providing the conceptual schemes or imaginative structures by which we make sense
of the world around us. My "perception" of the world is based in a
network of ever-forming assumptions about my environment, and
in a series of well-tested assumptions, shared by others with whom
I associate, about "the way the world works." Ambiguous data
may present different hypotheses, but my mind disambiguates that
data according to what I have learned to expect. That is, embodied
human life performs like a cultural, neuro-hermeneutic system,
locating (and, thus, making sense of) current realities in relation to
our grasp of the past and expectations of the future.[32]

Any number of phenomena display this neuro-hermeneutic system at work. In the U.S., for example, staunch Democrats and

---

[28] Mark Johnson, *The Body in the Mind: The Bodily Basis of Meaning, Imagination, and Reason* (Chicago: University of Chicago Press, 1987), xx.
[29] David J. Bryant, *Faith and the Play of Imagination: On the Role of Imagination in Religion* (StABH 5; Macon, GA: Mercer University Press, 1989), 5.
[30] Owen Flanagan, *The Problem of the Soul: Two Visions of Mind and How to
Reconcile Them* (New York: Basic, 2002), 27–55.
[31] Cf. Mark Johnson, *Moral Imagination: Implications of Cognitive Science
for Ethics* (Chicago: University of Chicago Press, 1993), ch. 8.
[32] See Stephen P. Reyna, *Connections: Brain, Mind, and Culture in a Social
Anthropology* (London: Routledge, 2002).

hard-core Republicans hear the same data but, predisposed to interpreting them differently, they walk away with opposing conclusions. In an fMRI study conducted at Emory University prior to the 2004 presidential election, Democrats and Republicans were given a reasoning task in which they were to evaluate damaging information about their own candidate. Notably absent among the subjects involved in this study was any activation of the neural circuits implicated in conscious reasoning once they were confronted with the damaging evidence. The researchers concluded that emotionally biased reasoning leads to the "stamping in" or reinforcement of a defensive belief, associating the participant's "revisionist" account of the data with positive emotion or relief and elimination of distress. The result is that partisan beliefs are calcified, and persons can learn very little from new data.[33]

The same can be said of racial bias, with its roots in a natural human alertness regarding members of unfamiliar groups.[34] And patients who have experienced selected lesions to the brain demonstrate the inability to see what they cannot believe to be true,[35] just as the rest of us operate normally with a strong hermeneutical bias on the basis of prior beliefs, so that we actually perceive stimuli when none are physically presented.[36]

[33] Drew Westen et al., "Neural Bases of Motivated Reasoning: An fMRI Study of Emotional Constraints on Partisan Political Judgment in the 2004 U.S. Presidential Election," *Journal of Cognitive Neuroscience* 18 (2006): 1947–58.
[34] E.g., Andreas Olsson et al., "The Role of Social Groups in the Persistence of Learned Fear," *Science* 309, no. 5735 (2005): 785–87; Jason P. Mitchell et al., "Dissociable Medial Prefrontal Contributions to Judgments of Similar and Dissimilar Others," *Neuron* 50 (2006): 655–63; cf. David M. Amodio and Chris D. Frith, "Meeting of Minds: The Medial Frontal Cortex and Social Cognition," *Nature Reviews Neuroscience* 7 (2006): 268–77.
[35] E.g., V.S. Ramachandran and Sandra Blakeslee, *Phantoms in the Brain: Probing the Mysteries of the Human Mind* (New York: William Morrow, 1998); V.S. Ramachandran, *A Brief Tour of Human Consciousness: From Imposter Poodles to Purple Numbers* (New York: Pi, 2004), ch. 2.
[36] See Aaron R. Seitz et al., "Seeing What Is Not There Shows the Costs of Perceptual Learning," *Proceedings of the National Academy of Sciences* 102, no. 25 (2005): 9080–85. More generally, see William Hirstein, *Brain Fiction: Self-Deception and the Riddle of Confabulation* (Cambridge, MA: The MIT Press, 2005).

In his latest book, *The Mindful Brain,* Daniel J. Siegel acknowledges the coercive power of ingrained brain states as they impinge
on human responses.[37] He uses the term "enslavement" to describe
large-scale dynamics established by earlier experience and embedded in beliefs in the form of patterns of judgments about good and
bad, right and wrong. This is not all bad, he notes. "We must make
summations, create generalizations, and initiate behaviors based
on a limited sampling of incoming data that have been shunted
through the filters of these mental models. Our learning brains
seek to find the similarities and differences, draw conclusions, and
act."[38] However, the consequence can be an internalized set of
"shoulds" that are actually destructive of personal well-being and
human community, the antidote to which he offers reflecting
thinking, mindful learning, and mindful awareness – that is,
refiguration of neuronal processes through conditional learning.

The irreducible collocation of conceptual, conative, and behavioral implications of conversion thus comes into focus.

Narrative hermeneutics

As in other instances of advance in neuroscience, so in the understanding of the human construction of the self progress has been
made in part through study of persons suffering some form of
insult to the brain. Particularly, persons with lesions to the neural
network responsible for the generation of narrative suffer from
deficits in the capacity to organize their experiences in terms of
past, present, and future, and accordingly suffer a loss in their
grasp of their own identities. So pivotal is narrative to the formation of identity, including the formation and articulation of beliefs,
that in the absence of memory humans will create stories by which
to make sense of their present situation. Indeed, "confabulating
amnestic individuals offer an unrivaled glimpse at the power of the

---

[37] Daniel J. Siegel, *The Mindful Brain: Reflection and Attunement in the Cultivation of Well-Being* (New York: Norton, 2007).
[38] Siegel, *The Mindful Brain,* 135.

human impulse to narrative."[39] For good reason, scientist-theologian Anne Foeret refers to humans as "*Homo Narrans Narrandus* – the storytelling person whose story has to be told," who tells stories to make sense of the world and to form personal identity and community; and this perspective has been ratified again and again in recent interdisciplinary study.[40] From neurobiology and its interactions with cultural anthropology and philosophy, then, we have a heightened interest in and recognition of *narrativity* as a human-forming, meaning-making enterprise.

No pure thinking

Finally, we may recall from Chapter 3 the impossibility of "pure reason" – that is, the error of imagining that we might engage in "thinking" or "rationality" or "cognition" apart from the influence of our emotions, as if our decisions might be made on the basis of "cool reason." There we noted the illogic of "cool reason" in decision-making, since so many options are available at any point in time that it is simply impossible to analyze each. Again, brain lesion studies have demonstrated that damage to the emotion-processing center of the brain impedes real-life rationality and decision-making. Why is this of interest here? In the literature on conversion in Lukan perspective, scholars have sometimes operated with distinctions between "thinking" and "feeling," "thinking" and "morality," "thinking" and "acting," and so on.

---

[39] Kay Young and Jeffrey L. Saver, "The Neurology of Narrative," *SubStance* 30 (2001): 72–84 (76). Feinberg (*Altered Egos*) and Hirstein (*Brain Fiction*) demonstrate the incredible lengths to which we will go to make storied sense of what we take to be true.

[40] Reported in S. Jennifer Leat, "Artificial Intelligence Researcher Seeks Silicon Soul," *Research News and Opportunities in Science and Theology* 3, no. 4 (2002): 7, 26 (7). See James B. Ashbrook and Carol Rausch Albright, *The Humanizing Brain: Where Religion and Neuroscience Meet* (Cleveland, OH: Pilgrim, 1997); and, for interdisciplinary work, e.g., Gary D. Fireman et al., eds., *Narrative and Consciousness: Literature, Psychology, and the Brain* (Oxford: Oxford University Press, 2003); Lewis P. Hinchman and Sandra K. Hinchman, eds., *Memory, Identity, Community: The Idea of Narrative in the Human Sciences* (Albany: State University of New York Press, 2001).

Accordingly, it might be imagined, conversion comprises an "intellectual" change, itself the consequence of a rational demonstration of the logic of the gospel. This is not the case.

Conclusion

Before returning to the Lukan narrative, it may be useful to summarize what we have seen. Among the important ramifications of these considerations are the following:

- the neurobiological correlates of moral formation and transformation;
- the importance of relationships for moral development;
- the construction of the self (and a community's identity) in narrative terms – grasping the present in terms of prior experiences and future expectations;
- an awareness of a person's behavior as the outcome of tracing well-worn grooves in his or her moral cognition – so that ongoing behavioral change is the correlate of transformation of his or her character; and
- the importance of formative practices in moral formation and reformation.

Luke-Acts and "Embodied Conversion"

As we have seen, the most basic and significant contribution of cognitive science is its irreducible emphasis on somatic existence as the basis and means of human existence, including the exercise of the mind. From this we might infer, for example, the fallacy of imagining that intellect and affect are separable, the fallacy of imagining that mind and behavior are separable, the fallacy of imagining that human life can be understood merely or primarily with respect to individuals, and the inescapable conclusion that human formation is a process. In important ways, these emphases correlate with NT perspectives on Christian conversion, so crucial to its depiction of the new humanity called forth in Christ. We turn then to a closer

examination of the two volumes in the NT attributed to Luke, the
Gospel of Luke and the Acts of the Apostles, or Luke-Acts, noted for
their emphasis on conversion.

That the Lukan writings support a heightened interest in conversion is widely acknowledged. Indeed, the importance of conversion is signaled immediately in Luke's first chapter, with Gabriel's
announcement to Zechariah that the son to be born to him, John,
would be a prophet. Gabriel summarizes the effect of John's ministry as a call to repentance:

> *He will turn* many of the people of Israel to the Lord their God . . .
> he will go before him,
> *to turn* the hearts of fathers to their children, and
> *[to turn]* the disobedient to the wisdom of the righteous,
> to make ready a people prepared for the Lord. (Luke 1:16–17
> [my translation])

In these words we discover immediately that repentance in Luke-
Acts will not be a theological abstraction, but rather aimed at a
transformation of day-to-day patterns of thinking, feeling, believing, and behaving. What begins with the angelic message in Luke 1
continues throughout the Lukan narrative, in which Jesus articulates his mission as calling sinners to repentance (Luke 5:32) and
reports rejoicing at the repentance of even one sinner (Luke 15:7,
10); in which the directed response to the good news is, "Repent,
and be baptized" (Acts 2:38); and in which Paul can summarize his
entire ministry as declaring "first to those in Damascus, then in
Jerusalem and throughout the countryside of Judea, and also to the
Gentiles, that they should repent and turn to God and do deeds
consistent with repentance" (Acts 26:20). Given its importance in
Luke-Acts, how does Luke develop this motif?

Repentance versus conversion

Some recent literature on conversion has focused on an understanding of conversion as a crossing of religious boundaries.

Accordingly, "repentance" would be expected of the Jewish people, "conversion" of Gentiles. Some evidence, especially within the speeches of Acts, might initially support such a distinction. Peter and Paul call their Jewish audiences not to serve a new God but to return to the God of their ancestors.[41] As Odil Steck has shown, prophetic speeches calling Israel to repentance follow a well-established tradition in Israel's Scriptures and the literature of Second Temple Judaism,[42] and the preaching of Peter and Paul among Jewish audiences in Acts conforms to this pattern.[43] Conversely, in those situations in which Paul addresses specifically Gentile audiences, he refers to "the living God" (as opposed to worthless idols – Acts 14:15) and proclaims that this God "commands all people everywhere to repent" (Acts 17:30). At Lystra and Athens, that is, Paul's concerns are more narrowly *theo*logical, while among Jews Peter and Paul alike proclaim that Jesus is the Christ. For Jews, the needed response is a reorientation toward the God of Israel and his purposes, known in the advent of Jesus Christ. For Gentiles, the needed response is a departure from idolatry in order to join the people of the God who raised Jesus from the dead.

As helpful as such a distinction might be, though, from the perspective of cognitive science it is phenomenologically unsustainable, since at the level of neuronal processes, the one metamorphosis is like the other. Moreover, this distinction fails as a representation of the perspective on converstion in Acts. 1) Many Gentiles within the narrative of Acts need no conversion to the God of Israel *per se* but, like the exemplary Cornelius (Acts

[41] Cf. Acts 2:38; 3:17–20; 5:31; 13:38–41. Martin Dibelius ("The Speeches in Acts and Ancient Historiography," in *Studies in the Acts of the Apostles* [London: SCM, 1956], 138–85 [165]) observes that the exhortation to repentance is stereotypical in the speeches in Acts; cf. Petr Pokorný, *Theologie der lukanischen Schriften* (FRLANT 174; Göttingen: Vandenhoeck & Ruprecht, 1998), 122–24.

[42] Cf. Jer 3:12–16; 7:3–25; 14:6–7; Ezek 18:30; Zech 1:3; 7:8–10; Mal 3:7; Odil Hannes Steck, *Israel und das gewaltsame Geschick der Propheten* (WMANT 23; Neukirchen-Vluyn: Neukirchener, 1967).

[43] So Hans F. Bayer, "The Preaching of Peter in Acts," in *Witness to the Gospel: The Theology of Acts* (ed. I. Howard Marshall and David Peterson; Grand Rapids, MI: Eerdmans, 1998), 257–74 (262–65).

10:1–4), already worship this God. They are recipients of the gift of repentance in the same way that the Jews are. Indeed, the Jerusalem leaders announce that "God has given even to the Gentiles the repentance that leads to life" (11:18), a claim that parallels Peter's pronouncement regarding Jesus, that "God exalted him at his right hand as Leader and Savior that he might give repentance to Israel and forgiveness of sins" (5:31). 2) A major component of conversion in Israel's Scriptures as well as in Acts is a turning from idolatry (e.g., Acts 14:15).[44] Importantly, then, Luke underscores the idolatry of even the Jewish people; the Jerusalem temple itself has become a manifestation of Jewish idolatry, according to Stephen's speech (cf. 7:48; 17:24–25). Indeed, membership among the people of God cannot be assumed simply on the basis of Abrahamic ancestry (Luke 3:7–14), with the result that the privilege of God's grace is no presumption of the Jewish people.[45] 3) When Paul recounts before King Agrippa his commission, he proclaims that Jesus sent him "to open their eyes so that they might turn from darkness to light and from the power of Satan to God" (Acts 26:17–18). In this case, Luke draws on the familiar language of religious conversion,[46] but interprets it so as to

---

[44] This is noted, e.g., by Christopher J.H. Wright, "Implications of Conversion in the Old Testament and the New," *International Bulletin of Missionary Research* 28 (2004): 14–19 (15, 18).

[45] To what degree is a conversion from idolatry the same for Jew and Gentile? For the Gentile, such conversion had immediate and far-reaching social consequences, since this entailed separation from ordinary socio-religious life (cf. Martin Goodman, *Mission and Conversion: Proselytizing in the Religious History of the Roman Empire* [Oxford: Clarendon, 1994], 104–5). This was less true for the Jew, at least in the period covered by Luke's narrative.

[46] Cf. *Joseph and Aseneth* 8:10; 15:12; 1 Thess 5:4–7; Col 1:12–13; Eph 5:8; 1 Pet 2:9; Dennis Hamm, "Sight to the Blind: Vision as Metaphor in Luke," *Bib* 67 (1986): 457–77. See also Isa 42:7, 16; Luke 2:32. Some scholars (e.g., Luke Timothy Johnson, *The Acts of the Apostle* [SP 5; Collegeville, MN: Liturgical, 1992], 436–37) take Luke's εἰς οὓς as a reference to the Gentiles alone, but a Pauline mission inclusive of Gentiles and Jews is supported by the Isaianic echoes, and by Luke 1:78–79; 2:32; Acts 9:15; 26:20, 23. Cf. Jacob Jervell, *Die Apostelgeschichte* [KEK 3; Göttingen: Vandenhoeck & Ruprecht, 1998), 594; Joseph A. Fitzmyer, *The Acts of the Apostles* (AB 31; New York: Doubleday, 1998), 759–60.

situate the redemptive purpose of God within the cosmic battle of competing kingdoms. It is an important component of this text that Gentiles and Jews alike need deliverance from darkness (cf. Luke 1:78–79). As Paul goes on to observe, obedience to the heavenly vision entailed declaring "first to those in Damascus, then in Jerusalem and throughout the countryside of Judea, and also to the Gentiles, that they should repent and turn to God and do deeds consistent with repentance" (Acts 26:19–20). The same response is expected of Jew and Gentile alike.[47] 4) Finally, we should note that in Israel's Scriptures the call to radical and ongoing conversion is addressed above all to God's people. They may serve as agents for the conversion of others, but they themselves have a continuous need for conversion.[48]

A new "conceptual scheme"

According to the first public address in Acts, the exaltation of Jesus and the consequent outpouring of the Holy Spirit have signaled a dramatic transformation in history (2:14–41). Here and elsewhere within the speeches of Acts, Jewish people might hear the familiar

---

[47] This is emphasized in Stenschke, *Luke's Portrait of Gentiles;* Méndez-Moratalla, *Paradigm of Conversion.*

[48] Wright, "Implications of Conversion"; see also Andrew F. Walls, "Converts or Proselytes? The Crisis over Conversion in the Early Church," *International Bulletin of Missionary Research* 29 (2004): 2–6 (3). It is especially on this point that Nave's study (*Role and Function of Repentance*) founders, since he rejects a connection between שוב in the Israel's Scripture and Luke's concept of repentance. The result is a useful emphasis on Greco-Roman background, which overturns earlier scholarly allegations about the uniqueness of the concept of repentance and/or conversion in Lukan or early Christian usage; but also a failure to recognize that שוב, נחם, μετανοέω, μετάνοια, and -στρεφω verbs belong to the same semantic domain (the LXX uses στρεφω to translate שוב and μετανοέω to translate נחם, but cf. references to the "turning" of Nineveh: μετανοέω in Luke 11:32; and, in Jonah 3:8, 10, שוב in the MT and ἀποστρέφω in the LXX); see the summary comments in Jonathan M. Lunde, "Repentance," in *DJG*, 669–73 (669). Nave thus denudes Luke's concept of its covenantal basis in Yahweh's initiative and call, emphasized recently in Ravens, *Luke and the Restoration of Israel*, 139–69; Pao, *Acts and the Isaianic New Exodus,* e.g., 118–20, 138–40.

stories borrowed from their Scriptures, but these stories have been cast in ways that advocate a reading of that history which underscores the fundamental continuity between the ancient story of Israel, the story of Jesus, and the story of the Way. Israel's past (and present) is understood correctly and embraced fully only in relation to the redemptive purpose of God, but this divine purpose can be understood only as articulated by authorized interpretive agents – first Jesus of Nazareth, and then his witnesses. Thus, for example, Paul's question to King Agrippa, "Do you believe the prophets?" (Acts 26:27), concerns not simply a commitment to the prophets, but to the prophets *as they have been expounded by Paul.* The coming of Jesus as Savior may signal the fresh offer of repentance and forgiveness of sins to Israel (Acts 5:31; 13:38–39), but the acceptance of this offer by Jewish people is dependent on their embracing *this interpretation of God's salvific activity.* Greek audiences, too, are asked to adopt a new way of viewing the world. Note how, at Athens, Paul distinguishes between how God worked in the past (17:30a; cf. 14:16) and how he will now operate (17:30b) – a distinction that calls for repentance.

For Luke, embracing this new conceptual scheme is a new way of seeing things, an opening of the mind to understand what was previously incomprehensible (cf. Luke 24:30–32, 44–48), that takes as its starting point the mission and message of Jesus, culminating in his death, resurrection, ascension, and outpouring of the Spirit at Pentecost. Among the scenes depicting this conceptual transformation, two are tied together by their common reference to "inspired speech" (ἀποφθέγγομαι, *apophengomai*), Acts 2:1–13 and 26:1–29. In the wake of the outpouring of the Spirit at Pentecost, Jesus' disciples are accused of drunken babbling (2:13) not because their words are incomprehensible ("we hear . . . in our own native languages," 2:8) but because of its preposterous content. Their doxology apparently includes among "the great things of God" (2:11) unexpected events and an alien representation of God's salvific intervention, centered on the death and resurrection of Christ (cf. 2:14–41, also the product of "inspired speech"). During Paul's speech before Herod Agrippa II and Porcius Festus,

Festus interrupts with this outburst, "You have lost your mind!"
Paul counters with a claim to inspired, sober speech (26:24–25).
The basis of Festus' interruption is not Paul's ecstatic or hysterical
speech (which one might expect, given Festus' characterization
of Paul – μαίνομαι/μανία (*mainomai/mania,* "to be crazy,"
"absurdly unlikely"), but rather Paul's exposition of Scripture as
witness to Jesus. As Fitzmyer observes, "Festus protests first over
Paul's erudition, his strange way of arguing, and his allusions to
Moses and the prophets. Festus has difficulty in following all this
argumentation and especially in admitting such a thing as resurrection."[49] That is, lacking the conceptual categories to make sense of
Paul's argument, Festus presumes that Paul is the one lacking in
cognitive equipment.

In the same way that, in a Gestalt shift, what was previously
seen as a duck is now seen as a rabbit, so conversion signals not
simply the introduction of new ideas into an old imaginative
framework, but a transformed imaginative framework within
which what was previously inconceivable is now matter-of-fact.
This emphasis is set out programmatically in Luke 4:18–19, where
Jesus' missionary program includes proclaiming "sight to the
blind" – a statement that anticipates the recovery of sight instigated by physical healing, to be sure (Luke 18:35–43; Acts 9:18–
19), but even more so portends the provision and reception of
divine revelation, the passage from darkness to light, the movement from ignorance to insight – and, so, entry into salvation and
inclusion in God's family (e.g., Luke 1:78–79; 2:9, 29–32; 3:6;
24:13–35; Acts 26:18).[50]

Conversion and socialization

If conversion is grounded in a fresh comprehension of the purpose
of God as this is plotted in Scripture, then it is manifest in the

---

[49] Fitzmyer, *Acts,* 763.
[50] See further, e.g., Hamm, "Sight to the Blind"; R. Alan Culpepper, "Seeing
the Kingdom of God: The Metaphor of Sight in the Gospel of Luke," *CurTM*
21 (1994): 424–33.

community of God's people who are constituted by this biblical narrative, and whose practices embody this spirituality and leverage the ongoing conversion of its membership. Conversion as an ongoing process of socialization needs particular emphasis here, both because it is often neglected in discourse about conversion in Luke-Acts and because it is so vital to the Lukan narrative. Seen from this vantage point, conversion entails autobiographical reconstruction.[51] Conversion shatters one's past and reassembles it in accordance with the new life of the converted; former understandings of one's self and one's experiences are regarded as erroneous and are provided new meaning (cf. Luke 9:23). Of course, the prime example of this emphasis in the Lukan narrative is Paul, and especially his narration of his experience on the road to Damascus (Acts 26:4–29). More pervasive are those instances where one's reformed allegiances and dispositions are expressed in terms that reflect a creative imagination, especially with regard to revisionist conceptualizations of the character of the people of God – and, thus, of Yahweh's purpose and Israel's history. Converts find explanations for phenomena in terms that are appropriate to the pattern of life they have embraced and that are often distinctive from the conceptual patterns held by persons outside the community of the converted.

Interestingly, this symbolic world comes to expression most fully in the context of one of the characteristic practices of the Christianity community. This is prayer, which provides the

---

[51] Cf. Peter L. Berger and Thomas Luckmann, *The Social Construction of Reality: A Treatise in the Sociology of Knowledge* (New York: Doubleday, 1966), 160: "Everything preceding the alternation is now apprehended as leading toward it . . . everything following it as flowing from its new reality. This involves a reinterpretation of past biography *in toto*, following the formula 'Then I *thought* . . . now I *know*.'" See further, David A. Snow and R. Machalek, "The Convert as a Social Type," in *Sociological Theory 1983* (ed. R. Collins; San Francisco: Jossey Bass, 1983), 259–89 (266–69); and, esp., Nicholas H. Taylor, "The Social Nature of Conversion in the Early Christian World," in *Modelling Early Christianity: Social-scientific Studies of the New Testament in Its Context* (ed. Philip F. Esler; London/New York: Routledge, 1995), 128–36.

opportunity for the disclosure of God's salvific purpose especially
at pivotal points in the mission. Acts portrays prayer as a community-defining practice that directs the expansion of the community.
This is because the habits of prayer counseled by Jesus serve as an
ongoing catalyst for the conformation of the community around
the unlimited mercy of God (cf. Luke 6:35–36; 11:1–13). Prayer of
this sort allows for the infusion of a life-world centered on the gracious God, on dependence on God, on the imitation of God, and on
the disclosure of God's purpose for humanity, all understood
against an eschatological horizon in which the coming of God in
sovereignty and redemption figures prominently.

In Acts conversion also entails incorporation into a new community, including adopting the rituals and behaviors peculiar to or
definitive of that new community. This is evident immediately in
Acts 2:42–47, the first in a series of summaries that dot the landscape of the narrative of Acts – this one serving the dual function of
exhibiting the communal dimension of the consequence of the outpouring of the Holy Spirit and demonstrating the quality of daily
life characteristic of those who are baptized in the name of Jesus
Christ.[52] The generalizations about the community of Jesus' followers sketched here amplify the response urged by Peter in 2:38,
"Repent and be baptized!" Baptism functions, on the one hand,
as the medium by which repentance comes to expression and, on
the other, as the sign that forgiveness has been granted.[53] To put it

---

[52] Cf. Henry J. Cadbury, "The Summaries in Acts," in *Additional Notes to the
Commentary* (vol. 5 of *The Acts of the Apostles;* ed. F.J. Foakes Jackson and
Kirsopp Lake; BChr 1; London: Macmillan, 1920), 392–402; Maria Anicia
Co, "The Major Summaries in Acts: Acts 2,42–47; 4,32–35; 5,12–16. Linguis-
tic and Literary Relationship," *ETL* 68 (1992): 49–85; Matthias Wenk, *Com-
munity-Forming Power: The Socio-Ethical Role of the Spirit in Luke-Acts*
(JPTSup 19; Sheffield: Sheffield Academic Press, 2000), 259–73.
[53] See Lars Hartman, *'Into the Name of the Lord Jesus': Baptism in the Early
Church* (SNTW; Edinburgh: T&T Clark, 1997), 130; Joel B. Green, "From
'John's Baptism' to 'Baptism in the Name of the Lord Jesus': The Significance
of Baptism in Luke-Acts," in *Baptism, the New Testament and the Church:
Historical and Contemporary Studies in Honour of R.E.O. White* (ed. Stanley
E. Porter and Anthony R. Cross; JSNTSup 171; Sheffield: Sheffield Academic
Press, 1999), 157–72.

differently, baptism serves a community-defining role – communicating on the part of the baptized an unswerving loyalty to the Lord and on the part of the church the full incorporation of the baptized into the community. Baptism is both response and gift. What is more, baptism in Acts has as its consequence, among other things, economic koinonia (e.g., 2:41–47) and the extension of hospitality (e.g., 10:47–48; 16:14–15, 28–34) – behaviors, then, that must be included under the heading of "fruits worthy of repentance" (Luke 3:7–14).

A community formed and forming

If repentance signals an essential reorientation of life, repentance is also something that persons "do." "Bear fruits worthy of repentance," John proclaims early in Luke's Gospel, before spelling out behavioral exemplars of repentance from the realm of socio-economic relations (Luke 3:7–14; cf. Acts 26:20). If we have learned in the last two or three centuries that "being" and "doing" are separable, we should not project such distinctions into the biblical materials, wherein the assumption that a person *is* one's behavior is more at home. We do what we are – that is, one's deepest commitments are unavoidably exhibited in one's practices, so that attention focuses on "embodied life," disallowing the possibility that the "real" person might be relegated to one's interior life.[54]

What are these community-constituting practices? Though they scarcely exhaust the possibilities resident in the Lukan narrative, three are of special interest for their pervasiveness and profundity: economic koinonia, prayer, and witness. *Economic koinonia* surfaces most explicitly in two summary statements, Acts 2:42–47 and 4:32–35, both of which exhibit the communal dimension of the consequences of the outpouring of the Spirit at the same time that they demonstrate how the message of Jesus' resurrection manifests itself in the nature of the community. Luke's portrait of God's people thus places a premium on care of the needy, portrays the

---

[54] See, e.g., Di Vito, "OT Anthropology"; Berger, *Identity and Experience*.

community of believers as an extended kin-group, and ties the life
of this community into the formation of God's people in exodus
(cf. Deut 15:1–18). Summaries, like these two texts in Acts, serve as
interpreting "headings," so it is not surprising that Acts also nar-
rates other instances of economic interest – for example, partner-
ship between communities of believers (e.g., 11:27–29), Paul's
claim that he was no lover of money (20:33–35), and especially the
persistent correlation of embracing the Christian message with
extension of hospitality (e.g., 10:44–48; 16:14–15, 30–34).

It is crucial that we recognize that, as "fruits worthy of repentance," practices of economic community and hospitality are not
"things to do" for the converted. Such practices are not simply
"logical consequences" of conversion, as some interpreters might
have it. The relationship is more organic, so that conversion gener-
ates such behaviors, is demonstrated in them, and is fueled by
them.

Among the Gospel writers, Luke devotes an inordinate amount
of attention to *prayer*, emphasizing especially the revelatory function of prayer.[55] This emphasis begins as early as Jesus' baptism
(Luke 3:21–22),[56] and continues into the book of Acts, where the
community of God's people likewise experiences the revelatory
function of prayer – that is, prayer as revelatory moment and as
invitation to align oneself with the aim of God thus revealed (e.g.,
Acts 9:10–16; 10:9–16; 22:17–21).

In the Gospel of Luke, prayer serves as a boundary marker,
employed by the Pharisees, for example, to identify themselves
over against others. In them we see that the habit of prayer is a catalyst for community formation. The question is, What sort of community? In Luke 5:27–39 and 18:9–14, prayer functions among
Pharisees as an identity marker oriented toward maintaining clear

[55] See esp., David Michael Crump, *Jesus the Intercessor: Prayer and Christol-
ogy in Luke-Acts* (WUNT 2:49; Tübingen: Mohr Siebeck, 1992); Joel B.
Green, "'Persevering Together in Prayer' (Acts 1:14): The Significance of
Prayer in the Acts of the Apostles," in *Into God's Presence: Prayer in the New
Testament* (ed. Richard N. Longenecker; MNTS; Grand Rapids, MI:
Eerdmans, 2001), 183–202.
[56] See also Luke 2:36–38; 9:18–27, 28–36; 10:21–22; 23:34, 46; 24:30–31.

lines of demarcation between groups – in these instances, as behaviors that separate Pharisees from toll collectors and sinners. Jesus' response is reminiscent of the prophetic criticism of pious acts when those acts are segregated from acts of justice and mercy (e.g., Isa 58:3–9; Jer 14:12; Zech 7:5–6). By way of contrast, the prayer of the toll collector demonstrates the reservoir of humility out of which flows hospitality and other signs of God's care to the marginal of society. For Luke, prayer is a practice that grows out and is formative of one's convictions and commitments. It is, for him, the conceptual scheme of the converted in practice. It is metonymic for one's character. Moreover, as we have already seen, prayer is for Christians in Acts a community-defining practice, leading to the conformation of the community around the gracious God.

The missionary portfolio Jesus gives to his followers in Acts 1:8 centers on practices of *witness:* "But you will receive power when the Holy Spirit has come upon you; and you will be my witnesses in Jerusalem, in all Judea and Samaria, and to the end of the earth." This mandate is especially interesting since it is self-evident that the significance of Jesus' words was not immediately obvious to his followers. The formation of disciples, as Luke develops it, is a process of conversion. It entails a reconstruction of one's self within a new web of relationships, a transfer of allegiances, and the embodiment of transformed dispositions and attitudes. The parade example of the interwoven nature of conversion and witness is the complex narration of the encounter between Peter and Cornelius and its aftermath in the Jerusalem church, in Acts 10:1–11:18. Cornelius is introduced first, with the result that we might gain the mistaken impression that this text centers on his conversion and that of his household. Instead, Luke's focus is on Peter and the Jerusalem church, and especially their ethnocentric practices. The significance of what transpires is accentuated by multiple evidences of the divine hand at work (e.g., 10:3–16, 44–47), which validate the practice of full fellowship between Jew and Gentile – the character of which was at stake in the protestations first of Peter (Acts 10:28a) and then of the circumcised in the Jerusalem church (Acts 11:2–3). Cornelius is converted, to be sure, but so are

Peter and those of the Jerusalem community – Cornelius, in that he moves from his position as a God-fearer on the margins of the Jewish religion to full membership within the community of God's people for whom Jesus is Lord; Peter and the Jerusalem community to a fuller embodiment of their newly embraced life-world, expressed in the confession that Jesus is, indeed, "Lord of all" (Acts 10:34–36).

In short, the practice of the church in Acts was, finally, to welcome Gentiles into their communities with a status equal to that of existing members, but this was so only as Jesus' followers involved themselves in witness, engaged with persons outside their own number, and came to embrace more fully the terms of their own faith. By engagement with persons at the "ends of the earth," they were pressed in the direction of an end-of-the-earth "conceptual scheme"; having embraced God's perspective on things, having relocated themselves in the story-line of God's ancient purpose, they found themselves in a process of transformation, being shaped so as more faithfully to incarnate this pattern of faith and life.

The rhetoric of conversion

The language Luke employs implements a strong bias in favor of the gospel of the kingdom of God. For example, he characterizes conversion as the movement from darkness to light – with "darkness" (σκότος, σκοτεινός, *skotos, skoteinos*) correlated with death, disease, the devil, cataclysm, and blindness; and "light" (ἐπιφαίνω, φῶς, φωτεινός, *epiphainō, phōs, phōteinos*) with revelation, understanding, health, the age of salvation, sight, and the coming of the Lord (e.g., Luke 1:79; 2:32; 11:33–36; 16:8; 22:53; 23:44; Acts 2:20; 9:3; 12:7; 13:11, 47; 26:18, 23). Hence, it is crucial that, in our analysis of the rhetoric of conversion, we account for more than "cool reason." When we do, other aspects of Lukan rhetoric can be grasped more fully.

Let me give two examples. First, it is clear that the speeches in Acts directed at Jewish audiences (e.g., in Acts 2:14–36; 7; 13:16–41), as well the Lukan narrative as a whole, renarrate the story of

Israel so as to demonstrate that the narrative of God's promises to Abraham comes to fruition in the advent of Jesus and continues in the life of the community of Jesus' followers. Given the ancient valuation of "antiquity" (Luke 5:39: "the old is good"),[57] Luke's revisionist historiography exhibits an attempt to reform long-held patterns of faith and thought by its appeal to the antiquity of the Christian movement and, then, to the purpose of God on display in the Christian movement. (A contemporary analogy is found in the opposite claim: "new and improved.") Luke's conversionist appeal thus trades on the hopes and longings of ancient people, on widely held cultural values, as well as on reasoning and logic. Second, we may think it enough that the phrase associated with the work of Jesus and his followers in the book of Acts, "signs and wonders" (e.g., 2:22, 43; 4:30; 5:12; 6:8; 8:6, 13; 14:3; 15:12), would signal images of well-being and wholeness in the service of conversionist rhetoric. However, this language is itself taken from the scriptural account of the exodus, where it broadcasts the actualization of God's redemptive purpose on behalf of his people and testifies to his commanding influence in history (e.g., Exod 7:3; Deut 4:34; 7:19; 26:8; 29:3; 34:11; cf. Acts 7:36). Accordingly, Luke portrays the hand of God on the side of the Jesus-movement – a powerful incentive favoring conversion to the Way. For those unfamiliar with Israel's Scriptures, analogous frames were available, since healing in Greco-Roman antiquity was associated with the ubiquitous gods, especially but not exclusively the cults and shrines honoring the healing deities (e.g., Hercules, Isis, Asclepius, Hygeia). (See Acts 14:8–13.) It almost goes without saying that evidence of healing would have been a profound validation of missionary testimony, not least for village and rural folk for whom the services of the "professional" physician were financially out of reach and who therefore would find the prospect of divine healing especially attractive. As Luke records of Paul and Barnabas in Iconium, "So they remained for a

---

[57] See Peter Pilhofer, *Presbyteron Kreitton: Der Altersbeweis der jüdischen und christlichen Apologeten und seine Vorgeschichte* (WUNT 2:39; Tübingen: Mohr Siebeck, 1990).

long time, speaking boldly for the Lord, who testified to the word of
his grace by granting signs and wonders to be done through them"
(Acts 14:3).

Conversion: Active and/or passive?

For Luke-Acts, "converts" might be "passive" (e.g., Acts 9:1–20)
or "active" (Luke 3:10, 12, 14; Acts 2:37; 16:30: "What should we
do?") – to use the paradigmatic categories of agency discussed by
Kilbourne and Richardson.[58] In the end, however, in Luke-Acts
passive and active flow together theologically, ecclesially, and
sociologically. Theologically, repentance is both divine gift
(passive) and call (active) (e.g., Luke 5:31–32; Acts 5:31; 11:18).
Ecclesially, repentance is signified by baptism – a quintessentially
passive act (one does not baptize oneself, but is baptized) for which
one must actively present oneself; and a ritual act by which the
converted are embraced within the community of believers.
Sociologically, conversion is not an event or static occurrence, but
must be understood in terms of embodiment within a community.
Converts require a community of reference and formation as they
(re-)learn how to think, believe, feel, and behave – that is, as they
embrace and embody fresh patterns for ordering life.[59]

Moment of decision and "movement"

Any emphasis on conversion as decision-making needs to be tem-
pered in two ways. First, for Luke, above all, conversion itself is the
gracious gift of God – as Peter announces in Jerusalem, "When
God raised up his servant, he sent him first to you, to bless you by
turning each of you from your wicked ways" (Acts 3:26; cf. 5:31;
11:18). Second, if the rhetoric of conversion in Luke-Acts is oriented at least in part to promote a response in favor of the gospel,

---

[58] Brock Kilbourne and James T. Richardson, "Paradigm Conflict, Types of
Conversion, and Conversion Theories," *Sociological Analysis* 50 (1988): 1–
21.
[59] See Kilbourne and Richardson, "Paradigm Conflict," 15.

this should not be taken as evidence that conversion is realized in a single point of decision-making. Instead, conversion is a journey, not an instantaneous metamorphosis; even though points of decision-making can be traced in the Lukan narrative, these provide points of beginning and milestones along the way, rather than conclusion. In this case, a *series* of transformations are compressed into a *single* moment, "conversion." But if this is so, one might then inquire, Who, then, is a convert? The simple answer would be, one who has undergone a redirectional rotation and is on the move in faithful service to the purpose of God as this is revealed in Jesus Christ and underwritten by the Spirit of God.

Conclusion

Previous study has indexed Luke's interest in conversion in a variety of ways, especially with reference to the vocabulary and related episodes of conversion in his narrative. Coming to the study of conversion in Luke-Acts from the perspective of cognitive science deepens our understanding of Luke's theology of conversion as it broadens our sense of what conversion entails. What is more, a number of the controverted issues surrounding the study of conversion in Acts find resolution when examined from the perspective of cognitive science.

Accordingly, conversion is inseparable from the human experience of embodiment, a reality that undermines claims that conversion is an "inner" change, or that conversion of individuals can be understood in individualistic terms, or that conversion might engage one's intellect but not one's affect (or vice versa), or that conversion might be pinpointed on a temporal map.

Conversion, then, is a transformation of conceptual scheme – conceptual, conative, and behavioral – by which life is reordered; and this highlights the eschatological context of conversion for Luke. For him, conversion is eschatologically driven in the sense that the outpouring of the Spirit marks the turn of the ages, motivates the Christian call to conversion, and fosters ongoing conversion. Accordingly, conversion is both gift and response. Luke's perspective on conversion thus takes seriously that the first and initiating act is God's.

Luke's perspective thus refuses any facile distinctions between conversion as act and process, between cognitive and moral change, between external and internal transformation, between movement from one religion to another and deepening commitment within one's religion, and between personal and community formation. "To welcome the word," as Acts 2:41 has it, is a transformative act that places embodied life in a new light, that leads one inexorably into a multiethnic and communal existence with others who incarnate and propagate this vision of God's restorative purpose, and that cannot but be exhibited in behaviors congruous with the way of Jesus Messiah.

Concluding Reflections

"Feed the soul or feed the hungry?"[60]
"Evangelicals should focus on saving souls, not the planet."[61]

Newspaper headlines like these make good sense in a world understood in dualistic terms. They make no sense at all in a world understood in the terms we have sketched in this chapter. Discussions of mission or portraits of the gospel must take seriously the message of a salvation oriented toward embodied human life. "Inner life" is not ruled out as a category, provided we understand that "inner" is not substantively different from "outer." "Individual" is not ruled out as a category, provided that emphases on the personal and on the nesting of persons within relationships are paramount. "Humanity" is not ruled out as a category, provided that it is never forgotten that the embodiedness (or "dustiness") of human life links moral development inexorably with the land ("dust") God created.

---

[60] Rich Copley, "Feed the Soul or Feed the Hungry?" *Lexington Herald Leader* (16 June 2002), D1, 5 (1).
[61] Cal Thomas, "Evangelicals Should Focus on Saving Souls, Not the Planet," *Lexington Herald Leader* (18 March 2005), A15.

Finally, the importance of neuro-hermeneutics noted in this chapter presses for further reflection. If our grasp of the world and construction of identity is inherently subjective, then the vision that guides that subjectivity advances in importance. The use of the term "truth" (ἀλήθεια, *alētheia*) in the NT is important here, since *alētheia* refers to conformity with the way things really are. On the one hand, this underscores the role of critical evaluation – testing beliefs for their coherence with other available data.[62] On the other, it highlights the importance of perspective – the way things really are according to whom? Here we return to the category of "imagination" or "conceptual scheme," and bring onto the table the metaphor of *enlightenment* as a way of portraying salvation in which the cross of Christ provides a way of comprehending life, orients a community around its identifying beliefs and values, and guides the actions of those whose lives carry its brand. The NT offers a range of images to describe salvation-as-embodied transformation, but none is more descriptive than Paul's testimony, "From now on, therefore, we regard no one from a human point of view. … So if anyone is in Christ, there is a new creation: everything old has passed away; see, everything has become new!" (2 Cor 5:16–17).

---

[62] The attendant philosophical and cognitive-scientific issues have begun to be explored by Jean-Pierre Changeux, *The Physiology of Truth: Neuroscience and Human Knowledge* (Cambridge, MA: Harvard University Press, 2002).

5

THE RESURRECTION OF
THE BODY

Jesus was resurrected to a new kind of bodily existence, thus affirming God's faithfulness to his creation and pointing to its deep transformation. ... The empty tomb validates God's willingness to deal with the bodily nature of human life. In addition, Christ's body becomes the visible medium for his memory. (Günter Thomas)[1]

When we die, there is a dichotomy of ego and earthly organism. We are constituted in such a way that we can survive "coming apart" at death, as unnatural as this may be. (John W. Cooper)[2]

---

[1] Günter Thomas, "Resurrection to New Life: Pneumatological Implications of the Eschatological Transition," in *Resurrection: Theological and Scientific Assessments* (ed. Ted Peters, Robert John Russell, and Michael Welker; Grand Rapids, MI: Eerdmans, 2002), 255–76 (263–64).
[2] Cooper, *Body, Soul, and Life Everlasting,* 163.

But someone will ask, "How are the dead raised? With what kind of body do they come?" (1 Cor 15:35)

"Lord, already there is a stench because he has been dead four days." Spoken by Martha, sister of the dead man Lazarus, in reply to Jesus' instruction to remove the stone from Lazarus' tomb (John 11:38–39), these words pinpoint the first of two central quandaries intrinsic to the historic confession of the Christian faith, "I believe in . . . the resurrection of the body." As Caroline Walker Bynum has demonstrated, Christian belief concerning the resurrection has stubbornly focused on the physicality of both resurrection and ultimate salvation.[3] As Martha recognizes, however, this belief flies in the face of the empirical observation that our physical bodies decay upon death; indeed, the warm climate and absence of embalming procedures in ancient Palestine necessitated both the use of spices to counter the repugnant odor of decomposition and the placement of the corpse on sand or salt to absorb the results of bodily disintegration.[4] The frailty of embodied existence seems to vacate the doctrine of (bodily) resurrection of all sensibility.

What is more, with the natural decay of the body, its constituent ingredients become so much a part of the fabric of the natural world that it would be impossible to reconstitute the body of one individual without violating the integrity of other bodies. This is because my body is made up of molecules that, in the long expanse of biological time, have belonged to other bodies, and are likely yet to be constitutive of still more bodies in the future. If resurrection requires the reassembly of our bodies at the end of the age, how will God adjudicate the inevitably competing claims to those basic

---

[3] Caroline Walker Bynum, *The Resurrection of the Body in Western Christianity, 200—1336* (New York: Columbia University Press, 1995). She concludes "that a concern for material and structural continuity showed remarkable persistence even where it seemed almost to require philosophical incoherence, theological equivocation, or aesthetic offensiveness. ... The materialism of [traditional Christian] eschatology expressed not body-soul dualism but rather a sense of self as psychosomatic unity" (11).

[4] See, e.g., Mark 15:46; John 19:40.

elements?[5] This problem is only heightened by the practice of
organ transplant and the prospect of organ cloning. Further, for
many of us, extending our current bodies into eternity would be a
prospect most unwelcome, given their infirmities, deformities, and
other deficits. What, then, might "resurrection of the body" entail?
This line of thinking introduces a second issue. If not through
persistence of this body, how might continuity of personal identity,
from death to life-after-death, be guaranteed?[6] How can I be sure
that the *me* that enjoys eternal life is really *me*? Here we raise the
question of personal identity in general, and the possibility of the
survival of personal identity in particular – an issue that has suggested to some that the hope of resurrection turns on a dualist
anthropology: mortal body, immortal soul. Given the self-evident
finality of death for the physical body, without recourse to a separate entity or personal "essence" (that is, a soul, which constitutes
the real *me*) that survives death, how can we maintain a reasonable
doctrine of the afterlife? If, instead of *possessing* a body, I *am* a
body, then when my body dies do I not likewise cease to exist?

Indeed, in his recent proposal of *The Emergent Self*, for example, William Hasker suggests that a physicalist account of human
nature finds some strong measure of support from biblical conceptions of the human person as "a single, integrated whole," but that
biblical visions of survival of death disallow an "ontological
holism" in favor of some form of disembodied personal existence
after death, however temporary. Hasker even goes so far as to
affirm that "the general pattern of New Testament eschatology (a
pattern already well established in first-century Judaism) involves
a three-stage progression: death, followed by a temporary state of

[5] This problem was grasped by Augustine, who wrote, "For all the flesh
which hunger has consumed finds its way into the air by evaporation, whence
... God almighty can recall it. That flesh, therefore, shall be restored to the
[one] in whom it first became human flesh. For it must be looked upon as borrowed by the other person, and, like a pecuniary loan, must be returned to the
lender" (*City of God* 22.20). Augustine's proposal breaks down, of course,
when the full extent of our biological interrelatedness is understood.
[6] For philosophical approaches to this issue, see Kevin J. Corcoran, ed., *Soul,
Body, and Survival: Essays on the Metaphysics of Human Persons* (Ithaca:
Cornell University Press, 2001).

disembodied existence, followed by the resurrection and judgment on the last day." On the basis of this alleged NT eschatology he goes on to argue for a portrait of the human person he dubs "emergent dualism."[7]

For us, what is crucial about Hasker's presentation is that, for his argument, a trail that at most points would lead to a physicalist account of the human person is rerouted in the direction of dualism on account of concerns with Christian eschatology, and more particularly with the notion of the intermediate state. Of interest, too, is that, for the teaching of the Bible on this matter, Hasker is apparently dependent, *en toto,* on the earlier work of the philosophical theologian John W. Cooper.[8] This hints at the surprising role Cooper's study of *Body, Soul, and Life Everlasting* has had,[9] and explains why I have constructed this chapter in part as a reply to Cooper's work.

I propose to explore the contribution of the NT message of the resurrection to Christian anthropology by pursuing three lines of inquiry. First, I will address issues of background by sketching the development and significance of resurrection in the Scriptures of Israel and raising questions against the idea of an "intermediate state." My aims here are to map something of the landscape within which we might locate resurrection texts in the NT, to broaden our vision of the significance of resurrection in God's redemptive plan, and to undermine what is for Cooper the self-evident place of the intermediate state in biblical faith.[10] Second, I will direct our

---

[7] Hasker, *Emergent Self,* 206–7.

[8] Cooper, *Body, Soul, and Life Everlasting.* Similarly, in their attempt to insist that the Bible supports substance dualism, J.P. Moreland and Scott B. Rae (*Body and Soul,* 23–40) focus on the intermediate state as a key piece of evidence, and build their case above all on Cooper's survey of the biblical materials.

[9] Surprisingly, without nuance or further exegetical analysis, Philip F. Esler assumes Cooper's analysis as the foundation for his view of the "communion of saints" (*New Testament Theology,* 241). This is an example of allowing substance metaphysics to set the terms of the discussion, without considering other interpretive options.

[10] Against the sort of proposal put forward by Cooper, see also Brian Edgar, "Biblical Anthropology and the Intermediate State," *EvQ* 74 (2002): 27–45, 109–21.

attention to three Lukan texts related to the ideas of intermediate state and resurrection: Luke 16:19–31; 23:40–43; and 24:36–49. This will allow me to question the basis for belief in an intermediate state as well as to press our thinking about the character of resurrection existence and the nature of personal identity (and, particularly, the persistence of personal identity beyond the grave). Third, I will turn to 1 Corinthians 15 (and, then, 2 Cor 5) as a way of focusing attention on Paul's understanding of a body suited for life-after-death. This will lead to some concluding, programmatic remarks about the nature of the human person as this relates to identity in this life and the life to come.

I intend to show that, with reference to the texts we will examine, an anthropology that posits an ontologically distinct soul, which constitutes the "real person" and which guarantees survival of personal identity from this life to the next, is not only unnecessary but actually stands in tension with key aspects of the resurrection message of the Scriptures. Personal identity with regard to both present life and life-after-death is narratively and relationally shaped and embodied, the capacity for life-after-death is not intrinsic to humanity but is divine gift, and resurrection signifies not rescue from the cosmos but transformation with it.

The perspective I will sketch underscores the miraculous character of resurrection by locating its possibility solely in God's gracious initiative. It takes seriously and is congruent with what we are learning from the neurosciences regarding the neural correlates of the dispositions and behaviors by which we identify our humanity, as well as the reality that, throughout our lives, nature and nurture sculpt our brains and shape our bodily existence in ways that form and reform who we are.

Resurrection in Israel's Scriptures

In the world of the NT, how might people have understood proclamation of the resurrection? That we should approach this question with caution is suggested by two NT texts. According to the first, when coming down the mountain following his transfiguration, Jesus directed his disciples, Peter, James, and John, "to tell no one about what they had seen, until after the Son of Man had risen from the dead. So they kept the matter to themselves, questioning what this rising from the dead could mean" (Mark 9:9–10). Though recipients of Jesus' prediction of resurrection, his own inner circle of disciples are said to have found his words about "rising from the dead" incomprehensible. This may have been because Jesus apparently spoke of the resurrection of an individual (that is, his own resurrection), whereas resurrection-belief in contemporary Judaism was corporate in its emphasis. Alternatively, the puzzle experienced by Jesus' followers might have reflected simply the lack of standardization in resurrection-talk in Second Temple Judaism.[11]

Another text, this one found in the Acts of the Apostles, has it, first, that the people of Athens mistook Paul's proclamation of the resurrection of Jesus as a message about two new deities, Jesus and Resurrection (17:18); and, second, that when those gathered on the Areopagus heard Paul announce that God had raised someone from the dead, some scoffed while others were curious to hear more (17:30–32). Luke had already identified the presence of Epicureans and Stoics, representatives of two philosophical schools whose views on the afterlife contrasted. Epicureans held that the soul was a substance of fine particles or atoms that dissipated at death; no belief in an afterlife would be consistent with this view. Stoic views of the afterlife are more difficult to summarize, and many Stoics seem to have believed that human souls could survive for an indefinite period after death. In his analysis, Kevin Anderson observes that "it is impossible to tell precisely what any given Stoic would have made of Paul's preaching concerning the resurrection – although few if any would have found *bodily* resurrection acceptable – but Stoic views of the afterlife seem to have been open to Platonic influences. Thus, Luke plausibly represents them as being

---

[11] Cf. Anthony Harvey, "'They discussed among themselves what this "rising from the dead" could mean' (Mark 9.10)," in *Resurrection: Essays in Honour of Leslie Houlden* (ed. Stephen Barton and Graham Stanton; London: SPCK, 1994), 69–78.

curious about this new doctrine of the resurrection, whereas the
Epicureans would have nothing to do with it."[12]
   Even if the language and idea of resurrection circulated widely
in the world of early Christianity, diverse views concerning the resurrection pervaded that world.[13] Depending on the context, for
example, talk of "resurrection" and "afterlife" might trigger
thoughts related to the resuscitation of a dead corpse, revivifica-
tion of the soul, flight of the immortal soul at the moment of death,
transformation of the body for afterlife, and more. What might resurrection signify for God's people in the first-century Roman
Mediterranean?

Life and death

The idea of resurrection from the dead belongs to the later horizons of Israel's faith, as this is witnessed in Israel's Scriptures.
Numerous texts record the burial of the dead (for example, Gen
50:13; Josh 24:32) without mentioning the fate of the dead. In fact,
when death is mentioned, it is generally treated with little more
profundity than as a reference to the cessation of life. As a whole,
the Scriptures of Israel are largely uninterested in the fate of the
dead.[14]

---

[12] K.L. Anderson, *Theology of Jesus' Resurrection*, 113.
[13] In addition to the surveys by Anderson (*Theology of Jesus' Resurrection*,
48–117) and N.T. Wright (*Resurrection of the Son of God*, 32–206), for orientation, see Jan Assmann, "Resurrection in Ancient Egypt," in *Resurrection:
Theological and Scientific Assessments* (ed. Ted Peters, Robert John Russell,
and Michael Welker; Grand Rapids, MI: Eerdmans, 2002), 124–35; Edwin
Yamauchi, "Life, Death, and the Afterlife in the Ancient Near East," in *Life in
the Face of Death: The Resurrection Message of the New Testament* (ed. Richard N. Longenecker; MNTS; Grand Rapids, MI: Eerdmans, 1998), 21–50;
Peter G. Bolt, "Life, Death, and the Afterlife in the Greco-Roman World," in
Life in the Face of Death, 51–79; and Richard Bauckham, "Life, Death, and
the Afterlife in Second Temple Judaism," in *Life in the Face of Death*, 80–95.
[14] Cf. the helpful, summary remarks in Kent Harold Richards, "Death:
Old Testament," *ABD* 2:108–10; and Philip S. Johnston, "Death and
Resurrection," *NDBT*, 443–47 (443–45). More lengthy treatments are
available in Robert Martin-Achard, *From Death to Life: A Study of the*

For Israel's Scriptures, death is never a question merely of biological cessation. Though the books of the OT provide some variation in their perspectives on death, we may nonetheless speak of
common threads. These would include at least three affirmations –
first, human existence is marked by finitude; second, death is abso-
lute; and third, death is regarded as the sphere within which fellowship with Yahweh is lost. As Stanley B. Marrow has recently
emphasized, in the OT death is the common destiny of all living
creatures; it allows no survivors – neither any persons nor any
parts of persons.[15] Scripture underscores the inescapable fact of
death itself ("We must all die"), and denies that death itself can be
revoked ("We are like water spilt on the ground, which cannot be
gathered again," citing 2 Sam 14:14). Thus does Joshua announce
his death, "I am about to go the way of all the earth" (Josh 23:14;
cf. 1 Kgs 2:2). If later it appears that Jesus cheats death through
raising up the dead (e.g., Luke 7:22), it should not be forgotten that
stories of resuscitation in the Gospels leave no room for thinking
that death has been finally overcome. Paradoxically, Jesus himself
dies – the very person who brought the dead back to life. Death is
the cessation of life in all of its aspects, and especially the severance
of all relationships – relationships with God and with every person
and with everything in the cosmos. This perspective on death is
grounded in the reality that the Hebrew Bible as a whole defines
the human person in relational rather than essentialist terms.
Human beings are assessed as genuinely human and alive only
within the family of humans brought into being by Yahweh and in
relation to the God who gives life-giving breath. Those who wor-
shiped Yahweh, then, could hardly venerate the dead or ascribe

---

Development of the Doctrine of the Resurrection in the Old Testament
(Edinburgh: Oliver and Boyd, 1960); Nicholas J. Tromp, *Primitive
Conceptions of Death and the Nether World in the Old Testament* (BibOr 21;
Rome: Pontifical Biblical Institute, 1969); and Philip S. Johnston, *Shades of
Sheol: Death and Afterlife in the Old Testament* (Downers Grove, IL:
InterVarsity, 2002).
[15] Cf. Stanley B. Marrow, "ΑΘΑΝΑΣΙΑ/ ΑΝΑΣΤΑΣΙΣ: The Road Not
Taken," *NTS* 45 (1999): 571–86.

ancestral powers to the dead, since they were cut off from him (cf. Pss 30:9; 115:17). Indeed, corpse impurity was a major contagion within the socio-religious economy of the people of God.[16] Accordingly, life beyond death would refer above all to restoration to Yahweh, and, then, to the reach of Yahweh's sovereignty even beyond that most potent of barriers to life, death itself.

Images of resurrection

Hints of resurrection faith occur in a handful of prophetic texts. For example, in Hosea 6:1–3 we read of the prospect of the revival of God's people:

Come, let us return to the LORD;
    for it is he who has torn, and he will heal us;
    he has struck down, and he will bind us up.
After two days he will revive us;
    on the third day he will raise us up,
    that we may live before him.
Let us know, let us press on to know the LORD;
    his appearing is as sure as the dawn;
    he will come to us like the showers,
    like the spring rains that water the earth.

This text attracted the attention of the church fathers, who read in it a prophecy of Jesus' resurrection on the third day, and early Jewish interpretation found here a reference to the end-time resurrection of Israel. In its own eighth-century context, this reading may not have been so clear, however. "Raising up" is more likely to have been heard as a metaphor for the restoration of the nation than as a reference to the literal raising up of persons whose life on this earth had ended.

Ezekiel 37:1–14, with its dramatic image of the valley of dry bones brought to life, also envisions Israel's restoration. This did

---

[16] Cf. Lev 11; Num 19; Hans Walter Wolff, *Anthropology of the Old Testament* (London: SCM, 1974), 102–5.

not keep later Jewish interpretation from finding here a graphic depiction of the resurrection, however. Note especially verses 12–13: "I am going to . . . bring you up from your graves!" In both of these texts – one from Hosea, the other from Ezekiel – we find the interweaving of the promise of Israel's restoration with the re-creative work of the Lord.

Many scholars find a more direct reference to resurrection in Isaiah 26:19:

> Your dead shall live,
>   their corpses shall rise.
> O dwellers in the dust,
>   awake and sing for joy!
> For your dew is a radiant dew,
>   and the earth will give birth to those long dead.

Like the vision in Ezekiel 37, Isaiah's words appear in a context that proposes Israel's restoration and, indeed, exaltation among the nations. With regard to the meaning of this text in particular, debate centers on whether a literal raising up of dead corpses is envisioned. At the very least, however, we have here in Isaiah a further text that relates the notion of resurrection to the activity of God by which he restores and exalts his people, and by which he pours upon them the totality of his covenant blessings.

The first unambiguous reference to the physical resurrection of the dead appears in Daniel 12:1–3:

> At that time Michael, the great prince, the protector of your people, shall arise. There shall be a time of anguish, such as has never occurred since nations first came into existence. But at that time your people shall be delivered, everyone who is found written in the book. Many of those who sleep in the dust of the earth shall awake, some to everlasting life, and some to shame and everlasting contempt. Those who are wise shall shine like the brightness of the sky, and those who lead many to righteousness, like the stars forever and ever.

This passage forms the climax of the revelation that began in Daniel 11:2, and marks the decisive triumph of God's people over the enemies of Israel. At last, Israel will experience salvation in its fullest sense. Not all will experience this deliverance, however, but only those found in "the book" (that is, the book of life – cf. Isa 4:3; Mal 3:16–18). Others will experience the resurrection as judgment. It is in this way that Daniel's concern with the vindication of God's righteous servants comes into clearest focus.

Even those texts that did not refer explicitly to resurrection of the dead would provide the raw material for a view of God that would blossom in the period of Second Temple Judaism. This view identified God as the source and sovereign over life, and this provided the ground for the affirmation of God's capacity to give back the life of the faithful tragically lost at the hands of Israel's enemies. Resurrection theology was profoundly *theocentric,* focused as it was on Israel's covenantal relationship with God; recognition on the part of the people of Israel of their own unfaithfulness to the covenant and, therefore, their experience of exile and foreign domination; and the hope of Israel that God's people might be "raised up" – that is, restored and established in a position of regency in the renewed cosmos. Resurrection-belief was thus cultivated in Israel's experience of exile, and in its radical understanding of God's justice. "The Old Testament God – the Creator, the Source of life, and the Lord of life – undoubtedly *could* raise the dead. That he *would* do so only became clear once death was perceived as contradicting God's righteousness and God's love."[17]

It is true, of course, that some Jews in the Second Temple period would not have shared hope in the resurrection. Luke, for example, distinguishes the Sadducees as persons who did not believe in the resurrection (Acts 23:8), and this characterization is echoed by the Jewish historian Josephus.[18] Nevertheless, we are able to

---

[17] Bauckham, "Life, Death, and the Afterlife," 86. For the continuity of Old and New Testaments with regard to the message of resurrection, see also Frank Crüsemann, "Scripture and Resurrection," in *Resurrection: Theological and Scientific Assessments,* 89–123.

[18] Josephus *JW* 2.8.14 §165; see also Matt 22:23; Mark 12:18; Luke 20:27.

identify the primary contours of resurrection-belief among the Jewish people, and these help us to know what categories of interpretation might have been available to those who first heard the Christian proclamation of resurrection.

First, resurrection signals the end-time restoration of Israel and triumph over its enemies. Resurrection marks God's vindication of the righteous who have suffered unjustly; having been condemned and made to suffer by a human court, the righteous will in the resurrection be vindicated in the divine court. That is, proclamation of "the resurrection" is synecdoche for the eschatological restoration of Israel and, then, the advent of the messianic age, with its implications for cosmic renewal, the "new heaven and new earth." Second, and closely related, resurrection marks the decisive establishment of divine justice, where rewards and punishments are meted out in relation to the character of one's life before death. Injustice and wickedness will not have the final word, but in the resurrection will be decisively repudiated. Third, although space must be carved out for a certain pluralism at this point, generally speaking, Jewish perspectives on life-after-death continued to embrace a view of the human person as a psychosomatic unity, so that belief in resurrection typically did not entail the expectation of the liberation of the immortal soul from the mortal body. At the same time, of course, we should recognize that this period of theological development spawned a variety of eschatological beliefs – some related more to the immortality of the soul, or the resurrection of the spirit, or the resurrection of the person understood as a unity, or to no afterlife whatsoever.[19]

---

[19] See John J. Collins, "The Afterlife in Apocalyptic Literature," in *Death, Life-after-Death, Resurrection and the World-to-Come in the Judaisms of Antiquity*, part 4 of *Judaism in Late Antiquity* (ed. Alan J. Avery-Peck and Jacob Neusner; Handbook of Oriental Studies – 1: The Near and Middle East 49; Leiden: Brill, 2000), 119–39; George W.E. Nickelsburg, "Judgment, Life-after-Death, and Resurrection in the Apocrypha and the Non-Apocalyptic Pseudepigrapha," in *Death, Life-after-Death, Resurrection and the World-to-Come*, 141–62; Philip R. Davies, "Death, Resurrection, and Life after Death in the Qumran Scrolls," in *Death, Life-after-Death, Resurrection and the World-to-Come*, 189–211; Lester L. Grabbe, *Judaic Religion in the*

An intermediate state?

By "intermediate state," I refer particularly to the temporary, disembodied existence of the human self, from the time of one's death
to the time of resurrection. By "intermediate state," I do not refer
(as Murray J. Harris does) to "the period that elapses *(from an
earthly viewpoint)* between the death of the individual believer and
the parousia of Christ or the consummation of all things."[20] This
latter notion of "intermediate state" may be granted without
requiring of a human self any temporary, disembodied existence
experienced for the duration of the period that elapses as time is
experienced "from an earthly viewpoint." The question is whether
the biblical materials anticipate a waiting period, experienced by
the dead person, between death and resurrection, or whether the
biblical materials anticipate for the dead an immediate resurrection, irrespective of how persons bound to time and space as we
know it mark the progression of the clock. As F.F. Bruce remarked
three decades ago, "The tension created by the postulated interval
between death and resurrection might be relieved today if it were
suggested that in the consciousness of the departed believer there is
no interval between dissolution and investiture, however long an
interval might be measured by the calendar of earth-bound human
history."[21] My focus here will be on John Cooper's work and, then,
the concept of Sheol and the related question of the nature of the
"shades" that inhabit Sheol in Israel's Scriptures.

    Cooper's dualistic interpretation of OT anthropology begins
with his examination of "the Old Testament view of existence after
death," and specifically with his claim that, from the perspective of
the OT, "personal existence is separable from earthly, bodily

---

Second Temple Period: Belief and Practice from the Exile to Yavneh (London:
Routledge, 2000), 257–70; Elledge, *Life after Death in Early Judaism*, esp. 5–
44.
[20] Murray J. Harris, *Raised Immortal: Resurrection and Immortality in the
New Testament* (Grand Rapids, MI: Eerdmans, 1983), 133; emphasis added.
[21] F.F. Bruce, *Paul: Apostle of the Heart Set Free* (Grand Rapids, MI:
Eerdmans, 1977), 312 n.40.

life."²² According to his analysis, the ancient Israelites shared a belief in the afterlife, but had their own term for "the departed" – namely, "*rephaim,*" often translated as "shades." These dwelt in Sheol in a kind of lethargic mode of existence marked by continuity of personal identity and the capacity for being awakened and engaging in interpersonal discourse. His survey of the relevant OT texts leads Cooper to the conclusion that OT teaching regarding existence in Sheol supports the affirmation that "persons are not merely distinguishable from their earthly bodies, they are separable from them and can continue to exist without them."²³

Readers of Cooper's analysis might be forgiven for imagining that the OT concerned itself pervasively with death and shaped a rather generous pattern of what happens after death. It is common, however mistaken, to imagine that the ancient Hebrews (as well as those persons who populated the first-century world of the Roman Mediterranean) were occupied with conversation around the question, What happens after we die? In fact, as I have already noted, death is not a major topic of OT theology, and the OT deals only incidentally with the subject. To speak of an OT *interest* in the "afterlife" thus raises important questions about how one might understand the nature of "life" and the character of "death," from within the Hebrew Scriptures.

It is important to note, then, that Sheol is only very rarely deployed in the OT as the common location of the dead. Rather, in most instances the term is used with reference to that human fate to which the ungodly are consigned and to which the godly declare their aversion; it is the antithesis of heaven. That is, the subterranean world of the dead is associated especially with the wicked, and this underscores the OT distinction between life (lived in this world, before and in relation to Yahweh) and death (in the underworld, separate from Yahweh).²⁴ This evidence coheres well with Israel's speech about human experience "in Sheol/in the Pit" and

---

²² Cooper, *Body, Soul, and Life Everlasting,* 58–80 (59).
²³ Cooper, *Body, Soul, and Life Everlasting,* 77.
²⁴ Cf. e.g., Pss 9:18; 16:10; 30:4; 31:18; 49:16; 55:16; 86:13; 88:6; Isa 5:14; Job 24:19; et al. See Desmond Alexander, "The Old Testament View of Life

"out of Sheol/out of the Pit," which Walter Brueggemann suggests has been informed by Israel's own life-story in and out of bondage in Egypt.[25] Israel's sense of the drama of human life is articulated in terms of death – that is, separation from Yahweh. As John Jarick observes, the general view of the Hebrew Bible is that Sheol is not only that "post-mortem realm devoid of all that pertains to life and hope," but also that "this realm is devoid of God as well."[26]

Even in those texts that speak of those who dwell in Sheol, we find no suggestion that some essential part of the human being (whether a soul or a spirit, or some other) has survived death.[27] This is a reminder that Israel's Scriptures as a whole do not define the human person in essentialist terms.

Before departing these more global comments on the issue of death and the afterlife, I should draw attention to alternative formulations of an "afterlife" found in the OT, even if they are never

---

after Death," *Themelios* 11 (1986): 41–46 (43–44); Philip S. Johnston, "The Underworld and the Dead in the Old Testament," *TynBul* 45 (1994): 415–19 (416); idem, *Shades of Sheol*. In his essay, "Beyond the Grave: Ezekiel's Vision of Death and Afterlife" (*BBR* 2 [1992]: 113–41), Daniel I. Block provides an extensive analysis of Ezekiel's vision of the netherworld. Although the term *rĕpa'îm* (see below) does not occur, he nevertheless notes with interest that Ezekiel speaks only of wicked persons and wicked nations as inhabiting Sheol, never of the state of the righteous in death (esp. 127–28).

[25] Brueggemann, *Theology of the Old Testament*, 483–85; compare Wolff, *Anthropology*, 106–7; Gerhard von Rad, *Old Testament Theology* (2 vols.; New York: Harper & Row, 1962–65), 2:349–50; Childs, *Old Testament Theology*, 245–46.

[26] John Jarick, "Questioning Sheol," in *Resurrection* (ed. Stanley E. Porter, Michael A. Hayes, and David Tombs; JSNTSup 186; Sheffield: Sheffield Academic Press, 1999), 22–32 (30). George E. Mendenhall comments that Sheol "can only be defined as the place where the dead are dead" ("From Witchcraft to Justice: Death and Afterlife in the Old Testament," in *Death and Afterlife: Perspectives of World Religions* [ed. Hiroshi Obayashi; Contributions to the Study of Religion 33; New York: Greenwood, 1992], 67–81 [68]).

[27] Cf. Richard Bauckham, "Life, Death, and the Afterlife." Bauckham observes that the older Jewish tradition portrays human beings as a "psychosomatic whole" whose "bodiliness is intrinsic to nature." Hence, there is no "soul" or "spirit" to survive death, and "existence *in death* is not the eternal life *beyond death* for which later Judaism hopes. That can only be conceived as a fully embodied life" (87).

generalized to the whole of God's people. God "took" Enoch (Gen 5:24) and Elijah "ascended in a whirlwind into heaven" on a chariot (2 Kgs 2:11), for example. These brief accounts provide no fodder for the notion of an intermediate state.

The term of more immediate interest, *rĕpā'îm* ("shades," often brought over into English as *rephaim* rather than translated), appears only eight times in the Hebrew Bible in the sense of "the dead."[28] Although the etymology and historical development of this term are both problematic,[29] its usage in the OT is more straightforward. *Rephaim* refers to those whose abode is Sheol, the place of the dead. Found in the OT only in poetic texts, the "shades" are portrayed through simple parallelism as "the dead." In Isaiah 26:14, 19 and Psalm 88:11, the *rephaim* are associated with "the dead"; in Proverbs 2:18 the term occurs in parallel with "death" (see the similar idea in Prov 21:16); and in Isaiah 14:9 and Proverbs 9:18 they appear in "the grave." That is, the *rephaim* are simply the human dead whose place is the grave. For Proverbs, references to the *rephaim* are used to dramatize the end of a way of life set in opposition to the righteous paths of God. Here the *rephaim* are associated with the place of the dead, Sheol or, simply, "death" (as "sphere of death"), in a manner characteristic of the teaching of the Two Ways found in the wisdom tradition.[30] In the single usage among the Psalms, the psalmist pleads for divine intervention, realizing that, if he dies, he will not be able to offer praise to God. Job 26:5 locates the *rephaim* under the waters, a portrait that plays on the mythological identification of the waters as a

---

[28] It is thus surprising to hear, then, that "the dead in Sheol are called *rephaim*, or shades" (Moreland and Rae, *Body and Soul*, 31). The dead are referred to as *repā'îm* only eight times, and as *'elôhîm* only twice. The typical term used to denote the dead is a participial form of *mwt* ("the dead"); cf. Heinz-Josef Fabry, K.-J. Illman, and Helmer Ringgren, "מות," *TDOT* 8:185–209 (204–5). *repa'îm* is also used as an indicator of ethnic identity, with reference to the ancient inhabitants of the northern Transjordan – e.g., Gen 14:5; 15:20; et al.

[29] Cf. Michael L. Brown, "רפא," *NIDOTTE* 3:1173–80 (1174–76). Cf. the earlier Tromp, *Primitive Conceptions of Death*, 176–80.

[30] Cf. Prov 5:5; 8:35–36; 11:19; 12:28; 13:14; 14:27; 16:14–15; 18:21. See also Deut 30:15, 19, where a similar choice is set before the people of Israel.

hostile, chaotic power (note the association with Sheol in 26:6).
Isaiah 26:14, 19, taken together, contrast the fate of the wicked,
who will be overtaken by death, and the righteous, whose death
will be overturned by Yahweh. This reading takes Isaiah 26:19 as a
prayer to Yahweh, so that "your dead" refers to Yahweh's dead,
and capitalizes on the portrait of Yahweh in Isaiah 25:7 as the one
who would "swallow up death forever." Old Testament scholars
have puzzled over whether this reference to resurrection is best
interpreted as a graphic metaphor for Israel's return from exile
(compare Ezek 37:1–14) or as perhaps the earliest reference in
Israel's Scriptures to the notion of the physical resurrection of the
righteous. Increasingly, however, this is regarded as a false choice,
since the latter comprises one of the means by which Yahweh
accomplishes the former.[31]

These instances of the term *rephaim* cohere well with more general comments on the fate of the dead (above), and help to particu-
larize those observations. No suggestion is found in any of these
texts that the *rephaim* might be regarded as "alive" or "living" or
otherwise as having some form of "personal existence."[32] Nor do

---

[31] So, e.g., Anderson, *Theology of Jesus' Resurrection*, 55–58; Brevard S.
Childs, *Isaiah* (OTL; Louisville: Westminster John Knox, 2001), 191–92; Ben
C. Ollenburger, "If Mortals Die, Will They Live Again? The Old Testament
and Resurrection," *Ex Auditu* 9 (1993): 29–44 (38–40).

[32] Moreland and Rae's claim, "For a number of reasons Old Testament teaching about life after death is best understood in terms of a diminished though
conscious form of disembodied personal survival in an intermediate state"
(*Body and Soul*, 32), rests on four lines of argumentation: 1) "life in Sheol
is often depicted as lethargic, inactive and resembling an unconscious coma";
2) "the practice of necromancy . . . is understood as a real possibility";
3) *nephesh* refers to "a conscious person without flesh and bone," which
"departs to God upon death"; and 4) "the Old Testament clearly teaches the
hope of resurrection beyond the grave." None of these lines of argument finds
warrant in texts dealing with the *rephaim*, only 3) requires an intermediate
state, and only 3) suggests "disembodied personal survival." (Communication
with the dead [2] requires existence beyond death, but neither an intermediate
state nor a disembodied person.) With regard to 3), not even James Barr's
recent attempt to rehabilitate a rendering of *nephesh* as "soul" (in the sense of
a separate metaphysical entity, distinct and separable from the body; in *The*

we find in these texts any speculation regarding what transpires between this life and the life to come, or with regard to what transpires between death and resurrection. Instead, we find that the *rephaim* are cut off from Yahweh.

The Gospel of Luke and the Intermediate State

Among the NT texts called upon to provide warrant for the concept of the intermediate state, two in the Gospel of Luke have become primary: Jesus' parable of the rich man and Lazarus (Luke 16:19–31); and the words of exchange between Jesus and the criminal at the crucifixion (Luke 23:40–43). Regarding the former, Cooper puts forward three reasons for his view that Jesus' parable provides a picture of the intermediate state: 1) the final resurrection, as Luke understands this event, has not yet taken place, since the rich man's brothers are still alive on earth; 2) Jesus' account has the rich man in Hades, an intermediate point on the way to Gehenna, in Luke's view; and 3) Jesus' depiction of the rich man as suffering bodily torment and thirst is consistent with the Second Temple Jewish representation of the intermediate state. Cooper also notes, however, that just because this parable uses popular images that signify an intermediate state does not mean that Jesus or Luke themselves actually affirmed the doctrine of the intermediate state.[33] More consequential for Cooper are Jesus' words to the criminal in Luke 23:42–43, "Today you will be with me in paradise": "He promised this repentant sinner the fellowship of paradise, the dwelling place of the faithful dead even before the resurrection, that very day." Because this text speaks so straightforwardly of the intermediate state, Cooper avers, we can presume

---

Garden of Eden and the Hope of Immortality [Minneapolis: Fortress, 1992], 36–47) convinces. As Di Vito summarizes, "However, with few unambiguous data to support Barr's analysis and numerous biblical texts that, on his admission, speak of the death of the נֶפֶשׁ, one is unlikely to infer the meaning 'immortal soul' from the use of נֶפֶשׁ in the OT without a predisposition to find it" ("OT Anthropology," 218; see more fully Seebass, "נֶפֶשׁ").

[33] Cooper, *Body, Soul, and Life Everlasting*, 136–39.

that the eschatological imagery of Luke 16:19–31 is theologically
relevant as well.[34]

More broadly, Cooper's treatment of the Lukan texts is shaped
by two interrelated and far-reaching presumptions. The first is
that, in the "intertestamental period" (i.e., the period of Second
Temple Judaism), testimony to an intermediate state was ubiquitous. The second is that this intermediate state was conceived in a
common way across Jewish literature of this era. Cooper also
imagines that the belief system regarding life after death that is
explicit in Second Temple Jewish writing draws out what was
already latent in the OT itself.

In fact, upon moving from the Scriptures of Israel into a NT text
like the Gospel of Luke, we find ourselves following new trails,
blazed within Second Temple Judaism. However, Cooper erroneously supposes that Jewish thought as it developed in this period
simply draws out the message present in embryonic form in the
Hebrew Bible, and on this shaky foundation he rests his assertion
that these later Jewish texts provide us with faithful commentaries
on OT perspectives. Although it is self-evident that Second Temple
Jewish literature reflects back on the Scriptures, whether we regard
their interpretations as "faithful" will depend on our hermeneutical theory. And irrespective of how this is adjudicated, we
would be mistaken were we to argue that a direct or simple line can
be drawn from OT texts to Second Temple Jewish interpretation.
Rather, with the onset of the fourth century BCE, Hebrew understandings of death and the afterlife were transformed under Greek
and later Roman influence. Ben Sira (2nd c. BCE) held to what we
might call a classical Hebrew position – affirming the creation of
human beings from the earth and their return to the earth upon
death (Sir 16:30; 17:1; 40:1, 11; 41:10), highlighting the inevitability of death (14:12–19), and denying human immortality (17:30;
44:9) – but, under the influence of hellenization, a position such as
his would be pulled in multiple directions. What can safely be said
about this period of theological development is that it spawned a

---

[34] Cooper, *Body, Soul, and Life Everlasting*, 139–42 (141).

variety of eschatological beliefs – some related more to the immortality of the soul, or the resurrection of the spirit, or the resurrection of the person understood as a unity, or to no afterlife whatsoever.[35] It is during this period that ideas of the intermediate state come into full bloom, and an intermediate state of some sort would certainly have had a place in popular conceptions of the afterlife among Luke's audience.

The parable of the rich man and Lazarus (Luke 16:19–31)

Within its narrative context, the parable of Luke 16:19–31 is told to Pharisees who have called into question Jesus' fidelity to the law (16:14–18). In this setting, the parable serves as a counter-challenge, indicating both Jesus' faithfulness before the law and Pharisaic duplicity. In one sense, the parable is concerned with wealth and its manifestations: a wealthy man engages in conspicuous consumption without regard for a poor man, in spite of the fact that this beggar who resides at his gate is quite literally his "neighbor" (vv. 19–21; cf. 10:29–37); and the rich and poor experience the eschatological reversal forecast in 6:20–24 (v. 25). In another sense, it is focused on the law (and, more broadly, the Scriptures) which, the parable informs us, is very much concerned with the state of the poor. In this case, a wealthy man comes to realize too late that he has ignored the words of Moses and the prophets concerning the poor. Our concerns here are more focused, however, on the eschatological picture painted by the parable – especially what it might say about an intermediate state and individual eschatology.

The stage is set by the extravagant parallelism resident in the depictions of the two main characters. The social distance between the two is continued through to the end, symbolized first by the gate, then by the "distance" ("far away," v. 23) and the "great chasm" fixed between them (v. 26). The rich man is depicted in

---

[35] Anderson, *Theology of Jesus' Resurrection*, 62; see, more broadly, 48–91; also Bauckham, "Life, Death, and the Afterlife"; and the sources listed above, n. 13.

outrageously affluent terms, while Lazarus is numbered among
society's "expendables," a man who had fallen prey to the ease
with which, even in an advanced agrarian society, persons without
secure land holdings might experience devastating downward
mobility. Jesus' comparison of these two characters in life continues in death. The unnamed rich man appears in Hades, Lazarus in
Abraham's bosom. Thus, while Lazarus is in a blissful state, the
wealthy man experiences torment and agony in Hades.

Whether Luke's parable envisions an intermediate state depends
on how one defines "state," whether in temporal or spatial terms,
or both. If one presumes time as experienced from an earthly point
of view, then it makes sense to speak of an intermediate state – that
is, a period that passes between the death of the individual and the
consummation of all things, as we, Luke's readers, experience time.
What is not obvious is that Lazarus (for example) experiences the
afterlife in this parable as a kind of waiting room between death
and final Judgment. Although it is common to read the Lukan parable against the backdrop of *1 Enoch* 22 (as Cooper does), this is
an erroneous exegetical move. Material from *1 Enoch* is of interest
insofar as it portrays Sheol with four different chambers, one for
each class of the dead, but irrelevant in that it imagines Sheol as a
place of detention, where people await their punishment at the
Judgment. Luke's parable (as well as additional Jewish texts from
the Second Temple period) depicts no period of detention, but has
the righteous already participating in rewards, the wicked already
suffering punishment.[36] Already present in Abraham's bosom,
where "there is no toil, no grief, no mourning, but peace, exulta-
tion and endless life" (*T. Ab.* 20:14),[37] Lazarus already shares in
Abraham's celebrated hospitality and participates in the heavenly

---

[36] See the discussion in Richard Bauckham, "Visiting Places of the Dead in the
Extra-Canonical Apocalypses," in *The Fate of the Dead: Studies on the Jewish and Christian Apocalypses* (NovTSup 93; Leiden: Brill, 1998), 81–96 (86–
90).

[37] ET in E.P. Sanders, "Testament of Abraham: A New Translation and Introduction," in *Old Testament Pseudepigrapha* (2 vols.; ed. James H.
Charlesworth; Garden City, NY: Anchor Bible, 1983/85), 1:871–902 (895).

banquet (see Luke 11:22–30). Similarly, the rich man is now suffering in Hades – not biding his time until the final Judgment. Also unclear is why this parable must be read as referring to a disembodied soul. Continuity of personal identity is obvious, the relationship between the character of one's earthly life and the nature of one's experience in the afterlife is highlighted, but these characters act as human agents with corporeal existence (who can thirst, speak, and, presumably, fetch water). As Turid Seim correctly observes, material-oriented ideas such as this were known in Luke's Greco-Roman setting, but were generally rejected in favor of spiritual ideas among the philosophically minded;[38] this makes Luke's emphasis on postmortem embodied existence all the more noticeable.

Here, the perspective of the Jewish *Apocalypse of Zephaniah* (probably from the early 1st c. CE) is of relevance. Here Hades is portrayed as the place of punishment for the wicked, visible from heaven, with the two, heaven and Hades, separated by a river. In 10:12–14, during his tour of heaven under the guidance of the great angel, the seer notes, "And I saw others with their hair on them. I said, 'Then there is hair and body in this place?' He said, 'Yes, the Lord gives body and hair to them as he desires.'"[39] This not only provides an interesting analog to the portrait painted in the Lukan parable, but points to a larger issue – namely, the impossibility of speaking of *the* concept of Hades in Second Temple Judaism, except in the broadest terms. Luke himself uses ᾅδης (*hadēs*) only four times; in addition to Luke 16:23, we find it twice in explicit dependence on the LXX (Acts 2:27, 31) and once in implicit dependence (Luke 10:15; cf. Isa 14:13–15). This way of accounting for the evidence gives us little assurance that the Lukan narrative speaks of Hades always in the same way, since it is at least as

---

[38] Turid Karlsen Seim, "In Heaven as on Earth? Resurrection, Body, Gender and Heavenly Rehearsals in Luke-Acts," in *Christian and Islamic Gender Models in Formative Traditions* (ed. Kari Elisabeth Børresen; Rome: Herder, 2004), 17–41 (18–21).

[39] ET in O.S. Wintermute, "Apocalypse of Zephaniah: A New Translation and Introduction," in *Old Testament Pseudepigrapha*, 1:497–515 (515).

likely, if not more so, that the intertextual use of the LXX con-
strains the meaning of Hades to its usage in the Scriptures of Israel
(i.e., as the general abode of the dead) while leaving open how
Hades might best be read in Jesus' parable in Luke 16:19–31. Evidence from the wider world of Luke would allow for readings of
Hades as the general abode of the dead; the intermediate abode for
all of the dead prior to the final Judgment; the intermediate abode
of the wicked and the righteous prior to the final Judgment, during
which time punishments and rewards are already being assessed;
and exclusively the place of punishment for the wicked.[40]

More obvious is how this text demonstrates a larger concern for
Luke with what Jacques Dupont referred to as "individual eschatology"[41] – that is, the fate of the individual immediately upon
death – even if Luke's interest here neither overshadows nor inter-
feres with his more thoroughgoing, corporate eschatology.[42] A similar perspective is found in the Testament of Abraham, usually
dated to the first century CE. In chapter 11 of the Testament we read

---

[40] Cf. the helpful summary in Richard Bauckham, "Hades, Hell," ABD 3:14–
15; and esp., idem, "Descents to the Underworld," in The Fate of the Dead, 9–
48; idem, "Early Jewish Visions of Hell," in The Fate of the Dead, 49–80; and
idem, "Visiting Places of the Dead." Bauckham notes that Hades and paradise
are within sight of each other in such texts as 4 Ezra 7:85, 93, just as Gehenna
and paradise appear within sight of each other (4 Ezra 7:36–38; 1 En.
108:14–15). Moreland and Rae (Body and Soul, 34) grossly oversimplify the
evidence when they assert that "in intertestamental Judaism, the intermediate
state was widely understood" to include 1) the belief that the dead were comprised of disembodied souls or spirits; 2) the dead were regarded as conscious
and active during the intermediate state; and 3) "resurrection was depicted as
the reunion of soul and body." This is due, apparently, to their
overdependence on Cooper (see Moreland and Rae, Body and Soul, 347
n.27).
[41] Jacques Dupont, "Die individuelle Eschatologie im Lukasevangelium und
in der Apostelgeschichte," in Orientierung an Jesus: Zur Theologie der
Synoptiker (ed. Paul Hoffman; Freiburg: Herder, 1973), 37–47. Cf. Luke
12:4–5, 16–21; 23:43; Acts 7:55–60; 14:22.
[42] See the discussion in John T. Carroll, Response to the End of History:
Eschatology and Situation in Luke-Acts (SBLDS 92; Atlanta: Scholars Press,
1988), 60–71; Walter Radl, Das Lukas-Evangelium (EdF 261; Darmstadt:
Wissenschaftliche Buchgesellschaft, 1988), 135–37.

of two gates, one for the righteous who enter paradise (or heaven, 20:12), the other for sinners destined for destruction and eternal punishment, with Judgment occurring at the moment of death and not at the End.

Given the pervasiveness of references to the intermediate state in contemporary Jewish literature, we should not be surprised to discover parallel ideas in a Lukan parable. However, given the diverse ways in which the intermediate state might be represented (in terms of temporality and spatiality, as well as with regard to the nature of human existence in this abode), we would be ill-advised to imagine that Jesus speaks in this account of disembodied existence in a place and time that stands between this life and the next. In fact, the evidence of the parable and of relevant parallels in Jewish literature actually moves in another direction, away from Cooper's reading of this material.

Jesus and the criminal at the crucifixion (Luke 23:40–43)

Luke alone records the exchange between the two criminals and Jesus at the scene of their crucifixion. The first criminal blasphemes Jesus while at the same time identifying himself with Jesus ("Save yourself, *and us!*"), whereas the second demonstrates astounding insight into Jesus' identity and status as God's agent of salvation. His plea, "Remember me!" is reminiscent of those words repeatedly spoken to Yahweh, whose memory is a source of divine blessing in keeping with his covenant.[43] Of particular interest here is Jesus' reply, "Truly I tell you, today you will be with me in Paradise," and especially the two words "today" and "Paradise." Although it is grammatically possible that "today" could be read with "Truly I tell you," its function as an adverb to denote when the criminal will join Jesus in Paradise is assured by the consistency with which Luke emphasizes the immediacy of salvation (e.g., Luke 4:21; 19:9). The point at issue, then, is Cooper's contention that "Paradise" denotes the intermediate resting place of the

---

[43] Cf. Ps 115:12; Judg 16:28; et al.

dead. The term itself, παράδεισος (*paradeisos*), originally referring to a "park" or "nobleman's estate," is used in the Greek versions of Genesis 2 for Eden. Given the idea in apocalyptic thought that the End would recapitulate the Beginning, the term came to be employed for the final, paradisal state enjoyed in the new creation. Is the referent of "paradise" the intermediate state enjoyed by the righteous, or is it the final reward? "Paradise" appears only three times in the NT (Luke 23:43; 2 Cor 12:4; Rev 2:7). Though we cannot assume that its usage in Luke should be measured in relation to other NT usage, it is of interest that, in Revelation, the term connotes the end-time consummation of God's purpose with its image of the restoration of divine presence and provision: "To everyone who conquers, I will give permission to eat from the tree of life that is in the paradise of God." Paul's description in 2 Corinthians 12 of being "caught up to the third heaven . . . caught up into Paradise" associates Paradise with the third heaven in a way that is reminiscent of several texts from Jewish apocalyptic, both in terms of the notion of a heavenly journey and with regard to the numbering of the heavens; this language is at home in a thought-world that presumes that the first Eden (Paradise) has been kept sealed in anticipation of the End, and, again, signifies life in the presence of God.[44] In the literature of Second Temple Judaism, Paradise could be used with reference simply to heaven, the divine abode and place of bliss, without temporal indicators.[45] It might refer to an intermediate abode of the righteous,[46] though most often it refers to the end-time dwelling of the righteous with God.[47] Interestingly, in the text outside of Luke's Gospel that contains the only known reference to the "bosom of Abraham" (see Luke 16:19–31), "Paradise" is also

---

[44] See Andrew T. Lincoln, *Paradise Now and Not Yet: Studies in the Role of the Heavenly Dimension in Paul's Thought with Special Reference to His Eschatology* (SNTSMS 43; Cambridge: Cambridge University Press, 1981), 77–84.

[45] Cf. 2 Esd 4:7–8; *T. Ab.* (B) 10:3.

[46] Cf. *1 En.* 37–71 (which most scholars now date to the late 1st c. CE).

[47] E.g., 2 Esd 7:36; 8:52; 2 *Bar.* 51:11; *T. Levi* 18:10–11. See the helpful summary of the evidence in James H. Charlesworth, "Paradise," *ABD* 5:154–55.

found, and is used with reference to dwelling in heaven immediately upon death (*T. Ab.* 20:14). This, together with what we have seen already with reference to Luke's "individual eschatology," undermines any suggestion that Jesus' promise to the criminal at his execution might provide the basis for a doctrine of the intermediate state.

In short, attempts to locate in the Gospel of Luke an eschatological pattern that requires or includes an intermediate state cannot be sustained. The reasons for this are several, and include: 1) a definition of "intermediate state" that presumes that time experienced by the dead and by those still living is identical; 2) failure to take seriously Luke's own concern to include in his eschatological portrait an emphasis on what happens to persons upon death; and 3) lack of sufficient nuance with regard to the nature and diversity of perspectives on death and the afterlife represented within the literature of Second Temple Judaism. As we have seen, Luke 16:19–31 self-evidently refers to an intermediate state *insofar as "intermediate" refers to the linear marking of time from the perspective of the rich man's brothers still alive in this world.* Whether the rich man and Lazarus experience their existence beyond death as "intermediate" is an altogether different question, however. A more nuanced reading of the evidence of the Second Temple period than Cooper has provided reveals the variety of ways in which Hades can be envisaged, and associates Jesus' parable most closely with an image of Hades as the immediate (not intermediate) abode of the wicked and the righteous who already experience the assessment of punishments and rewards. Similarly, Cooper's reading of Luke 23:40–43 presumes an insufficiently nuanced description of Jewish speculation concerning paradise in the world of Luke's Gospel. In the thought-world of Luke, Cooper's position is a possible option, but neither required nor favored within the world of Luke's Gospel; nor is it supported by the Lukan narrative itself. Indeed, Luke's texts find their closest parallels in that literature wherein the dead experience neither a period nor a place of waiting but enter their eternal reward immediately upon death.

The Disciples and the Resurrected Jesus
(Luke 24:36–49)

Our concerns with the nature of life beyond the grave and continuity of personal identity from life to life-after-death are not of recent vintage, but are woven into the fabric of Luke's account of the post-resurrection appearances. This is signaled, first, in the priority given the (in)ability of people to recognize Jesus (see Luke 24:16, 31, 35); and, second, by Jesus' emphatic claim, "It is I myself," or "It is really me!" (24:39, my translation).

Luke's presentation of the resurrected Jesus takes two routes at once, so as to demonstrate his corporeality without allowing his physicality to determine exhaustively the form of his existence.[48] On one side of the ledger we find evidence that Jesus' post-resurrection, bodily existence was out of the ordinary. He disappears and appears suddenly (24:31, 36), in the same way that an angel appears to Cornelius (Acts 10:30) and reminiscent of angels in Israel's Bible (e.g., Gen 18:2; Dan 8:15; 12:5).[49] His appearance is elusive, both to the two disciples on the Emmaus road (24:15–16) and to his followers gathered in Jerusalem (24:36–37). Indeed, the latter regard him as a "spirit," a "ghostly apparition," the disembodied residue of a dead person. It is difficult not to see in the disciples' responses a dualist anthropology; accordingly, in their imaginative categories, they were encountering a disembodied spirit, a phantasm. This analysis of things is flatly contradicted by Jesus, who immediately demonstrates that he is no ghost.

---

[48] More broadly, see Robert H. Gundry, "The Essential Physicality of Jesus' Resurrection according to the New Testament," in *Jesus of Nazareth: Lord and Christ: Essays on the Historical Jesus and New Testament Christology* (ed. Joel B. Green and Max Turner; Grand Rapids, MI: Eerdmans, 1994), 204–19.

[49] On the connections of this material with angelophanies, see Crispin H.T. Fletcher-Louis, *Luke-Acts: Angels, Christology and Soteriology* (WUNT 2:94; Tübingen: Mohr Siebeck, 1997), 62–70. Fletcher-Louis helpfully analyzes Luke's presentation of Jesus in these scenes as both more divine than angels and more human.

On the other side of the ledger, Jesus goes to great lengths to establish his physicality. As Luke will later observe, here Jesus begins to present himself "alive to them by many convincing proofs" (Acts 1:3; cf. 10:40–41; 13:30–31) – an observation that urges our contemplation of the essential physicality of "life." Importantly, then, Jesus grounds the continuity of his identity ("It is really me!"), first, in his materiality, his physicality – in the constitution of flesh and density of bones: "Look at my hands and my feet; see that it is I myself. Touch me and see; for a ghost does not have flesh and bones as you see that I have" (24:39). Here is no phantom, no vision, no spirit-being. Jesus presses further, requesting something to eat, then consuming broiled fish in the presence of his disciples (24:41–43). Do angels eat? David Goodman asks this question, noting that, from the second century BCE, it was axiomatic that angels did not eat ordinary, earthly food.[50] Thus, for example, speaking to Tobit and Tobias, "Raphael, one of the seven angels who stand ready and enter before the glory of the Lord," observes, "Although you were watching me, I really did not eat or drink anything – but what you saw was a vision" (Tob 12:15, 19). In Luke's report of Jesus' post-resurrection existence, we find no witness to resurrection as escape from bodily existence (as one would expect if a Platonic dualism were presumed here), nor is it possible to confuse Jesus' postmortem existence with that of an angel; his, rather, is a transformed materiality, a full bodily resurrection.

The meal scene Luke briefly recounts serves a further purpose, however. It bears witness to Jesus' physicality, then serves to guarantee the postmortem persistence of Jesus' personal identity in yet another way – namely, by re-establishing within the Lukan narrative Jesus' fellowship with his disciples at the table. Within the Third Gospel, meal scenes often provided Jesus with opportunity for disclosure of his mission (e.g., Luke 5:27–32; 14–15; 19:1–10) and, in the Emmaus episode, of his identity (24:30–31, 35). The

---

[50] David Goodman, "Do Angels Eat?" *JJS* 37 (1986): 160–70. See also *T. Ab.* 4:9.

eating scene Luke mentions here (see also Acts 1:3; 10:41) invites
multiple layers of significance: restored fellowship with Jesus,
Jesus' self-disclosure, material evidence of his resurrected status,
and opportunity for teaching and discussion.[51] He is not only capable of eating, but actually initiates a resumption of the table fellowship that had characterized Jesus' ministry in Galilee and en route
to Jerusalem. Hence, the post-resurrection persistence of Jesus'
identity is established, first, with reference to his physicality and,
second, with reference to relationality and mission.

Luke thus navigates between two popular views for imaging the
afterlife – the one more barbaric, the other more sophisticated.
First, he shows that Jesus' disciples did not mistake him for a
cadaver brought back to life, a reanimated corpse. Luke distinguishes Jesus' resurrected body from the resuscitated bodies of the
widow's son in Nain (7:11–17), Jairus' daughter (8:40–42, 49–56),
Tabitha (Acts 9:36–43), and Eutychus (20:7–12). Second, he certi-
fies that neither is Jesus an "immortal soul" free from bodily existence. Jesus is present to his disciples, beyond the grave, as a fully
embodied person. What is more, his affirmation concerning himself could not be more emphatic: "It is I myself!" "It is really me!" –
intimating the profound continuity between these phases of his
life: before crucifixion and after resurrection.

To Luke's readers, the evidence marshaled thus far may seem to
be enough, but the narrator gives no indication that, to this point,
the doubts of Jesus' disciples have been laid to rest. Instead, Jesus
moves immediately to a third kind of evidence: "Then he said to
them, 'These are my words that I spoke to you while I was still with
you – that everything written about me in the law of Moses, the
prophets, and the psalms must be fulfilled'" (Luke 24:44). Here is
the move Jesus makes: He weaves a story; or, rather, he picks up the
story that is already present, the one in the Scriptures, within
which, throughout his ministry, he has sought to inscribe himself.
In an essential sense, his identity is lodged there, in the grand story

---

[51] See the helpful analysis of this scene in John Paul Heil, *The Meal Scenes in
Luke-Acts: An Audience-Oriented Approach* (SBLMS; Atlanta: Society of
Biblical Literature, 1999), 219–26.

of God. What is more, he shows that the Scriptures themselves can be read aright only with reference to him, only insofar as they are actualized in the continuity of his person from life to crucifixion and afterlife, in resurrection.

This Lukan emphasis may seem strange to people of the West in the early twenty-first century, accustomed as we have become to notions of personhood that place a premium on self-actualization and self-legislation. As Jürgen Moltmann helpfully summarizes, our anthropology is "dominated by the will to give the conscious mind power over the instrument of the body," but this emphasis stands in stark contrast to concerns with embodiment, relationship, and narrative so at home in the world of Israel's Scriptures.[52] The Israelite has a sense of self above all in relation to the people of God, and this in relation to the covenant and promises of the God of Israel. Personal identity is found in the historical narrative within which people live, in relation to the divine vocation given that people.

As Luke presents it, Jesus' identity is not grounded simply in his existence as a human being, but in terms of his relationship to God, his vocation within the purpose of God, and his place within the community of God's people – past, present, and future. And all of this comes together in a grand convergence in his resurrection. This is not death leading to the flight of the soul, freed from the encumbrance of a physical body, but the means by which the people of God would experience end-time restoration as God's people. This is not resurrection understood as escape, but as embrace; in his career we find Jesus embracing the whole of God's work, from creation to exodus to exile and, now, New Exodus, as God's purpose working itself out in the world. Jesus' identity is lodged profoundly in the grand story of God – which, then, can only be grasped in reference to his crucifixion and resurrection. Resurrection is not soulflight, but the exclamation point and essential affirmation that Jesus has placed on display for all to see a life of service, even the service of life-giving death, and that this life carries with it the

---

[52] Moltmann, *God in Creation*, 244–75 (245).

divine imprimatur, actualizing as it does God's own redemptive project.

The "Resurrection Body" at Corinth

Within the Pauline corpus, 2 Corinthians 5:1–10 is usually regarded as providing the most pressing evidence in Paul for a body-soul dualism realized in an intermediate state. Attention often focuses on verses 1–3: "For we know that if our earthly tent is dismantled, we have a house from God – a dwelling not made with human hands, eternal in the heavens. In view of this we sigh, longing to put on our heavenly house, assuming, of course, that when we take it off we will not be found naked" (my translation). According to many interpreters, Paul presents here a thanatology concerned with freeing the soul from the body for a higher destiny. According to Ben Witherington, "Paul speaks of three states: the present condition in the tent-like frame, the intermediate state of nakedness, which he does not find desirable, and the future condition in which a further frame will have been put on, hopefully, over the present one."[53] In their defense of substance dualism, J.P. Moreland and Scott B. Rae observe that Paul addresses the question "What sort of hope do we have if the body itself is destroyed?" by "teaching about the intermediate state and its relationship to the future resurrection" – an interpretation that "has obvious dualistic implications."[54]

It is worth noticing at the outset how distant Paul's perspective is from an eschatology grounded in a Greek dualism. A Greek dualist might look forward to death, which allowed for soul-flight to the desirable goal of immortality, but this is not Paul's understanding here. Even if we were to imagine that Paul writes of a bodiless, interim period, he looks upon the possibility of this

---

[53] Ben Witherington III, *Conflict and Community in Corinth: A Socio-Rhetorical Commentary on 1 and 2 Corinthians* (Grand Rapids, MI: Eerdmans, 1995), 391.
[54] Moreland and Rae, *Body and Soul*, 38–39.

"nakedness" (γυμνός, *gymnos*) with abhorrence. This attitude reflects a wider, Jewish perspective, wherein to be found "naked" was to suffer humiliation, and to lose one's status as a human.[55]

Paul's opening comment in 2 Corinthians 5:1, "For we know that," reminds us that Paul is not trail-blazing here, but calling to mind former instruction given in 1 Corinthians 15. Resurrection-belief constitutes an important battleground in the Paul-Corinth correspondence, and this controversy comes into focus above all in 1 Corinthians 15. Here, then, is Paul's most sustained discussion of the resurrection.

Why Paul engages in an extended discourse on the resurrection at the end of 1 Corinthians remains a matter of debate, though we should presume with most scholars today that Paul's theological concerns are motivated by issues intrinsic to the situation in Corinth and otherwise on display in his correspondence with them. Since Paul's primary stated objective in 1 Corinthians is to restore unity (1:10), the proposal made by Dale Martin concerning the nature of the Corinthian situation is especially attractive.[56] Following customary practice in the Roman world, persons of high status in Corinth, Martin suggests, would have extended hospitality to itinerant philosophers and thus have been exposed to more sophisticated notions about the afterlife. For them, Paul's talk of the raising of the dead would have been reminiscent of fables about the resuscitation of corpses, the stuff of popular myths. Taught to degrade the body, they would have found Paul's teaching about the resurrection incomprehensible, even ridiculous. Indeed, for them, salvation would have constituted escape from the physical world, not an eschatological affirmation of bodily existence. Those of lower status, to whom Paul can refer as "those who have nothing" (11:22), on the other hand, would have been incapable of welcoming itinerant philosophers into their homes and, thus, would have lived apart from their influence. They would have had closer

---

[55] Cf. Gladas Hamel, *Poverty and Charity in Roman Palestine, First Three Centuries C.E.* (Berkeley: University of California Press, 1990), 73–75.

[56] Martin, *Corinthian Body;* this is true even if his understanding of the nature of the resurrection body is problematic.

contact with superstitions and popular myths, including those
relating the resuscitation of corpses and the endowment of those
corpses with immortality. Remembering the aim of this letter to
catalyze unity, Paul's challenge is to represent the resurrection-
belief of early Christianity with enough sophistication to communicate effectively with those of high status while not alienating
those of lower status. Even if Martin's position might deserve further nuance, it nevertheless makes good sense that Paul is strug-
gling with a Corinthian Christian community within which
something of the diversity of Greco-Roman views surrounding the
afterlife was present and that this lack of agreement was playing
havoc both with the integrity of the church and with this central
claim of the Christian gospel.

   In 1 Corinthians 15, Paul defended belief in the future resurrection by: 1) appeal to what had already become Christian tradition
(vv. 1–11); 2) observing that a denial of the future resurrection was
tantamount to denying the resurrection of Christ, and moving on
to an affirmation of Christ's resurrection as "first fruits" of the
future resurrection (vv. 12–34); and 3) sketching how one might
plausibly conceive of the resurrection of the dead (vv. 35–58). Of
particular importance to us is this last subsection, 15:35–38, where
Paul turns from the "what" of the resurrection to the "how," and,
among other things, affirms the following: 1) There is a profound
continuity between present life in this world and life everlasting
with God. For human beings, this continuity has to do with
embodied existence. 2) Present human existence, however, is
marked by frailty, deterioration, weakness, and is therefore
unsuited for eternal life. Therefore, in order for Christian believers
to share in eternal life, their bodies must be transformed. Paul does
not here think of "immortality of the soul." Neither does he proclaim a resuscitation of dead bodies that might serve as receptacles
for souls that had escaped the body in death. Instead, he sets before
his audience the promise of their transformation into glorified
bodies (cf. Phil 3:21). 3) Paul's ideas are, in part, rooted in images
from the natural world and, in part, related to the resurrection of
Jesus Christ. As it was with Christ's body, Paul insists, so it will be

with ours: the same, yet not the same; transformed for the new conditions of life with God forever. 4) For Paul, this has important meaning for the nature of Christian life in the present. For example, this message underscores the significance of life in this world, which many Christians at Corinth had not taken seriously. We should not imagine that our bodies are unimportant, then, or that what we do to our bodies or with our bodies is somehow unrelated to eternal life (cf. Col 1:24).

For our purposes, a key concern revolves around the nature of the resurrection body, to which the NRSV unfortunately refers as "a spiritual body" in contrast to "a physical body" (15:44).[57] At the very least, Paul underscores an essential continuity grounded in the import of the body (σῶμα, sōma) to human existence and identity in this life and in life-after-death. The distinction Paul draws is between the σῶμα ψυχικόν (sōma psychikon) and the σῶμα πνευματικόν (sōma pneumatikon). The first expression is drawn from Genesis 2:7, which has it that Adam was created a living ψυχή (psychē, "life" or "vitality," often translated as "soul"); hence, the first Adam was a psychikos body. (Note: neither Paul nor Genesis communicates that Adam had such a body, but rather that he was one.) However, as is manifestly evident, this body was subject to death and decay on account of sin and, therefore, was ill-suited to eternal life with God. What is needed, then, is a different form of existence, which is given us by the last Adam, Christ, who does not simply receive life (as did the first Adam), but actually gives it. "Thus it is written, 'The first man, Adam, became a living being (ψυχήν ζῶσαν, psychēn zōsan; citing Gen 2:7); the last Adam [Christ] became a life-giving spirit'" (1 Cor 15:45). As a consequence, whereas the sōma psychikon is a body provided by God and well-suited for this age, the sōma pneumatikon, also provided by God, is well-suited for the age to come.

Characterizing the resurrection body in contrast to ordinary bodily existence in this world, Paul observes, "What is sown is perishable, what is raised is imperishable. It is sown in dishonor, it is

---

[57] For an important corrective to the dualism suggested by this language, see Wright, *Resurrection of the Son of God,* 348–56.

raised in glory. It is sown in weakness, it is raised in power. It is sown a physical body, it is raised a spiritual body" (15:42–44). This helps further to distinguish the ordinary human body (perishable, inglorious, weak) from the resurrection body (imperishable, glorious, powerful) at the same time that it presses the question, What is the source of this new body? How is it constituted?

Paul insists that the first Adam was dusty, the second Adam heavenly, and in doing so makes use of the physical science of his world (15:47–49).[58] That is, ἐ γῆς χοικός (*ek gēs choikos*, "[of] dust of the earth") and ἐξ οὐρανοῦ (*ex ouranou*, "of heaven") refer to the nature of two kinds of body – the one made up of the stuff of the earth, dust, and thus well-suited to earthly life; the other made up of heavenly stuff, and thus well-suited to life in the heavens. This portrait of resurrection was not unique to Paul. A belief in astral immortality was widely held by the time of the Roman Empire. This is abundantly attested in such epitaphs as this one: "Mother, do not weep for me. What is the use? You ought rather to reverence me, for I have become an evening star, among the gods."[59] In the tradition of Israel, too, stars could be associated with heavenly beings or angels, so that eternal life might be cast as an angel-like existence. In Daniel 12:3, "those who are wise shall shine like the brightness of the sky, and those who lead many to righteousness, like the stars forever and ever." Star imagery was deployed to indicate royal position, so that we should hardly imagine that Daniel's expectation centers on an actual celestial transformation. Rather, the restoration of Israel is effected through resurrection, with astral imagery evoking enthronement.[60] Paul's description of the resurrection body, "raised in glory" (15:43), easily finds a home among these ideas.

---

[58] See Alan G. Padgett, "The Body in Resurrection: Science and Scripture on the 'Spiritual Body' (1 Cor 15:35–58)," *WW* 22 (2002): 155–63.

[59] Richard Lattimore, *Themes in Greek and Latin Epitaphs* (Illinois Studies in Language and Literature 28.1–2; Urbana: University of Illinois Press, 1942), 35 (see 32–35).

[60] Anderson, *Theology of Jesus' Resurrection*, 58–61. On the association of stars with heavenly beings, cf. Dan 8:10; Judg 5:20; Job 38:7. On the association of eternal life with angelic existence, cf. *1 En.* 39:5; 104:2–6;

What is more, by referring to the resurrected body with the modifier *pneumatikon*, Paul clarifies that the form of embodied existence in the resurrection is given through Christ (himself a "life-giving spirit") and determined by the Spirit of God. As Anthony Thiselton translates it, God has provided for this age "an ordinary human body," "a body for the human realm," but, in the resurrection, God will provide "a body for the realm of the Spirit."[61]

In this way, Paul speaks to the nature of the resurrection body (i.e., one chosen by God, free from decay and weakness) and the agency through whom the body is transformed (it is God's doing), while holding in tension his vision of both a transformed body and an organic continuity between our present, mortal existence and our transformed existence. Even if, as Paul avers, "flesh and blood cannot inherit the kingdom of God" (15:50), it remains the case that the world-to-come will be inhabited by embodied persons. What is more, the transformation leading to a nonperishable existence is the consequence of (and not preparation for) resurrection. That is, nothing in the created human being is intrinsically immortal.[62] Resurrection and embodied afterlife are God's doing, divine gift.

Returning now to 2 Corinthians 5, Paul has just admitted that present existence is marked by suffering, dying, and death (2 Cor 4)[63] – not a very promising reality for persons anticipating bodily,

---

2 *Bar.* 51:10–11; *T. Mos.* 10:9; cf. 4 Ezra 7:97, 125. On the regnant connotations of star imagery, cf. Num 24:17; Judg 5:20; Isa 14:12–13; Dan 8:10; Wis 13:2; 2 Macc 9:10. For the enthronement motif, cf. Isa 14:12–14; *Ps. Sol.* 1:5; *T. Levi* 18:3; *T. Jud.* 24:1.

[61] Anthony C. Thiselton, *The First Epistle to the Corinthians: A Commentary on the Greek Text* (NIGTC; Grand Rapids, MI: Eerdmans, 2000), 1276–81.

[62] See further, Murray J. Harris, "Resurrection and Immortality in the Pauline Corpus," in *Life in the Face of Death*, 147–70; Richard N. Longenecker, "Is There Development in Paul's Resurrection Thought?" in *Life in the Face of Death*, 171–202.

[63] On the contrast between the "inner" and "outer human being" (2 Cor 4:16), see Hans Dieter Betz, "The Concept of the 'Inner Human Being' (ὁ ἔσω ἄνθρωπος) in the Anthropology of Paul," *NTS* 46 (2000): 315–41. Although Betz disagrees with Heckel (*Der innere Mensch*) as to the *source* of Paul's

heavenly existence. Paul's response is that death is not the end of
hope but a transition, and to make this point he employs two seemingly incongruous metaphors: the tent-like house ("earthly tent...
dismantled," "a house from God," and "our heavenly house") and
"being clothed" ("longing to be clothed," "when we have taken it
off we will not be found naked," "we wish not to be unclothed but
to be further clothed").

The metaphor of "tent" is reminiscent of
Israel's past, in which the "tent" or tabernacle gave way to a temple, which was itself destroyed and replaced; indeed, for Paul's
audience, the temple had been replaced yet again, this time by the
Christian community itself, a temple "not made with human
hands." In its present context, though, the "tent" that is "falling
apart" is associated with the "outer human being" that is "wasting
away" (2 Cor 4:16) – that is, with bodily existence. What Paul
anticipates, then, is a new form of bodily existence, one that is well-
suited to eternity with God in heaven. This language is then correlated with another metaphor, "putting on" or "being clothed," the
opposite of "nakedness." Given that nakedness functioned metaphorically for moral shame (cf., e.g., Isa 20:2–4; 47:3; Ezek 23:28–
29; Matt 22:11; Rev 16:15; note Paul's references to baptism as
being clothed in Christ – e.g., Rom 13:11–14; Gal 3:23–29; Col
3:9–10), we can see Paul operating on two fronts at once. On the
one hand, he categorically rejects the notion that the answer to
human frailty is escape from bodily life. On the other, he anticipates the new form of bodily existence that God will provide – not
to be traded for the old (which, after all, is for Christians a "being
clothed in Christ"), but to subsume the old.[64] Thus, Paul's language
is indeed dualistic but not in an anthropological sense. He thinks of
an eschatological dualism, contrasting the now and the not-yet:
Having put on Christ in baptism, we now yearn for a life that conforms to his. In this case, our hope that we not be found naked
refers to the time of the final Judgment (see v. 10), when we will

---

language, both agree that Paul distances his usage from Platonic categories
that portray an immortal soul entombed in a material body.
[64] ἐπενδύομαι (ependuomai): "to put one garment over another."

experience the consummation of our new life in Christ rather than the "exposure" that comes in condemnation.[65]

In short, Paul's focal concern is not with thanatology, but with resurrection hope. Both in 1 Corinthians 15 and in 2 Corinthians 5:1–10, he affirms that transformation and immortality are the consequence of (and not preparation for) resurrection. Although often read against the backdrop of body-soul dualism, and thus taken as further support for body-soul dualism, 2 Corinthians 5:1–10 actually points in a different direction. The dualism with which it is concerned is eschatological rather than anthropological. When read in relation to Paul's earlier teaching in 1 Corinthians 15 (an interpretive move invited by the text itself), this passage thus provides no warrant for disembodied, human existence in an intermediate state.

One final issue: If *continuity* is marked by embodied existence in this life and in the resurrection, the question remains how the "me" that is really "me" makes the transition into resurrected life. That is, if the question for the Corinthians must have focused above all on the nature of the *body* ("But someone will ask, 'How are the dead raised? With what kind of body do they come?'" [15:35]), we may nevertheless wonder, How does what "dies" "come to life"? (15:36). How can continuity of personal identity be sustained? We have seen that, in Luke 24, physicality, relationality, and narrativity comprise an answer to this question. What of Paul?

Importantly, when Paul's thought moves into this arena, he does not use the language we might expect, had we imagined that he had been decisively influenced by a dualist anthropology; words like "spirit" or "soul," which we might have anticipated from a dualist anthropology, are not found in these contexts.[66] Rather, he uses

---

[65] Cf. Anthony E. Harvey, *Renewal through Suffering: A Study of 2 Corinthians* (SNTW; Edinburgh: T&T Clark, 1996), 66–69.

[66] See the similar reflections in Peter Lampe, "Paul's Concept of a Spiritual Body," in *Resurrection: Theological and Scientific Assessments,* 103–14. Lampe, however, presumes that, with this language, Paul introduces an intermediate state, but this is not at all clear (cf., e.g., Markus Bockmuehl, *The Epistle to the Philippians* [BNTC; London: A&C Black, 1998], 91–93).

personal pronouns, together with the notable phrase σὺν Χριστῷ
(sun Christō, "with Christ"; e.g., Phil 1:23; cf. 2 Cor 5:8) or ἐν
Χριστῷ (en Christō, "in Christ"; e.g., 1 Thess 4:16). These are not
phrases descriptive of an essentialist ontology; they do not address
issues of substance. Rather, they express "my" existence, the persistence of personal identity, in profoundly relational terms.[67]

Conclusion

By way of conclusion, let me tease out some ways in which these
exegetical and theological reflections bear on our portrait of the
human person. In doing so, it will be useful to begin in conversation with a relevant consideration from the neurosciences. First,
even for the non-dualist, it is problematic to imagine that human
identity is constructed or sustained solely in material terms. This is
because, right up to the moment of death itself, the body is con-
stantly remaking itself, with cells being sloughed off and replaced
at sometimes astonishing speeds. Even if the genesis of new brain
cells, neurons, in adults is comparatively limited,[68] this does not
mean that the brain is static throughout our lives. At a basic level,
formative influences are encoded in the synapses of the central nervous system, those points of communication among our neurons,
as those neural connections that are used are maintained and
remodeled, those that fall into disuse are eliminated, and fresh connections are generated in response to our experiences. Even if our
genes bias the way we think and behave, the systems responsible
for much of what we do and how we do it are shaped by our experiences, our relationships, by learning. If this is true, then how can
we speak of continuity of personal identity?

Taking seriously the relevant considerations from our exegetical
work, together with the evidence we have from the neurosciences,

---

[67] See the useful discussion of the theological significance of this "withness" in
Shults, Reforming Theological Anthropology, 184–88.
[68] See Elizabeth Gould and Charles G. Gross, "Neurogenesis in Adult Mammals: Some Progress and Problems," Journal of Neuroscience 22 (2002):
619–23.

let me propose that our identity is formed and found in self-conscious *relationality* with its neural correlates and embodied *narrativity* or formative histories. By "formative histories," I do not mean "history" in an objective sense as "what really happened," but the stories within and by which we come to make sense of the events of our lives and world; hence, I prefer the term "narrative," which suggests a particular way of telling the stories of our lives. What I want especially to underscore here, though, is that who we are, our personhood, is inextricably bound up in our physicality, and so is inextricably tied to the cosmos God has created, and in the sum of our life experiences and relationships. This perspective coheres well with Nancey Murphy's argument that personal identity focuses on human moral character and social relations, with their neural substrate; and with Charles Gutenson's perspective, which accords privilege to "my nested existence in a web of relationships as well as the profound impact those relationships have on my own identity."[69]

This means, second, that death must be understood not only in biological terms, as merely the cessation of one's body, but as the conclusion of embodied life, the severance of all relationships, and the fading of personal narrative. It means that, at death, the person *really dies;* from the perspective of our humanity and sans divine intervention, there is no part of us, no aspect of our personhood, that survives death.

Third, we have seen in the NT material we have examined that belief in life-after-death requires embodiment – that is, re-embodiment. And this provides the basis for relational and narrative continuity of the self. It also begs the question, How are we capable of traversing from life to life-after-death? Simply put, we

---

[69] Nancey Murphy, "The Resurrection Body and Personal Identity: Possibilities and Limits of Eschatological Knowledge," in *Resurrection: Theological and Scientific Assessments,* 202–18; Charles E. Gutenson, "Time, Eternity, and Personal Identity," in *What about the Soul? Neuroscience and Christian Anthropology* (ed. Joel B. Green; Nashville: Abingdon, 2004), 117–32. Cf. the fascinating argument of Caroline Walker Bynum concerning the coalescing of (bodily) shape and (embodied) story in personal identity (*Metamorphosis and Identity* [New York: Zone, 2001]).

are not. The capacity for resurrection, for transformed existence, is not a property intrinsic to the human person (nor to the created cosmos). This is, as Paul emphasizes, God's doing. Even if our transformed lives in Christ in this world anticipate, they do not constitute eschatological existence. The glorious, bodily transformation of which Paul speaks is the consequence of resurrection, not preparation for it. How, then, is personal identity sustained from this world to the world-to-come? On the one hand, Paul locates the answer to this problem under the category of "mystery" (1 Cor 15:51–57). On the other, he hints at a relational ontology – that is, the preservation of our personhood, "you" and "me," in relational terms: *with Christ, in Christ.* This suggests that the relationality and narrativity that constitute who I am are able to exist apart from neural correlates and embodiment only insofar as they are preserved in God's own being, in anticipation of new creation.

This reminds us, again, that the capacity for "afterlife" is not a property of humanity, but is a divine gift, divinely enacted. It also underscores the reality that, in eschatological salvation, we are not rescued from the cosmos in resurrection, but transformed with it in new creation.

SUGGESTED READING

Berger, Klaus. *Identity and Experience in the New Testament*. Minneapolis: Fortress, 2003.

Brown, Warren S., Nancey Murphy, and H. Newton Maloney, eds. *Whatever Happened to the Soul? Scientific and Theological Portraits of Human Nature*. Theology and the Sciences. Minneapolis: Fortress, 1998.

Corcoran, Kevin J. *Rethinking Human Nature: A Christian Materialistic Alternative to the Soul*. Grand Rapids, MI: Baker Academic, 2006.

Di Vito, Robert A. "Old Testament Anthropology and the Construction of Personal Identity." *Catholic Biblical Quarterly* 61 (1999): 217–38.

Green, Joel B., ed. *What about the Soul? Neuroscience and Christian Anthropology*. Nashville: Abingdon, 2004.

Green, Joel B., and Stuart L. Palmer, eds. *In Search of the Soul: Four Views of the Mind-Body Problem*. Downers Grove, IL: InterVarsity, 2005.

Jeeves, Malcolm, ed. *From Cells to Souls – And Beyond: Changing Portraits of Human Nature*. Grand Rapids, MI: Eerdmans, 2004.

Middleton, J. Richard. *The Liberating Image: The Imago Dei in Genesis 1*. Grand Rapids, MI: Brazos, 2005.

Murphy, Nancey. *Bodies and Souls, or Spirited Bodies?* Current Issues in Theology. Cambridge: Cambridge University Press, 2006.

Peterson, Gregory R. *Minding God: Theology and the Cognitive Sciences.* Theology and the Sciences. Minneapolis: Fortress, 2003.

Schweizer, Eduard. "Body." *Anchor Bible Dictionary* 1:767–72.

Shults, F. LeRon. *Reforming Theological Anthropology: After the Philosophical Turn to Relationality.* Grand Rapids, MI: Eerdmans, 2003.

Watts, Fraser. *Theology and Psychology.* Ashgate Science and Religion Series. Aldershot: Ashgate, 2002.

Wright, John P., and Paul Potter, eds. *Psyche and Soma: Physicians and Metaphysicians on the Mind-Body Problem from Antiquity to Enlightenment.* Oxford: Clarendon, 2000.

Wright, N.T. *The Resurrection of the Son of God.* Christian Origins and the Question of God. Vol. 3. Minneapolis: Fortress, 2003.

BIBLIOGRAPHY

Alexander, Denis. *Rebuilding the Matrix: Science and Faith in the 21st Century.* Grand Rapids, MI: Zondervan, 2003.

Alexander, Desmond. "The Old Testament View of Life after Death." *Themelios* 11 (1986): 41–46.

Amodio, David M., and Chris D. Frith. "Meeting of Minds: The Medial Frontal Cortex and Social Cognition." *Nature Reviews Neuroscience* 7 (2006): 268–77.

Anderson, Kevin L. *'But God Raised Him from the Dead': The Theology of Jesus' Resurrection in Luke-Acts.* PBM. Carlisle: Paternoster, 2006.

Anderson, Steven W., et al. "Impairment of Social and Moral Behavior Related to Early Damage in Human Prefrontal Cortex." *Nature Neuroscience* 2 (1999): 1032–37.

Anderson, V. Elving. "A Genetic View of Human Nature." In *Whatever Happened to the Soul? Scientific and Theological Portraits of Human Nature*, ed. Warren S. Brown et al., 49–72. TSc. Minneapolis: Fortress, 1998.

Ashbrook, James B., and Carol Rausch Albright. *The Humanizing Brain: Where Religion and Neuroscience Meet.* Cleveland, OH: Pilgrim, 1997.

Asimov, Isaac. *I, Robot*. New York: Doubleday, 1950.

Assmann, Jan. "Resurrection in Ancient Egypt." In *Resurrection: Theological and Scientific Assessments*, ed. Ted Peters, Robert John Russell, and Michael Welker, 124–35. Grand Rapids, MI: Eerdmans, 2002.

Aune, David E. *Revelation*. Vol. 3. WBC 52c. Nashville: Thomas Nelson, 1998.

Ayala, Francisco J. "Biological Evolution and Human Nature." In *Human Nature*, ed. Malcolm Jeeves, 46–64. Edinburgh: The Royal Society of Edinburgh, 2006.

Barr, James. *The Garden of Eden and the Hope of Immortality*. Minneapolis: Fortress, 1992.

_____. *The Semantics of Biblical Language*. Oxford: Oxford University Press, 1961.

Barth, Karl. *Church Dogmatics*. Vol. 3: *The Doctrine of Creation*. Part one. Edinburgh: T&T Clark, 1958.

_____. "The Strange New World within the Bible." In *The Word of God and the Word of Man*, 28–50. Gloucester: Peter Smith, 1978.

Bauckham, Richard. *The Bible in Politics: How to Read the Bible Politically*. Louisville: Westminster John Knox, 1989.

_____. "Descents to the Underworld." In *The Fate of the Dead: Studies on the Jewish and Christian Apocalypses*, 9–48. NovTSup 93. Leiden: Brill, 1998.

_____. "Early Jewish Visions of Hell." In *The Fate of the Dead: Studies on the Jewish and Christian Apocalypses*, 49–80. NovTSup 93. Leiden: Brill, 1998.

_____. "The Economic Critique of Rome in Revelation 18." In *The Climax of Prophecy: Studies on the Book of Revelation*, 338–83. Edinburgh: T&T Clark, 1993.

_____. "Hades, Hell." *ABD* 3:14–15.

_____. "Life, Death, and the Afterlife in Second Temple Judaism." In *Life in the Face of Death: The Resurrection Message of the New Testament*, ed. Richard N. Longenecker, 80–95. MNTS. Grand Rapids, MI: Eerdmans, 1998.

_____. "Visiting Places of the Dead in the Extra-Canonical Apocalypses." In *The Fate of the Dead: Studies on the Jewish and Christian Apocalypses*, 81–96. NovTSup 93. Leiden: Brill, 1998.

Bayer, Hans F. "The Preaching of Peter in Acts." In *Witness to the Gospel: The Theology of Acts*, ed. I. Howard Marshall and David Peterson, 257–74. Grand Rapids, MI: Eerdmans, 1998.

Beauregard, Mario, and Vincent Paquette. "Neural Correlates of a Mystical Experience in Carmelite Nuns." *Neuroscience Letters* 405 (2006): 186–90.

Bechara, Antoine, et al. "Emotion, Decision Making and the Orbitofrontal Cortex." *Cerebral Cortex* 10 (2000): 295–307.

Beckman, Mary. "Crime, Culpability, and the Adolescent Brain." *Science* 305 (2004): 596–98.

Berger, Klaus. *Identity and Experience in the New Testament*. Minneapolis: Fortress, 2003.

Berger, Peter L., and Thomas Luckmann. *The Social Construction of Reality: A Treatise in the Sociology of Knowledge*. New York: Doubleday, 1966.

Berry, R.J. *God's Book of Works: The Nature and Theology of Nature*. Glasgow Gifford Lectures. London: T&T Clark, 2003.

Betz, Hans Dieter. "The Concept of the 'Inner Human Being' (ὁ ἔσω ἄνθρωπος) in the Anthropology of Paul." *NTS* 46 (2000): 315–41.

Biddle, Mark E. *Missing the Mark: Sin and Its Consequences in Biblical Theology*. Nashville: Abingdon, 2005.

Blakeslee, Sandra. "Cells That Read Minds." *New York Times* (10 January 2006); {http://www.nytimes.com/2006/01/10/science/10mirr.html?_r=1&oref=login&pagewanted=all}; accessed 10 January 2007.

———. "Humanity? Maybe It's All in the Wiring." *New York Times* (9 December 2003): F1.

Blocher, Henri. *Original Sin: Illuminating the Riddle*. NSBT. Grand Rapids, MI: Eerdmans, 1997).

Block, Daniel I. "Beyond the Grave: Ezekiel's Vision of Death and Afterlife." *BBR* 2 (1992): 113–41.

Bockmuehl, Markus. *The Epistle to the Philippians*. BNTC. London: A&C Black, 1998.

Bolt, Peter G. "Life, Death, and the Afterlife in the Greco-Roman World." In *Life in the Face of Death: The Resurrection Message of the New Testament*, ed. Richard N. Longenecker, 51–79. MNTS. Grand Rapids, MI: Eerdmans, 1998.

Bovon, François. *L'œuvre de Luc: Études d'exégèse et de théologie*. Paris: Cerf, 1987.

Boyle, Robert. *A Free Inquiry into the Vulgarly Received Notion of Nature*, ed. Edward B. Davis and Michael Hunter. CTHP. Cambridge: Cambridge University Press, 1996 [1686].

Bratsiotis, N.P. "בשר." *TDOT* 2:313–32.

Brown, Michael L. "רפים." *NIDOTTE* 3:1173–80.

Brown, Warren S. "Cognitive Contributions to Soul." In *Whatever Happened to the Soul? Scientific and Theological Portraits of Human Nature*, ed. Warren S. Brown, Nancey Murphy, and H. Newton Malony, 99–125. TSc. Minneapolis: Fortress, 1998.

Brown, Warren S., Nancey Murphy, and H. Newton Malony, eds. *Whatever Happened to the Soul? Scientific and Theological Portraits of Human Nature*. TSc. Minneapolis: Fortress, 1998.

Bruce, F.F. *Paul: Apostle of the Heart Set Free*. Grand Rapids, MI: Eerdmans, 1977.

———. "Paul on Immortality." *SJT* 24 (1971): 457–72.

Brueggemann, Walter. *Theology of the Old Testament: Testimony, Dispute, Advocacy*. Minneapolis: Fortress, 1997.

Bryant, David J. *Faith and the Play of Imagination: On the Role of Imagination in Religion*. StABH 5. Macon, GA: Mercer University Press, 1989.

Bultmann, Rudolf. *Theology of the New Testament*. 2 vols. New York: Charles Scribner's Sons, 1951–55.

Burns, Jeffrey M., and Russell H. Swerdlow. "Right Orbitofrontal Tumor with Pedophilia Symptom and Constructional Apraxia Sign." *Archives of Neurology* 60, no. 3 (2003): 437–40.

Bynum, Caroline Walker. *The Resurrection of the Body in Western Christianity, 200–1336*. New York: Columbia University Press, 1995.

———. *Metamorphosis and Identity*. New York: Zone, 2001.

Cadbury, Henry J. "The Summaries in Acts." In *Additional Notes to the Commentary*. Vol. 5 of *The Acts of the Apostles*, ed. F.J. Foakes Jackson and Kirsopp Lake, 392–402. BChr 1. London: Macmillan, 1920.

Cargal, Timothy B. *Restoring the Diaspora: Discursive Structure and Purpose in the Epistle of James*. SBLDS 144. Atlanta: Scholars Press, 1993.

Carroll, John T. *Response to the End of History: Eschatology and Situation in Luke-Acts*. SBLDS 92. Atlanta: Scholars Press, 1988.

Chalmers, David J. *The Conscious Mind: In Search of a Fundamental Theory*. Oxford: Oxford University Press, 1996.

Chamblin, J. Knox. "Psychology." In *DPL*, 765–75.

Changeux, Jean-Pierre. *The Physiology of Truth: Neuroscience and Human Knowledge*. Cambridge, MA: Harvard University Press, 2002.

Charlesworth, James H. "Paradise." *ABD* 5:154–55.

Chester, Andrew, and Ralph P. Martin. *The Theology of the Letters of James, Peter, and Jude*. NTT. Cambridge: Cambridge University Press, 1994.

Cheung, Luke L. *The Genre, Composition and Hermeneutics of James.* PBM. Carlisle: Paternoster, 2003.

Childs, Brevard S. *Biblical Theology of the Old and New Testaments: Theological Reflection on the Christian Bible.* Minneapolis: Fortress, 1992.

————. *Isaiah.* OTL. Louisville: Westminster John Knox, 2001.

————. *Old Testament Theology in a Canonical Context.* Philadelphia: Fortress, 1985.

Churchland, Patricia Smith. *Brain-Wise: Studies in Neurophilosophy.* Cambridge, MA: The MIT Press, 2002.

————. *Neurophilosophy: Toward a Unified Science of the Mind-Brain.* Cambridge, MA: The MIT Press, 1986.

Clayton, Philip. *Mind and Emergence: From Quantum to Consciousness.* Oxford: Oxford University Press, 2005.

Co, Maria Anicia. "The Major Summaries in Acts: Acts 2,42–47; 4,32–35; 5,12–16. Linguistic and Literary Relationship." *ETL* 68 (1992): 49–85.

Collins, John J. "The Afterlife in Apocalyptic Literature." In *Judaism in Late Antiquity.* Part 4: *Death, Life-after-Death, Resurrection and the World-to-Come in the Judaisms of Antiquity,* ed. Alan J. Avery-Peck and Jacob Neusner, 119–39. Handbook of Oriental Studies – 1: The Near and Middle East 49. Leiden: Brill, 2000.

Cooper, John W. *Body, Soul, and Life Everlasting: Biblical Anthropology and the Monism-Dualism Debate.* Grand Rapids, MI: Eerdmans, 1989; 2nd ed., 2000.

————. "Response to *In Search of the Soul:* 'I Don't Think It's Lost.'" Paper presented at the annual meeting of the Society of Christian Philosophers. Philadelphia, 20 November 2005.

Copley, Rich. "Feed the Soul or Feed the Hungry?" *Lexington Herald Leader* (16 June 2002), D1, 5.

Corcoran, Kevin J. *Rethinking Human Nature: A Christian Materialistic Alternative to the Soul.* Grand Rapids, MI: Baker Academic, 2006.

————, ed. *Soul, Body, and Survival: Essays on the Metaphysics of Human Persons.* Ithaca: Cornell University Press, 2001.

Cordoso, Silvia Helena, and Renato M.E. Sabbatini. "What Makes Us Singularly Humans?" *Brain & Mind* (2000); {http://www.epub.org.br/cm/n10/editorial-n10_i.htm}; accessed 21 January 2002.

Coricelli, Giorgio, et al. "Regret and Its Avoidance: A Neuroimaging Study of Choice Behavior." *Nature Neuroscience* 8 (2005): 1255–62.

Cranefield, Paul F. "A Seventeenth-century View of Mental Deficiency and Schizophrenia: Thomas Willis on 'Stupidity or Foolishness'." *Bulletin of the History of Medicine* 35 (1961): 291–316.

Crick, Francis H. *The Astonishing Hypothesis: The Scientific Search for the Soul.* New York: Simon & Schuster, 1994.

Crump, David Michael. *Jesus the Intercessor: Prayer and Christology in Luke-Acts.* WUNT 2:49. Tübingen: Mohr Siebeck, 1992.

Crüsemann, Frank. "Scripture and Resurrection." In *Resurrection: Theological and Scientific Assessments,* ed. Ted Peters, Robert John Russell, and Michael Welker, 89–123. Grand Rapids, MI: Eerdmans, 2002.

Culpepper, R. Alan. "Seeing the Kingdom of God: The Metaphor of Sight in the Gospel of Luke." *CurTM* 21 (1994): 424–33.

Cunningham, Andrew. "Sir Thomas Browne and his *Religio Medici*: Reason, Nature and Religion." In *Religio Medici: Medicine and Religion in Seventeenth-Century England,* ed. Ole Peter Grell and Andrew Cunningham, 12–61. Aldershot: Scolar, 1996.

Dalley, Jeffrey W. "Nucleus Accumbens D2/3 Receptors Predict Trait Impulsivity and Cocaine Reinforcement." *Science* 315, no. 5816 (2007): 1267–70.

Damasio, Antonio R. *Descartes' Error: Emotion, Reason, and the Human Brain.* New York: Avon, 1994.

d'Aquili, Eugene G., and Andrew B. Newberg. "The Neuropsychological Basis of Religions, or Why God Won't Go Away." *Zygon* 33 (1998): 187–201.

Davies, Philip R. "Death, Resurrection, and Life after Death in the Qumran Scrolls." In *Judaism in Late Antiquity.* Part 4: *Death, Life-after-Death, Resurrection and the World-to-Come in the Judaisms of Antiquity,* ed. Alan J. Avery-Peck and Jacob Neusner, 189–211. Handbook of Oriental Studies – 1: The Near and Middle East 49. Leiden: Brill, 2000.

Dawkins, Richard, and Steven Pinker. "Is Science Killing the Soul?" The Guardian-Dillons Debate. Chaired by Tim Radford. London, 10 February 1999. *Edge* 53 (8 April 1999); {http://www.edge.org/documents/archive/edge53.html}; accessed 2 January 2004.

Destro, Adriana, and Mauro Pesce. "Self, Identity, and Body in Paul and John." In *Self, Soul and Body in Religious Experience,* ed. Albert I. Baumgarten, J. Assmann, and G.G. Stroumsa, 184–97. SHR 78. Leiden: Brill, 1998.

de Waal, Francis. *Good Natured: The Origins of Right and Wrong in Humans and Other Animals.* Cambridge, MA: Harvard University Press, 1996.

_____. *Peacemaking among Primates.* Cambridge, MA: Harvard University Press, 1989.

Dibelius, Martin. "The Speeches in Acts and Ancient Historiography." In *Studies in the Acts of the Apostles,* 138–85. London: SCM, 1956.

Di Vito, Robert A. "Here One Need Not Be One's Self: The Concept of 'Self' in the Old Testament." In *The Whole and Divided Self: The Bible and Theological Anthropology,* ed. David E. Aune and John McCarthy, 49–88. New York: Crossroad, 1997.

_____. "Old Testament Anthropology and the Construction of Personal Identity." *CBQ* 61 (1999): 217–38.

Dolan, Raymond J. "On the Neurology of Morals." *Nature Neuroscience* 2 (1999): 927–29.

Domning, Daryl P., and Monika K. Hellwig. *Original Selfishness: Original Sin and Evil in the Light of Evolution.* Aldershot: Ashgate, 2006.

Dunn, James D.G. *The Theology of Paul the Apostle.* Grand Rapids, MI: Eerdmans, 1998.

Dupont, Jacques. "Conversion in the Acts of the Apostles." In *The Salvation of the Gentiles: Essays on the Acts of the Apostles,* 61–84. New York: Paulist, 1979.

_____. "Die individuelle Eschatologie im Lukasevangelium und in der Apostelgeschichte." In *Orientierung an Jesus: Zur Theologie der Synoptiker,* ed. Paul Hoffman, 37–47. Freiburg: Herder, 1973.

Eaves, Lindon. "Genetic and Social Influences on Religion and Values." In *From Cells to Souls – And Beyond: Changing Portraits of Human Nature,* ed. Malcolm Jeeves, 102–22. Grand Rapids, MI: Eerdmans, 2004.

Eco, Umberto. *Semiotics and the Philosophy of Language.* AS. Bloomington: University of Indiana Press, 1984.

Edgar, Brian. "Biblical Anthropology and the Intermediate State." *EvQ* 74 (2002): 27–45, 109–21.

Ehrman, Bart D., ed. *The Apostolic Fathers.* 2 vols. LCL 24–25. Cambridge, MA: Harvard University Press, 2003.

Eisenberger, Naomi I., et al. "Does Rejection Hurt? An fMRI Study of Social Exclusion." *Science* 302, no. 5643 (2003): 290–92.

Elledge, C.D. *Life after Death in Early Judaism: The Evidence of Josephus.* WUNT 2:208. Tübingen: Mohr Siebeck, 2006.

Esler, Philip F. *New Testament Theology: Communion and Community.* Minneapolis: Fortress, 2005.

Everson, Stephen. "Psychology." In *The Cambridge Companion to Aristotle*, ed. Jonathan Barnes, 168–94. Cambridge: Cambridge University Press, 1995.

Fabry, Heinz-Josef. "גויה." *TDOT* 2:433–38.

———. "לב." *TDOT* 7:399–437.

Fabry, Heinz-Josef, K.-J. Illman, and Helmer Ringgren. "מות." *TDOT* 8:185–209.

Feinberg, Todd E. *Altered Egos: How the Brain Creates the Self.* Oxford: Oxford University Press, 2001.

Feldman, Louis. *Jew and Gentile in the Ancient World.* Princeton, NJ: Princeton University Press, 1993.

Feldmeier, Reinhard. "Seelenheil: Überlegungen zur Soteriologie und Anthropologie des 1. Petrusbriefes." In *The Catholic Epistles and the Tradition*, ed. J. Schlosser, 291–306. BETL 176. Leuven: Leuven University Press, 2004.

Finn, Thomas M. *From Death to Rebirth: Ritual and Conversion in Antiquity.* New York: Paulist Press, 1997.

Fireman, Gary D., et al., eds. *Narrative and Consciousness: Literature, Psychology, and the Brain.* Oxford: Oxford University Press, 2003.

Fitzmyer, Joseph A. *The Acts of the Apostles.* AB 31. New York: Doubleday, 1998.

Flanagan, Owen. *The Problem of the Soul: Two Visions of Mind and How to Reconcile Them.* New York: Basic, 2002.

Fletcher-Louis, Crispin H.T. *Luke-Acts: Angels, Christology and Soteriology.* WUNT 2:94. Tübingen: Mohr Siebeck, 1997.

Frede, Michael. "On Aristotle's Conception of the Soul." In *Essays on Aristotle's De anima*, ed. Martha C. Nussbaum and Amélie Oksenberg Rorty, 93–107. Oxford: Clarendon, 1992.

Froehlich, Karlfreid. "'Take up and Read': Basics of Augustine's Biblical Interpretation." *Int* 58 (2004): 5–16.

Fuller, Michael. "A Typology for the Theological Reception of Scientific Innovation." *S&CB* 12 (2000): 115–25.

Garrison, John C. *The Psychology of the Spirit: A Contemporary System of Biblical Psychology.* Xlibris, 2001.

Gaventa, Beverly Roberts. *From Darkness to Light: Aspects of Conversion in the New Testament.* OBT 20. Philadelphia: Fortress, 1986.

Gazzaniga, Michael S. *The Ethical Brain.* New York: Dana, 2005.

Gibbs Jr., Raymond W. *Embodiment and Cognitive Science.* Cambridge: Cambridge University Press, 2006.

Glimcher, Paul W. *Decisions, Uncertainty, and the Brain: The Science of Neuroeconomics.* Cambridge, MA: The MIT Press, 2003.

Goldberg, Elkhonon. *The Executive Brain: Frontal Lobes and the Civilized Mind.* Oxford: Oxford University Press, 2001.

Goodman, David. "Do Angels Eat?" *JJS* 37 (1986): 160–70.

Goodman, Martin. *Mission and Conversion: Proselytizing in the Religious History of the Roman Empire.* Oxford: Clarendon, 1994.

Gorman, James. "Fishing for Clarity in the Waters of Consciousness." *New York Times* (13 May 2003); {http://query.nytimes.com/gst/fullpage.html?res=9800E0D6133FF930A25756C0A9659C8B63& sec=&spon=&partner=permalink&exprod=permalink}; accessed 6 June 2003.

Gould, Elizabeth, and Charles G. Gross, "Neurogenesis in Adult Mammals: Some Progress and Problems." *Journal of Neuroscience* 22 (2002): 619–23.

Grabbe, Lester L. *Judaic Religion in the Second Temple Period: Belief and Practice from the Exile to Yavneh.* London: Routledge, 2000.

Grant, Edward. *Science and Religion, 400 BC to AD 1550: From Aristotle to Copernicus.* Baltimore: Johns Hopkins University Press, 2004.

Green, Joel B. *1 Peter.* THNTC. Grand Rapids, MI: Eerdmans, 2007.

_____. "From 'John's Baptism' to 'Baptism in the Name of the Lord Jesus': The Significance of Baptism in Luke-Acts." In *Baptism, the New Testament and the Church: Historical and Contemporary Studies in Honour of R.E.O. White,* ed. Stanley E. Porter and Anthony R. Cross, 157–72. JSNTSup 171. Sheffield: Sheffield Academic Press, 1999.

_____. "'Persevering Together in Prayer' (Acts 1:14): The Significance of Prayer in the Acts of the Apostles." In *Into God's Presence: Prayer in the New Testament,* ed. Richard N. Longenecker, 183–202. MNTS. Grand Rapids, MI: Eerdmans, 2001.

_____. *Salvation.* UBT. St. Louis, MO: Chalice, 2003.

_____. "Science, Religion, and the Mind-Brain Problem: The Case of Thomas Willis (1621–1675)." *S&CB* 15 (2003): 165–85.

Greene, Joshua D. "From Neural 'Is' to Moral 'Ought': What Are the Moral Implications of Neuroscientific Moral Psychology?" *Nature Reviews Neuroscience* 4 (2003): 847–50.

_____, et al. "The Neural Bases of Cognitive Conflict and Control in Moral Judgement." *Neuron* 44 (2004): 389–400.

Greenfield, Susan. "Soul, Brain and Mind." In *From Soul to Self,* ed. M. James C. Crabbe, 108–25. London: Routledge, 1999.

Grenz, Stanley J. *The Social God and the Relational Self: A Trinitarian Theology of the Imago Dei.* The Matrix of Christian Theology. Louisville: Westminster John Knox, 2001.

Grigsby, Jim, and David Stevens. *Neurodynamics of Personality*. New York: Guilford, 2000.

Gundert, Beate. "Soma and Psyche in Hippocratic Medicine." In *Psyche and Soma: Physicians and Metaphysicians on the Mind-Body Problem from Antiquity to Enlightenment*, ed. John P. Wright and Paul Potter, 13–35. Oxford: Clarendon, 2000.

Gundry, Robert H. "The Essential Physicality of Jesus' Resurrection according to the New Testament." In *Jesus of Nazareth: Lord and Christ: Essays on the Historical Jesus and New Testament Christology*, ed. Joel B. Green and Max Turner, 204–19. Grand Rapids, MI: Eerdmans, 1994.

———. *Sōma in Biblical Theology with Emphasis on Pauline Anthropology*. SNTSMS 29. Cambridge: Cambridge University Press, 1976.

Gunton, Colin E. *Christ and Creation*. Grand Rapids, MI: Eerdmans, 1992.

———. "Trinity, Ontology and Anthropology: Towards a Renewal of the Doctrine of the *Imago Dei*." In *Persons Divine and Human: King's College Essays on Theological Anthropology*, ed. Christoph Schwöbel and Colin E. Gunton, 47–61. Edinburgh: T&T Clark, 1991.

Gutenson, Charles E. "Time, Eternity, and Personal Identity." In *What about the Soul? Neuroscience and Christian Anthropology*, ed. Joel B. Green, 117–32. Nashville: Abingdon, 2004.

Hahn, Ferdinand. *Theologie des Neuen Testaments*. 2 vols. Tübingen: Mohr Siebeck, 2001/05.

Hallett, Mark. "Volitional Control of Movement: The Physiology of Free Will." *Clinical Neurophysiology* 118 (2007): 117–92.

Hamel, Gladas. *Poverty and Charity in Roman Palestine, First Three Centuries C.E.* Berkeley: University of California Press, 1990.

Hamm, Dennis. "Sight to the Blind: Vision as Metaphor in Luke." *Bib* 67 (1986): 457–77.

Harris, Murray J. *Raised Immortal: Resurrection and Immortality in the New Testament*. Grand Rapids, MI: Eerdmans, 1983.

———. "Resurrection and Immortality in the Pauline Corpus." In *Life in the Face of Death: The Resurrection Message of the New Testament*, ed. Richard N. Longenecker, 147–70. MNTS. Grand Rapids, MI: Eerdmans, 1998.

Harrison, Peter. *The Bible, Protestantism, and the Rise of Natural Science*. Cambridge: Cambridge University Press, 1998.

Hartman, Lars. *'Into the Name of the Lord Jesus': Baptism in the Early Church*. SNTW. Edinburgh: T&T Clark, 1997.

Hartmann, Dirk. "Neurophysiology and Freedom of the Will." *Poiesis &
Praxis* 2 (2004): 275–84.

Harvey, Anthony E. *Renewal through Suffering: A Study of 2 Corinthians.* SNTW. Edinburgh: T&T Clark, 1996.

————. "'They discussed among themselves what this "rising from the
dead" could mean' (Mark 9.10)." In *Resurrection: Essays in Honour
of Leslie Houlden*, ed. Stephen Barton and Graham Stanton, 69–78.
London: SPCK, 1994.

Hasker, William. *The Emergent Self.* Ithaca: Cornell University Press,
1999.

Hays, Richard B. "Made New by One Man's Obedience." In *Proclaiming
the Scandal of the Cross: Contemporary Images of the Atonement*,
ed. Mark D. Baker, 96–102. Grand Rapids, MI: Baker Academic,
2006.

Heckel, Theo K. "Body and Soul in Saint Paul." In *Psyche and Soma: Physicians and Metaphysicians on the Mind-Body Problem from Antiquity to Enlightenment*, ed. John P. Wright and Paul Potter, 117–31.
Oxford: Clarendon, 2000.

————. *Der innere Mensch: Die Paulinische Verarbeitung eines
Platonischen Motivs.* WUNT 2:53. Tübingen: Mohr Siebeck, 1993.

Hefner, Philip. *The Human Factor: Evolution, Culture, and Religion.*
TSc. Minneapolis: Fortress, 1993.

Heil, John Paul. *The Meal Scenes in Luke-Acts: An Audience-Oriented
Approach.* SBLMS. Atlanta: Society of Biblical Literature, 1999.

Hengel, Martin. *Judaism and Hellenism: Studies in their Encounter in
Palestine during the Early Hellenistic Period.* 2 vols. in 1. Philadelphia: Fortress, 1974.

Herzfeld, Noreen L. *In Our Image: Artificial Intelligence and the Human
Spirit.* TSc. Minneapolis: Fortress, 2002.

Hinchman, Lewis P., and Sandra K. Hinchman, eds. *Memory, Identity,
Community: The Idea of Narrative in the Human Sciences.* Albany:
State University of New York Press, 2001.

Hirstein, William. *Brain Fiction: Self-Deception and the Riddle of Confabulation.* Cambridge, MA: The MIT Press, 2005.

Holt, Jim. "Of Two Minds." *The New York Times Magazine*, 8 May
2005, 11–13.

Howell, Kenneth J. *God's Two Books: Copernican Cosmology and Biblical Interpretation in Early Modern Science.* Notre Dame, IN: University of Notre Dame Press, 2002.

Huttenlocher, Peter R. *Neural Plasticity: The Effects of Environment on the Development of the Cerebral Cortex.* Perspectives in Cognitive Neuroscience. Cambridge, MA: Harvard University Press, 2002.

Huxley, Thomas H. "On the Hypothesis that Animals Are Automata, and its History." In *Methods and Results: Essays*, 199–250. New York: D. Appleton, 1894.

Ito, Shigehiko, et al. "Performance Monitoring by the Anterior Cingulate Cortex during Saccade Countermanding." *Science* 302, no. 5642 (2003): 120–22.

Jackson-McCabe, Matt A. *Logos and Law in the Letter of James: The Law of Nature, the Law of Moses, and the Law of Freedom.* NovTSup 100. Leiden: Brill, 2001.

Jarick, John. "Questioning Sheol." In *Resurrection*, ed. Stanley E. Porter, Michael A. Hayes, and David Tombs, 22–32. JSNTSup 186. Sheffield: Sheffield Academic Press, 1999.

Jeeves, Malcolm A. "Human Nature: An Integrated Picture." In *What about the Soul? Neuroscience and Christian Anthropology*, ed. Joel B. Green, 171–89. Nashville: Abingdon, 2004.

_____. *Human Nature at the Millennium: Reflections on the Integration of Psychology and Christianity.* Grand Rapids, MI: Baker Academic, 1997.

Jeeves, Malcolm A., ed. *From Cells to Souls – And Beyond: Changing Portraits of Human Nature.* Grand Rapids, MI: Eerdmans, 2004.

Jenson, Robert W. *Systematic Theology.* 2 vols. Oxford: Oxford University Press, 1997–99.

Jervell, Jacob. *Die Apostelgeschichte.* KEK 3. Göttingen: Vandenhoeck & Ruprecht, 1998.

Jewett, Paul K. *Who We Are: Our Dignity as Human: A Neo-Evangelical Theology.* With Marguerite Shuster. Grand Rapids, MI: Eerdmans, 1996.

Jewett, Robert. *Paul's Anthropological Terms: A Study of Their Use in Conflict Settings.* AGJU 10. Leiden: Brill, 1971.

Johnson, Luke Timothy. *The Acts of the Apostle.* SP 5. Collegeville, MN: Liturgical, 1992.

_____. "Friendship with the World and Friendship with God: A Study of Discipleship in James." In *Brother of Jesus, Friend of God: Studies in the Letter of James*, 202–20. Grand Rapids, MI: Eerdmans, 2004.

_____. *The Letter of James: A New Translation with Introduction and Commentary.* AB 37A. New York: Doubleday, 1995.

Johnson, Mark. *The Body in the Mind: The Bodily Basis of Meaning, Imagination, and Reason.* Chicago: University of Chicago Press, 1987.

_____. *Moral Imagination: Implications of Cognitive Science for Ethics.* Chicago: University of Chicago Press, 1993.

Johnston, Philip S. "Death and Resurrection." In *NDBT*, 443–47.

_____. "Humanity." In *NDBT*, 564–65.

_____. *Shades of Sheol: Death and Afterlife in the Old Testament.* Downers Grove, IL: InterVarsity, 2002.

_____. "The Underworld and the Dead in the Old Testament." *TynBul* 45 (1994): 415–19.

Kandel, Eric R. "Free Will Is Exercised Unconsciously, without Awareness." *Edge* 176 (12 January 2006); {http://www.edge.org/q2006/q06_5.html}; accessed 26 January 2006.

Keller, Julia C. "Sacred Minds." *Science and Theology News* 6, no. 4 (2005): 18.

Kilbourne, Brock, and James T. Richardson. "Paradigm Conflict, Types of Conversion, and Conversion Theories." *Sociological Analysis* 50 (1988): 1–21.

King-Casas, Brooks, et al. "Getting to Know You: Reputation and Trust in a Two-Person Economic Exchange." *Science* 308, no. 5718 (2005): 78–82.

Koch, Christof. *The Quest for Consciousness: A Neurobiological Approach.* Englewood, CO: Roberts, 2004.

Koenig, Michael, et al. "Damage to the Prefrontal Cortex Increases Utilitarian Moral Judgements." *Nature* (21 March 2007); {http://www.nature.com/nature/journal/vaop/ncurrent/abs/nature05631.html}; accessed 22 March 2007.

Kolb, Bryan, and Ian Q. Whishaw. *An Introduction to Brain and Behavior.* New York: Worth, 2001.

Konradt, Matthias. *Christliche Existenz nach dem Jakobusbrief: Eine Studie zu seiner soteriologischen und ethischen Konzeption.* SUNT 22. Göttingen: Vandenhoeck & Ruprecht, 1998.

Konstan, David. *Friendship in the Classical World.* Cambridge: Cambridge University Press, 1997.

Koontz, Dean. *Watchers.* New York: Berkley, 1987.

Kornell, Nate, et al. "Transfer of Metacognitive Skills and Hint Seeking in Monkeys." *Psychological Science* 18 (2007): 64–71.

Kringelbach, Morten L. "The Human Orbitofrontal Cortex: Linking Reward to Hedonic Experience." *Nature Reviews Neuroscience* 6 (2005): 691–702.

Kumari, Veena. "Do Psychotherapies Produce Neurobiological Effects?" *Acta Neuropsychiatrica* 18 (2006): 61–70.

Kümmel, Werner Georg. *Man in the New Testament.* London: Epworth, 1963.

Laidlaw, J. "Body." In *Dictionary of the Bible,* 5 vols., ed. James Hastings, 1:309. New York: Charles Scribner's Sons, 1903.

Lakoff, George. "How the Body Shapes Thought: Thinking with an All-Too-Human Brain." In *The Nature and Limits of Human Understanding,* ed. Anthony J. Sanford, 49–73. The 2001 Gifford Lectures. London: T&T Clark, 2003.

———. "How to Live with an Embodied Mind: When Causation, Mathematics, Morality, the Soul, and God Are Essentially Metaphorical Ideas." In *The Nature and Limits of Human Understanding,* ed. Anthony J. Sanford, 75–108. The 2001 Gifford Lectures. London: T&T Clark, 2003.

Lambert, J.C. "Body." In *Dictionary of the Apostolic Church,* 3 vols., ed. James Hastings, 1:154–56. New York: Charles Scribner's Sons, 1922.

———. "Soul." In *A Dictionary of Christ and the Gospels,* 2 vols., ed. James Hastings, 1:520. New York: Charles Scribner's Sons, 1908.

Lampe, Peter. "Paul's Concept of a Spiritual Body." In *Resurrection: Theological and Scientific Assessments,* ed. Ted Peters, Robert John Russell, and Michael Welker, 103–14. Grand Rapids, MI: Eerdmans, 2002.

Lattimore, Richard. *Themes in Greek and Latin Epitaphs.* Illinois Studies in Language and Literature 28.1–2. Urbana: University of Illinois Press, 1942.

Leat, S. Jennifer. "Artificial Intelligence Researcher Seeks Silicon Soul." *Research News and Opportunities in Science and Theology* 3, no. 4 (2002): 7, 26.

LeDoux, Joseph. *The Emotional Brain: The Mysterious Underpinnings of Emotional Life.* London: Weidenfeld & Nicolson, 1998.

———. *Synaptic Self: How Our Brains Become Who We Are.* New York: Viking Penguin, 2002.

Levine, Joseph. "Materialism and Qualia: The Explanatory Gap." *PPQ* 64 (1983): 354–61.

Libet, Benjamin. "Do We Have Free Will?" In *The Volitional Brain: Towards a Neuroscience of Free Will,* ed. Benjamin Libet et al., 47–57. Thorverton: Imprint Academic, 1999.

———. *Mind Time: The Temporal Factor in Consciousness.* Cambridge, MA: Harvard University Press, 2004.

―――, et al. "Time of Conscious Intention to Acts in Relation to Onset of Cerebral Activity (Readiness-Potential)." *Brain* 106 (1983): 623–42.

―――, et al., eds., *The Volitional Brain: Towards a Neuroscience of Free Will.* Thorverton: Imprint Academic, 1999.

Lincoln, Andrew T. *Paradise Now and Not Yet: Studies in the Role of the Heavenly Dimension in Paul's Thought with Special Reference to His Eschatology.* SNTSMS 43. Cambridge: Cambridge University Press, 1981.

Loewenstein, George. "The Pleasures and Pain of Information." *Science* 312 (2006): 704–6.

Longenecker, Richard N. "Is There Development in Paul's Resurrection Thought?" In *Life in the Face of Death: The Resurrection Message of the New Testament,* ed. Richard N. Longenecker, 171–202. MNTS. Grand Rapids, MI: Eerdmans, 1998.

Looy, Heather. "Embodied and Embedded Morality: Divinity, Identity, and Disgust." *Zygon* 39 (2004): 219–35.

Lunde, Jonathan M. "Repentance." In *DJG*, 669–73.

MacDonald, Paul S. *History of the Concept of Mind: Speculations about Soul, Mind and Spirit from Homer to Hume.* Aldershot: Ashgate, 2003.

Macmillan, Malcolm. "Restoring Phineas Gage: A 150th Retrospective." *Journal of the History of the Neurosciences* 9 (2000): 46–66.

MacMullen, Ramsey. *Paganism in the Roman Empire.* New Haven: Yale University Press, 1981.

Maguire, E.A., et al. "Navigation-related Structural Change in the Hippocampi of Taxi Drivers." *Proceedings of the National Academy of Sciences* 97 (2000): 4398–403.

Malina, Bruce J. *The New Testament World: Insights from Cultural Anthropology.* Rev. ed. Louisville: Westminster John Knox, 1993.

Markham, Paul N. *Rewired: Exploring Religious Conversion.* DDCT. Eugene, OR: Pickwick, 2007.

Marrow, Stanley B. "ΑΘΑΝΑΣΙΑ / ΑΝΑΣΤΑΣΙΣ: The Road Not Taken." *NTS* 45 (1999): 571–86.

Martin, Dale B. *The Corinthian Body.* New Haven: Yale University Press, 1995.

Martin-Achard, Robert. *From Death to Life: A Study of the Development of the Doctrine of the Resurrection in the Old Testament.* Edinburgh: Oliver and Boyd, 1960.

McCoy, Allison N., and Michael L. Platt. "Risk-sensitive Neurons in Macaque Posterior Cingulate Cortex." *Nature Neuroscience* 8 (2005): 1220–27.

McGrath, Alister E. *A Scientific Theology.* Vol. 1: *Nature.* Grand Rapids, MI: Eerdmans, 2001.

Mendenhall, George E. "From Witchcraft to Justice: Death and Afterlife in the Old Testament." In *Death and Afterlife: Perspectives of World Religions,* ed. Hiroshi Obayashi, 67–81. Contributions to the Study of Religion 33. New York: Greenwood, 1992.

Méndez-Moratalla, Fernando. *The Paradigm of Conversion in Luke.* JSNTSup 252. London: T&T Clark, 2004.

Metzinger, Thomas. "The Forbidden Fruit Intuition." *Edge* 176 (12 January 2006); {http://www.edge.org/q2006/q06_7.html#metzinger}; accessed 26 January 2006.

_____. "Introduction: Consciousness Research at the End of the Twentieth Century." In *Neural Correlates of Consciousness: Empirical and Conceptual Questions,* ed. Thomas Metzinger, 1–12. Cambridge, MA: The MIT Press, 2000.

Meyrick, F., and J.C. Lambert. "Body." In *A Dictionary of Christ and the Gospels,* 2 vols., ed. James Hastings, 1:217–18. New York: Charles Scribner's Sons, 1908.

Middleton, J. Richard. *The Liberating Image: The Imago Dei in Genesis 1.* Grand Rapids, MI: Brazos, 2005.

Miller, Greg. "Reflecting on Another's Mind." *Science* 308, no. 5724 (2005): 945–47.

Miller, Patrick D. "What Is a Human Being? The Anthropology of Scripture." In *What about the Soul? Neuroscience and Christian Anthropology,* ed. Joel B. Green, 63–73. Nashville: Abingdon, 2004.

Mitchell, Jason P., et al. "Dissociable Medial Prefrontal Contributions to Judgments of Similar and Dissimilar Others." *Neuron* 50 (2006): 655–63.

Moll, Jorge, et al. "The Neural Basis of Human Moral Cognition." *Nature Reviews Neuroscience* 6 (2005): 799–809.

_____. "The Neural Correlates of Moral Sensitivity: A Functional Magnetic Resonance Imaging Investigation of Basic and Moral Emotions." *Journal of Neuroscience* 22, no. 7 (2002): 2730–36.

Moltmann, Jürgen. *God in Creation: A New Theology of Creation and the Spirit of God.* The Gifford Lectures 1984–85. San Francisco: Harper & Row, 1985.

Moreland, J.P. "Restoring the Substance to the Soul of Psychology." *JPsyT* 26 (1998): 29–43.

_____, and Scott B. Rae. *Body and Soul: Human Nature and the Crisis in Ethics.* Downers Grove, IL: InterVarsity, 2000.

Mullin, Paul. "Can the Image of God Ever Be Artificial?" *Research News and Opportunities in Science and Theology* 3, no. 6 (2003): 7, 27.

Murphy, Nancey. *Bodies and Souls, or Spirited Bodies?* CIT. Cambridge: Cambridge University Press, 2006.

_____. "The Resurrection Body and Personal Identity: Possibilities and Limits of Eschatological Knowledge." In *Resurrection: Theological and Scientific Assessments,* ed. Ted Peters, Robert John Russell, and Michael Welker, 202–18. Grand Rapids, MI: Eerdmans, 2002.

Nave Jr., Guy D. *The Role and Function of Repentance in Luke-Acts.* SBLAB 4. Atlanta: Society of Biblical Literature, 2002.

Nee, Watchman. *The Spiritual Man.* 3 vols. New York: Christian Fellowship, 1968.

Newberg, Andrew B., and Bruce Y. Lee. "The Neuroscientific Study of Religious and Spiritual Phenomena: Or Why God Doesn't Use Biostatistics." *Zygon* 40 (2005): 469–89.

Newberg, Andrew, et al. "Cerebral Blood Flow during Meditative Prayer: Preliminary Findings and Methodological Issues." *Perceptual and Motor Skills* 97 (2003): 625–30.

_____. "The Measurement of Regional Cerebral Blood Flow during the Complex Cognitive Task of Meditation: A Preliminary SPECT Study." *Psychiatry Research: Neuroimaging* 106 (2001): 113–22.

_____. "The Measurement of Regional Cerebral Blood Flow during Glossolalia: A Preliminary SPECT Study." *Psychiatry Research: Neuroimaging* 148 (2006): 67–71.

Nickelsburg, George W.E. "Judgment, Life-after-Death, and Resurrection in the Apocrypha and the Non-Apocalyptic Pseudepigrapha." In *Judaism in Late Antiquity. Part 4: Death, Life-after-Death, Resurrection and the World-to-Come in the Judaisms of Antiquity,* ed. Alan J. Avery-Peck and Jacob Neusner, 141–62. Handbook of Oriental Studies – 1: The Near and Middle East 49. Leiden: Brill, 2000.

Obhi, Sukhvinder S., and Patrick Haggard. "Free Will and Free Won't." *American Scientist* 92 (2004): 358–65.

Ollenburger, Ben C. "If Mortals Die, Will They Live Again? The Old Testament and Resurrection." *Ex Auditu* 9 (1993): 29–44.

Olson, Richard G. *Science and Religion, 1450–1900: From Copernicus to Darwin.* Baltimore: Johns Hopkins University Press, 2004.

Olsson, Andreas, et al. "The Role of Social Groups in the Persistence of Learned Fear." *Science* 309, no. 5735 (2005): 785–87.

Osborne, Grant R. *Revelation.* . Grand Rapids, MI: Baker Academic, 2002.

O'Toole, Robert F. *The Unity of Luke's Theology: An Analysis of Luke-Acts.* GNS 9. Wilmington, DE: Michael Glazier, 1984.

Overbye, Dennis. "Free Will: Now You Have It, Now You Don't." *The New York Times,* 2 January 2007; {http://select.nytimes.com/search/restricted/article?res=F10616F73D540C718CDDA80894DF404482#}; accessed 2 January 2007.

Padgett, Alan G. "The Body in Resurrection: Science and Scripture on the 'Spiritual Body' (1 Cor 15:35–58)." *WW* 22 (2002): 155–63.

Panksepp, Jaak. "Beyond a Joke: From Animal Laughter to Animal Joy?" *Science* 308, no. 5718 (2005): 62–63.

Pannenberg, Wolfhart. *Systematic Theology.* 3 vols. Grand Rapids, MI: Eerdmans, 1991–98.

Pao, David W. *Acts and the Isaianic New Exodus.* WUNT 2:130. Tübingen: Mohr Siebeck, 2000.

Parkin, Jon. *Science, Religion and Politics in Restoration England: Richard Cumberland's De legibus naturae.* SH ns. Woodbridge: Boydell, 1999.

Peace, Richard V. *Conversion in the New Testament: Paul and the Twelve.* Grand Rapids, MI: Eerdmans, 1999.

Peacock, Andrew. "The Relationship between the Soul and the Brain." In *Historical Aspects of the Neurosciences: A Festschrift for Macdonald Critchley,* ed F. Clifford Rose and W.F. Bynum, 83–98. New York: Raven, 1982.

Pennisi, Elizabeth. "Are Our Primate Cousins 'Conscious'?" *Science* 284, no. 5423 (1999): 2073–76.

———. "Why Do Humans Have So Few Genes?" *Science* 39, no. 5731 (2005): 80.

Peters, Ted. "The Soul of Trans-Humanism." *Dialog* 44 (2005): 381–95.

Peterson, Gregory R. "Do Split Brains Listen to Prozac?" *Zygon* 39 (2004): 555–76.

———. *Minding God: Theology and the Cognitive Sciences.* TSc. Minneapolis: Fortress, 2003.

———. "Minding *Minding God*: A Response to Spezio and Bielfeldt." *Zygon* 39 (2004): 605–14.

Pilhofer, Peter. *Presbyteron Kreitton: Der Altersbeweis der jüdischen und christlichen Apologeten und seine Vorgeschichte.* WUNT 2:39. Tübingen: Mohr Siebeck, 1990.

Pockett, Susan, et al., eds., *Does Consciousness Cause Behavior?* Cambridge, MA: The MIT Press, 2006.

Pokorný, Petr. *Theologie der lukanischen Schriften.* FRLANT 174. Göttingen: Vandenhoeck & Ruprecht, 1998.

Preuss, Horst Dietrich. *Old Testament Theology.* 2 vols. OTL. Louisville: Westminster John Knox, 1992.

Radl, Walter. *Das Lukas-Evangelium.* EdF 261. Darmstadt: Wissenschaftliche Buchgesellschaft, 1988.

Ramachandran, V.S. *A Brief Tour of Human Consciousness: From Imposter Poodles to Purple Numbers.* New York: Pi, 2004.

————. "Mirror Neurons and Imitation Learning as the Driving Force behind 'the Great Leap Forward' in Human Evolution." *Edge* 69 (1 June 2000) {http://www.edge.org/documents/archive/edge69.html}; accessed 17 September 2007.

Ramachandran, V.S., and Sandra Blakeslee. *Phantoms in the Brain: Probing the Mysteries of the Human Mind.* New York: William Morrow, 1998.

Ravens, David. *Luke and the Restoration of Israel.* JSNTSup 119. Sheffield: Sheffield Academic Press, 1995.

Reyna, Stephen P. *Connections: Brain, Mind, and Culture in a Social Anthropology.* London: Routledge, 2002.

Richards, Kent Harold. "Death: Old Testament." *ABD* 2:108–10.

Riese, Walther. *A History of Neurology.* New York: MD Publications, 1959.

Roberts, Alexander, et al., eds. *Ante-Nicene Fathers.* 10 vols. Buffalo, NY: Christian Literature, 1885–87; reprint ed., Peabody, MA: Hendrickson, 1994.

Robinson, H. Wheeler. *The Christian Doctrine of Man.* 3rd ed. Edinburgh: T&T Clark, 1926.

————. "Man." In *Dictionary of the Apostolic Church,* 3 vols., ed. James Hastings, 2:3–6. New York: Charles Scribner's Sons, 1922.

Robinson, John A.T. *The Body: A Study in Pauline Theology.* SBT 5. London: SCM, 1952.

Robinson, T.M. "The Defining Features of Mind-Body Dualism in the Writings of Plato." In *Psyche and Soma: Physicians and Metaphysicians on the Mind-Body Problem from Antiquity to Enlightenment,* ed. John P. Wright and Paul Potter, 37–55. Oxford: Clarendon, 2000.

Rolston III, Holmes. "Kenosis and Nature." In *The Work of Love: Creation as Kenosis,* ed. John Polkinghorne, 43–65. Grand Rapids, MI: Eerdmans, 2001.

Rousseau, Philip. "Conversion." *OCD,* 386–87.

Rynkiewich, Michael A. "What about the Dust? Missiological Musings on Anthropology." In *What about the Soul? Neuroscience and*

Christian Anthropology, ed. Joel B. Green, 133–44. Nashville: Abingdon, 2004.

Sanders, E.P. "Testament of Abraham: A New Translation and Introduction." In *Old Testament Pseudepigrapha*, 2 vols., ed. James H. Charlesworth, 1:871–902. Garden City, NY: Anchor Bible, 1983/85.

Schall, Jeffrey D. "Neural Basis of Deciding, Choosing and Acting." *Nature Reviews Neuroscience* 2 (2001): 33–42.

Schnelle, Udo. *Neutestamentliche Anthropologie: Jesus, Paulus, Johannes.* BThS 18. Neukirchen-Vluyn: Neukirchener, 1991. ET: *The Human Condition: Anthropology in the Teachings of Jesus, Paul, and John.* Minneapolis: Fortress, 1996.

Schwartz, Jeffrey M., and Sharon Begley. *The Mind and the Brain: Neuroplasticity and the Power of Mental Force.* New York: HarperCollins, 2002.

Schweizer, Eduard. "Body." *ABD* 1:767–72.

Sebanz, Natalie, and Wolfgang Prinz, eds. *Disorders of Volition.* Cambridge, MA: The MIT Press, 2006.

Seebass, H. "נֶפֶשׁ." *TDOT* 9:497–519.

Seim, Turid Karlsen. "In Heaven as on Earth? Resurrection, Body, Gender and Heavenly Rehearsals in Luke-Acts." In *Christian and Islamic Gender Models in Formative Traditions*, ed. Kari Elisabeth Børresen, 17–41. Rome: Herder, 2004.

Seitz, Aaron R., et al. "Seeing What Is Not There Shows the Costs of Perceptual Learning." *Proceedings of the National Academy of Sciences* 102, no. 25 (2005): 9080–85.

Seitz, Christopher R. *Word without End: The Old Testament as Abiding Theological Witness.* Grand Rapids, MI: Eerdmans, 1998.

Shults, F. LeRon. *Reforming Theological Anthropology: After the Philosophical Turn to Relationality.* Grand Rapids, MI: Eerdmans, 2003.

Siegel, Daniel J. *The Developing Mind: How Relationships and the Brain Interact to Shape Who We Are.* New York: Guilford, 1999.

_____. *The Mindful Brain: Reflection and Attunement in the Cultivation of Well-Being.* New York: Norton, 2007.

Smalley, Stephen S. *The Revelation to John: A Commentary on the Greek Text of the Apocalypse.* Downers Grove, IL: InterVarsity, 2005.

Snow, David A., and R. Machalek. "The Convert as a Social Type." In *Sociological Theory 1983*, ed. R. Collins, 259–89. San Francisco: Jossey Bass, 1983.

Sorabji, Richard. "Soul and Self in Ancient Philosophy." In *From Soul to Self*, ed. M. James C. Crabbe, 8–32. London: Routledge, 1999.

Spence, Sean A. "The Cycle of Action: A Commentary on Garry Young (2006)." *Journal of Consciousness Studies* 13 (2006): 69–72.

———. "Prefrontal White Matter – the Tissue of Lies?" *British Journal of Psychiatry* 187 (2005): 326–27.

Steck, Odil Hannes. *Israel und das gewaltsame Geschick der Propheten.* WMANT 23. Neukirchen-Vluyn: Neukirchener, 1967.

Stenschke, Christoph W. *Luke's Portrait of Gentiles Prior to Their Coming to Faith.* WUNT 2:108. Tübingen: Mohr Siebeck, 1999.

Stone, James L. "Transcranial Brain Injuries Caused by Metal Rods or Pipes over the Past 150 Years." *Journal of the History of the Neurosciences* 8 (1999): 227–34.

Stone, Lawson G. "The Soul: Possession, Part, or Person? The Genesis of Human Nature in Genesis 2:7." In *What about the Soul? Neuroscience and Christian Anthropology,* ed. Joel B. Green, 47–61. Nashville: Abingdon, 2004.

Suddendorf, Thomas. "Foresight and Evolution of the Human Mind." *Science* 312, no. 5776 (2006): 1006–7.

Swedenborg, Emanuel. *The Interaction of the Soul and Body.* London: The Swedenborg Society, 2005 [1769].

Taeger, J.W. *Der Mensch und sein Heil: Studien zum Bild des Menschen und zur Sicht der Bekehrung bei Lukas.* SNT 14. Gütersloh: Gerd Mohn, 1982.

Talbert, Charles H. "Conversion in the Acts of the Apostles: Ancient Auditors' Perceptions." In *Literary Studies in Luke-Acts: Essays in Honor of Joseph B. Tyson,* ed. Richard O. Thompson and Thomas E. Phillips, 141–53. Macon, GA: Mercer University Press, 1998.

Tancredi, Laurence. *Hardwired Behavior: What Neuroscience Reveals about Morality.* Cambridge: Cambridge University Press, 2005.

Taylor, Charles. *Sources of the Self: The Making of the Modern Identity.* Cambridge, MA: Harvard University Press, 1989.

Taylor, John. "Humanity as a Species among the Species." In *The Dynamics of Human Life,* ed. Mark Elliott, 1–33. Carlisle: Paternoster, 2001.

Taylor, Nicholas H. "The Social Nature of Conversion in the Early Christian World." In *Modelling Early Christianity: Social-scientific Studies of the New Testament in Its Context,* ed. Philip F. Esler, 128–36. London/New York: Routledge, 1995.

Thielicke, Helmut. *Being Human . . . Becoming Human: An Essay in Christian Anthropology.* Garden City, NY: Doubleday, 1984.

Thiselton, Anthony C. *The First Epistle to the Corinthians: A Commentary on the Greek Text.* NIGTC. Grand Rapids, MI: Eerdmans, 2000.

Thomas, Cal. "Evangelicals Should Focus on Saving Souls, Not the Planet." *Lexington Herald Leader* (18 March 2005), A15.

Thomas, Günter. "Resurrection to New Life: Pneumatological Implications of the Eschatological Transition." In *Resurrection: Theological and Scientific Assessments*, ed. Ted Peters, Robert John Russell, and Michael Welker, 255–76. Grand Rapids, MI: Eerdmans, 2002.

Thuan, Trinh Xuan. *Chaos and Harmony: Perspectives on Scientific Revolutions of the Twentieth Century*. Oxford: Oxford University Press, 2001.

Towner, W. Sibley. "Clones of God: Genesis 1:26–28 and the Image of God in the Hebrew Bible." *Int* 59 (2005): 341–56.

Tromp, Nicholas J. *Primitive Conceptions of Death and the Nether World in the Old Testament*. BibOr 21. Rome: Pontifical Biblical Institute, 1969.

van der Eijk, Philip J. "Aristotle's Psycho-physiological Account of the Soul-Body Relationship." In *Psyche and Soma: Physicians and Metaphysicians on the Mind-Body Problem from Antiquity to Enlightenment*, ed. John P. Wright and Paul Potter, 57–77. Oxford: Clarendon, 2000.

Vierkant, Tillmann. "Owning Intentions and Moral Responsibility." *Ethical Theory & Moral Practice* 8 (2005): 507–34.

von Rad, Gerhard. *Old Testament Theology*. 2 vols. New York: Harper & Row, 1962/65.

von Staden, Heinrich. "Body, Soul, and Nerves: Epicurus, Herophilus, Erasistratus, the Stoics, and Galen." In *Psyche and Soma: Physicians and Metaphysicians on the Mind-Body Problem from Antiquity to Enlightenment*, ed. John P. Wright and Paul Potter, 79–116. Oxford: Clarendon, 2000.

Walls, Andrew F. "Converts or Proselytes? The Crisis over Conversion in the Early Church." *International Bulletin of Missionary Research* 29 (2004): 2–6.

Walter, Henrik. *Neurophilosophy of Free Will: From Libertarian Illusions to a Concept of Natural Autonomy*. Cambridge, MA: The MIT Press, 2001.

Warne, Graham J. *Hebrew Perspectives on the Human Person in the Hellenistic Era: Philo and Paul*. MBPS 35. Lewiston, NY: Mellen, 1995.

Watts, Fraser. *Theology and Psychology*. ASRS. Aldershot: Ashgate, 2002.

Wegner, Daniel M. *The Illusion of Conscious Will*. Cambridge, MA: The MIT Press, 2002.

————, and Betsy Sparrow. "Authorship Processing." In *The Cognitive Neurosciences*, 3rd ed., ed. Michael S. Gazzaniga, 1201–9. Cambridge, MA: The MIT Press, 2004.

————, and Thalia Wheatley. "Apparent Mental Causation: Sources of the Experience of Will." *American Psychologist* 54 (1999): 480–92.

————, et al. "Vicarious Agency: Experiencing Control over the Movements of Others." *Journal of Personality and Social Psychology* 86 (2004): 838–48.

Wenk, Matthias. *Community-Forming Power: The Socio-Ethical Role of the Spirit in Luke-Acts.* JPTSup 19. Sheffield: Sheffield Academic Press, 2000.

————. "Conversion and Initiation: A Pentecostal View of Biblical and Patristic Perspectives." *JPT* 17 (2000): 56–80.

Wesley, John. *Explanatory Notes upon the New Testament.* London: Epworth, 1976 (1754).

Westen, Drew, et al. "Neural Bases of Motivated Reasoning: An fMRI Study of Emotional Constraints on Partisan Political Judgment in the 2004 U.S. Presidential Election." *Journal of Cognitive Neuroscience* 18 (2006): 1947–58.

Wheeler, E. "Man." In *A Dictionary of Christ and the Gospels*, 2 vols., ed. James Hastings, 2:107–110. New York: Charles Scribner's Sons, 1908.

Wilckens, Ulrich. *Die Missionsreden der Apostelgeschichte: Form- und traditionsgeschichtliche Untersuchungen.* 3rd ed. WMANT 5. Neukirchener-Vluyn: Neukirchener, 1974.

————. *Theologie des Neuen Testaments.* 4 vols. Neukirchener-Vluyn: Neukirchener, 2002–05.

Wilkes, K.V. "*Psuchē* versus the Mind." In *Essays on Aristotle's De anima*, ed. Martha C. Nussbaum and Amélie Oksenberg Rorty, 109–27. Oxford: Clarendon, 1992.

Wilkinson, John. *The Bible and Healing: A Medical and Theological Commentary.* Edinburgh: Handsel; Grand Rapids, MI: Eerdmans, 1998.

Williams, Patricia A. *Doing without Adam and Eve: Sociobiology and Original Sin.* TSc. Minneapolis: Fortress, 2001.

Willis, Thomas. *The Anatomy of the Brain and Nerves.* Translated by Samuel Pordage. Ed. William Feindel. CML. Birmingham: McGill-Queens University Press, 1978 (1681).

————. *Two Discourses concerning the Soul of Brutes, Which Is That of the Vital and Sensitive of Man.* Gainesville, FL: Scholars' Facsimiles and Reprints, 1971 (1683).

Wilson, Walter T. "Sin as Sex and Sex with Sin: The Anthropology of James 1:12–15." *HTR* 95 (2002): 147–68.

Wintermute, O.S. "Apocalypse of Zephaniah: A New Translation and Introduction." In *Old Testament Pseudepigrapha*, 2 vols., ed. James H. Charlesworth, 1:497–515. Garden City: New York, 1983/85.

Witherington III, Ben. *Conflict and Community in Corinth: A Socio-Rhetorical Commentary on 1 and 2 Corinthians.* Grand Rapids, MI: Eerdmans, 1995.

Wolfe, Tom. "Sorry, but Your Soul Just Died." In *Hooking Up*, 89–109. New York: Farrar, Strauss & Giroux, 2000.

Wolff, Hans Walter. *Anthropology of the Old Testament.* London: SCM, 1974.

Wright, Christopher J.H. "Implications of Conversion in the Old Testament and the New." *International Bulletin of Missionary Research* 28 (2004): 14–19.

———. "Old Testament Ethics: A Missiological Perspective." *Catalyst* 26, no. 2 (2000): 5–8.

Wright, John P., and Paul Potter, eds. *Psyche and Soma: Physicians and Metaphysicians on the Mind-Body Problem from Antiquity to Enlightenment.* Oxford: Clarendon, 2000.

Wright, N.T. *The New Testament and the People of God.* Vol. 1 of Christian Origins and the Question of God. Minneapolis: Fortress, 1992.

———. *The Resurrection of the Son of God.* Vol. 3 of Christian Origins and the Question of God. Minneapolis: Fortress, 2003.

Yamauchi, Edwin. "Life, Death, and the Afterlife in the Ancient Near East." In *Life in the Face of Death: The Resurrection Message of the New Testament*, ed. Richard N. Longenecker, 21–50. MNTS. Grand Rapids, MI: Eerdmans, 1998.

Yang, Yaling, et al. "Prefrontal White Matter in Pathological Liars." *British Journal of Psychiatry* 187 (2005): 320–25.

Young, Garry. "Preserving the Role of Conscious Decision Making in the Initiation of Intentional Action." *Journal of Consciousness Studies* 13 (2006): 51–68.

Young, Kay, and Jeffrey L. Saver. "The Neurology of Narrative." *SubStance* 30 (2001): 72–84.

Zeman, Adam. *Consciousness: A User's Guide.* New Haven: Yale University Press, 2002.

Zhu, Jing. "Reclaiming Volition: An Alternative Interpretation of Libet's Experiment." *Journal of Consciousness Studies* 10 (2003): 61–77.

Zimmer, Carl. *Soul Made Flesh: The Discovery of the Brain – and How It Changed the World.* New York: Free Press, 2004.

Modern Authors

Scripture and Other Ancient Literature